CW01183315

Reading Communities from Salons to Cyberspace

Reading Communities from Salons to Cyberspace

Edited by
DeNel Rehberg Sedo

palgrave
macmillan

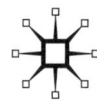

Introduction, selection and editorial matter © DeNel Rehberg Sedo 2011
Individual contributions © contributors 2011

All rights reserved. No reproduction, copy or transmission of this publication may be made without written permission.

No portion of this publication may be reproduced, copied or transmitted save with written permission or in accordance with the provisions of the Copyright, Designs and Patents Act 1988, or under the terms of any licence permitting limited copying issued by the Copyright Licensing Agency, Saffron House, 6–10 Kirby Street, London EC1N 8TS.

Any person who does any unauthorized act in relation to this publication may be liable to criminal prosecution and civil claims for damages.

The authors have asserted their rights to be identified as the authors of this work in accordance with the Copyright, Designs and Patents Act 1988.

First published 2011 by
PALGRAVE MACMILLAN

Palgrave Macmillan in the UK is an imprint of Macmillan Publishers Limited, registered in England, company number 785998, of Houndmills, Basingstoke, Hampshire RG21 6XS.

Palgrave Macmillan in the US is a division of St Martin's Press LLC,
175 Fifth Avenue, New York, NY 10010.

Palgrave Macmillan is the global academic imprint of the above companies and has companies and representatives throughout the world.

Palgrave® and Macmillan® are registered trademarks in the United States, the United Kingdom, Europe and other countries.

ISBN 978–0–230–29988–7

This book is printed on paper suitable for recycling and made from fully managed and sustained forest sources. Logging, pulping and manufacturing processes are expected to conform to the environmental regulations of the country of origin.

A catalogue record for this book is available from the British Library.

Library of Congress Cataloging-in-Publication Data
Reading communities from salons to cyberspace / edited by DeNel Rehberg Sedo.
  p. cm.
Includes bibliographical references and index.
ISBN 978–0–230–29988–7 (alk. paper)
 1. Books and reading—Social aspects—History. 2. Book clubs (Discussion groups)—History. 3. Group reading—History. 4. Reading promotion—History. 5. Books and reading—Social aspects—Great Britain—History. 6. Books and reading—Social aspects—United States—History.   I. Rehberg Sedo, DeNel, 1965–
  Z1003.R295 2011
  028'.9—dc22   2011012461

10 9 8 7 6 5 4 3 2 1
20 19 18 17 16 15 14 13 12 11

Printed and bound in the United States of America

This collection is dedicated to the founding members of the Society for the History of Authorship, Reading and Publishing (SHARP)

Contents

List of Figures and Tables	ix
Acknowledgements	x
Notes on Contributors	xi
An Introduction to Reading Communities: Processes and Formations DeNel Rehberg Sedo	1
1 Reading in an Epistolary Community in Eighteenth-Century England Betty A. Schellenberg	25
2 Nineteenth-Century Reading Groups in Britain and the Community of the Text: an Experiment with *Little Dorrit* Jenny Hartley	44
3 Reading Across the Empire: the National Home Reading Union Abroad Robert Snape	60
4 Utopian Civic-Mindedness: Robert Maynard Hutchins, Mortimer Adler, and the Great Books Enterprise Daniel Born	81
5 'I Used to Read Anything that Caught My Eye, But...': Cultural Authority and Intermediaries in a Virtual Young Adult Book Club DeNel Rehberg Sedo	101
6 The Growth of Reading Groups as a Feminine Leisure Pursuit: Cultural Democracy or Dumbing Down? Anna Kiernan	123
7 Speaking Subjects: Developing Identities in Women's Reading Communities Linsey Howie	140
8 Leading Questions: Interpretative Guidelines in Contemporary Popular Reading Culture Anna S. Ivy	159

9 Marionettes and Puppeteers? The Relationship between
  Book Club Readers and Publishers   181
  Danielle Fuller, DeNel Rehberg Sedo and Claire Squires

Bibliography   200

Index   213

List of Figures and Tables

Figures

I.1 Dickens and group read *Dombey*. Illustrated by Fred Barnard in the Household Edition of John Forster's *Life of Charles Dickens*, reprinted in *Scenes and Characters from the Works of Charles Dickens, Being 865 Drawings by Fred Barnard, Phiz and others*, Chapman and Hall, London 1908: available online at http://www.archive.org/details/scenescharacters00londuoft, p. 571 — 4

3.1 An indicative map of the geographical spread of National Home Reading Union activity in the 1890s — 65

4.1 'The 102 Great Ideas'. Photo celebrating the making of the Syntopicon — 82

7.1 Book club members meet author Loranne Brown — 144

Tables

3.1 Geographical spread of the Australasian Home Reading Union and distribution of its membership — 69

5.1 TYABC titles that are also YA Book Award winners (USA), 2002–05 — 111

Acknowledgements

I remember clearly the day I came up with the idea of this collection; it was soon after another invigorating SHARP annual conference several years back. As one usually feels after meeting scholars who inspire and whose work is relevant to your own, I wanted to continue the momentum I experienced at the meeting. I felt the motivation of bringing together those of us who spend our research time and effort on better understanding historical and contemporary reading communities. Much to my surprise, every single author I approached agreed to be part of the project.

It is to these authors that I feel the most gratitude. They were patient throughout an extremely long gestation period for the collection, which included not only a move across the country, but also the completion and defence of my PhD thesis, and then my promotion process. They endured reviews and revisions with grace and haste. Their dedication, perseverance and rigour are evident within these pages. I am honoured to bring their work together under one cover.

I appreciate the funding provided by MSVU, the Nova Scotia Research Innovation Trust and the Canadian Foundation for Innovation. Over the years, I have had the assistance of three burgeoning reading researchers. My sincere appreciation goes to Julie Van Huyse, Leslie Carson and Janine Basha for their astute proofreading skills, unending energy and good humour. Thanks also go to Ian Colford, who offered excellent prose advice for my introduction, and to the anonymous readers who read earlier versions of the manuscript. I appreciate the support and professionalism of Paula Kennedy and Benjamin Doyle at Palgrave Macmillan; I had no idea the publishing process could be so enjoyable! Another reason that process has been pleasant is because of the close eye and enthusiasm of Barbara Slater. Thank you. My research partner, Danielle Fuller, has provided close readings of my own contributions, offered advice when solicited, and has laughed and cried with me through the ups and downs of the entire process. No one could have a smarter colleague or a better friend to work with, and I thank her for sticking with me throughout the years. To Brent, my husband, editor, proofreader, idea-bouncer, jokester and best reader: Mil gracias, mi amor. No lo podría haber hecho sin ti.

Notes on Contributors

Daniel Born is the author of *The Birth of Liberal Guilt in the English Novel: Charles Dickens to H.G. Wells* (1995). He earned his doctorate at the Graduate Center of the City University of New York, where he studied with Irving Howe and Alfred Kazin. He was a vice president and chief of staff at the Great Books Foundation, and he also edited the Foundation's quarterly magazine, *The Common Review*. He is currently a lecturer in Northwestern University's School of Continuing Studies, MA literature program, and an academic chair in Kaplan University's School of Legal Education. He lives in Chicago.

Danielle Fuller is Director, Regional Centre for Canadian Studies, and Senior Lecturer, University of Birmingham, UK. She is the author of various articles about Canadian literary culture, contemporary reading cultures and of *Writing the Everyday: Women's Textual Communities in Atlantic Canada* (2004), which won the Gabrielle Roy Prize (English-language). She is currently collaborating with DeNel Rehberg Sedo on a monograph arising from an Arts and Humanities Research Council-funded interdisciplinary project that investigated contemporary mass-mediated reading events in three nation-states.

Jenny Hartley is Professor of English Literature at Roehampton University, London. Her book *Reading Groups* (2000) was the first survey of reading groups in the United Kingdom. She has been running reading groups in prisons since 1999. Her most recent book is *Charles Dickens and the House of Fallen Women* (2008).

Linsey Howie is an Associate Professor in the School of Occupational Therapy at La Trobe University in Melbourne Australia. Linsey has a PhD in sociology and she is trained in a Gestalt approach to psychotherapy. She has a particular interest in groups in therapy, community-based groups and the power of groups to sustain and nurture people in their local communities. She is also interested in promoting the link between what people do and their subjective experience of health and well-being; book groups and other leisure groups appear to play an important role in this area.

Anna S. Ivy is a Senior Lecturer in English at the University of Illinois, Urbana-Champaign. She received her PhD from the University of

Pennsylvania; her dissertation, titled *From Princeton to Paradise: Women's Reading in Academic and Popular Culture*, deals with contemporary struggles over the function and value of women's reading at that confluence of the critical and the personal that is the site of so much feminist scholarship.

Anna Kiernan is Head of the Department of Writing at University College Falmouth. Previously, she was Course Leader of the MA in Publishing at Kingston University. She is doing a PhD in Life Writing at Goldsmiths College. Her most recently published book is the anthology *Bit on the Side: Work, Sex, Love, Loss and Own Goals* (2007).

DeNel Rehberg Sedo is an Associate Professor in the Department of Communication Studies and a Lecturer in the Cultural Studies Program at Mount Saint Vincent University in Halifax, Nova Scotia. Along with Danielle Fuller, she is co-director of the 'Beyond the Book: Mass Reading Events in the UK, Canada and the USA' research project, and has published a variety of articles, chapters and encyclopedia entries on contemporary and historical reading communities. She is also the Director of the Atlantic Canada Communication Issues Research Lab, which was funded by the Nova Scotia Research Innovation Trust and the Canadian Foundation for Innovation.

Betty A. Schellenberg is Professor and Chair of English at Simon Fraser University, where she is one of the founding members of the Print Culture Studies group. Her recent publications include *Reconsidering the Bluestockings* (2003; co-edited with Nicole Pohl) and *The Professionalization of Women Writers in Eighteenth-Century Britain* (2005). She is currently editing a volume of *The Cambridge Edition of the Correspondence of Samuel Richardson* and writing a book on the interface between manuscript and print literary cultures in eighteenth-century Britain.

Robert Snape works in the Centre for Worktown Studies at the University of Bolton. He has published widely on the social and cultural history of leisure in Britain between 1850 and 1939. He discovered the National Home Reading Union while researching his doctoral thesis on fiction provision in British public libraries between 1850 and 1914. He later published a history of the NHRU in the *Journal of Victorian Culture*, an account of the contribution of the NHRU to the development of rational and improving holidays in *Leisure Studies* and most recently a paper in the *Journal of Tourism History* that traced the influence of the North American Chautauqua movement on the NHRU and subsequently on the development of serious holidays in Britain.

Claire Squires is Professor of Publishing Studies and Director of the Stirling Centre for Publishing and Communication at the University of Stirling. Her publications include *Marketing Literature: the Making of Contemporary Writing in Britain* (Palgrave, 2007) and *Philip Pullman: Master Storyteller* (2007). She is co-editor of the *Cambridge History of the Book in Britain Volume 7: The Twentieth Century and Beyond* (forthcoming).

An Introduction to Reading Communities: Processes and Formations

DeNel Rehberg Sedo

> In reconstructing sociable forms of reading, book historians make one reader knowable to another.
>
> Leah Price[1]

> Books cannot be understood apart from the society that creates them, and conversely, no literate society can be understood without some study of the book it produces.
>
> Cathy N. Davidson[2]

Bringing together scholarship on reading communities that traverses three centuries and numerous cultural contexts, the chapters collected in *Reading Communities from Salons to Cyberspace* illustrate the cross-disciplinary nature of scholarship in the history of reading. In its own way, each of the pieces in this book addresses Davidson's call to reflect upon the private and social interactions that occur between texts and their readers. But while the collection as a whole incorporates the perspectives of authors working in a range of disciplines – and who, because of this, engage in a variety of research methods – a common thread runs through all these chapters: the assumption that shared reading is both a *social process* and a *social formation*. Each author conceives differently the social dimensions of reading. However, by locating reading communities in literary salons, author-reader relationships, face-to-face book clubs, television programmes, online chat rooms, and formal reading programmes designed by cultural authorities, the collection also acknowledges Price's proposition by reconstructing sociable forms of reading.

2 *Reading Communities from Salons to Cyberspace*

The study of book clubs, reading groups or literary societies can be described as a study of interdependencies. Building upon the influential work of book historians who question the assumption of the isolated individual reader, the authors in this collection draw attention to the relationships readers forge with one another and demonstrate how these social interactions influence the very personal relationship one enjoys with a book.[3] The collection is not meant to be an exhaustive survey of reading communities from the eighteenth to the twenty-first centuries nor does it encompass the developing world. Rather, it is designed to focus on more recent reading groups while recognizing the importance of the reading-group phenomenon within a broader historical framework. Several exemplary essays establish the context of early reading groups, allowing readers to see the phenomenon as a long-standing practice that has served different functions in various places and times. One of these chapters examines the era of literary salons; another looks at readers of the works of Charles Dickens; the remaining seven bring us from the turn of the last century to the contemporary reader who is influenced by various forms of media convergence. Collectively, then, the authors whose work is printed in this volume offer a range of insights into the social structures that influence both collective and private reading practices. And in turn, each piece illustrates how 'the private' and 'the collective' cannot be considered as isolated phenomena. That is, we cannot arrive at a full understanding of private reading practices without at the same time considering the role of social relationships and institutions.

Along with the assumption that shared reading is both a social process and a social formation, there are three distinct links evident in the reading communities presented in this collection. The first is the notion of community. This is introduced in the first section below with an overview of shared reading that is meant to illustrate neither a simplistic move from oral (pre-literate) to textual (literate) societies, nor a historical process that only took place in the west during the Middle Ages, but aims rather to give the reader a brief glimpse at the early processes and formations of shared reading practices. The chapter continues with a discussion of current reading community scholarship because evident in this scholarship is the role of education, which is the second link between most of the pieces in *Reading Communities from Salons to Cyberspace*. The final section offers a discussion of the third link: the rich repertoire of research methods available to book historians. Each contribution's method of enquiry is highlighted in an effort to illustrate the wealth of tools that can be used to interrogate collective reading practices.

A brief historical introduction to shared reading

During the Middle Ages, the practice of gathering together to read or to listen to someone read from a text grew in popularity and eventually became commonplace. Though illiteracy was the norm and few people owned books, travelling entertainers and troubadours roamed the countryside reading out loud to those who wanted to listen. In the homes of the privileged minority, educated servants read to their masters. The gatherings were frequently utilitarian in nature; labour of some sort would accompany the reading from the book. One example of this can be found in the fifteenth-century story of a learned old man who is asked by a group of women to act as a reader while the women spin and talk with one another.[4]

By the late eighteenth century, the members of small 'book societies', 'reading societies', 'book clubs' and 'literary societies' were discussing books and socializing while the group also acted as a lending and circulating library.[5] Some of the groups had women members, but it was not until the early 1800s that women started forming literary societies in any great numbers for the purpose of discussing books, and it was only after the Civil War that the movement took hold in the United States. At this point in history, in both Canada and the United States, literacy was expanding at a great rate, and access to books and other literature was growing to answer an increasing demand. Women were slowly gaining access to public spaces.[6] As more middle-class women gained leisure time as a result of the changes brought on by the Industrial Revolution, they gathered to practise religion, gradually gaining access to public spaces that were traditionally open only to men. As Thomas Augst has illustrated, for example, gender, class and race were often barriers to education, but through libraries, books and knowledge were useful in institutionalizing a more democratic print culture.[7]

Nineteenth-century literary societies were the descendants of the seventeenth-century European salons that were the gathering spots for those – mainly men – who wanted to discuss literature, politics or culture. But the membership of these North American 'literary societies' was comprised mainly of white females and in practice they were modelled after the familial reading sessions that took place in some homes, in which books or magazines were read and discussed, for both educational and entertainment purposes.[8] There is also evidence of mixed-gender African-American literary societies, whose members read to and for one another.[9] These readers sought not leisure, but to gain cultural capital in an increasingly literate society. As education improved and literacy spread, the

READING "DOMBEY" AT THE SNUFF SHOP—Book 5, chap. vii.

Figure I.1 Dickens and group read *Dombey*. Illustrated by Fred Barnard in the Household Edition of John Forster's *Life of Charles Dickens*, reprinted in *Scenes and Characters from the Works of Charles Dickens, Being 865 Drawings by Fred Barnard, Phiz and others*, Chapman and Hall, London 1908: available online at http://www.archive.org/details/scenescharacters00londuoft, p. 571

members of literary societies came more often than not from the burgeoning middle class.[10] Anne Ruggles Gere estimates that by the end of the nineteenth century, there were more than two million American women in literary societies,[11] and Barbara Sicherman estimates that 75 per cent of US public libraries were founded by these types of women's groups.[12] Most of these reading women turned their attention to charity work because at the time, it was assumed their sensitivity as ladies lent itself to the study of societal concerns, and they could do this without abandoning domestic duties.[13] Although literary societies may not have directly encouraged their members to join suffragist and temperance movements, they also often acted as training grounds for women who later became involved in those movements.[14] Interestingly, many women who became involved in social movements reported becoming more active readers and writers.[15]

Under the guise of helping people in need, American, Canadian,[16] European and colonial[17] women overcame the resistance of spouses, society and perhaps even their own sense of familial duty. As is the case in contemporary women's book clubs, literary society meetings of the previous century provided the framework for a woman's sense of order and understanding; they were spaces in which women's wisdom and knowledge could be articulated, validated and appreciated.[18] The discussions 'provided a common language and a medium of intellectual and social exchange that helped the women define themselves and formulate responses to the larger world'.[19] Group membership and reading practices provided a community that often connected readers in similar groups across North America and in Great Britain in a real or imagined way.[20] The communication networks between the different readers and the groups to which they belonged complicates Benedict Anderson's oft-cited notion of imagined literary community membership in *Imagined Communities: Reflections on the Origin and Spread of Nationalism*.[21] According to Anderson, an imagined community is created, in part, through the ritual of reading the daily newspaper. He argues that readers know that the act of reading the newspaper is being replicated by hundreds or thousands of other readers, leading to shared but imagined identities, lifestyles and interests. In this collection, we show that not only does the *act* of reading function as a community-building exercise, but also that exchanges of letters, books and interpretations serve as both real and imagined community building blocks, taking their place as markers of membership of a community but also acting as barriers.

Reading communities of the past often exposed their members to learning opportunities that were not available within the institutionalized education system.[22] In the early part of the century, formal study groups established by universities, government agencies and religious institutions reflected the growing momentum of the adult education movement, which had begun in the late 1870s and which continued well into the middle of the twentieth century.[23] These groups, whose size varied according to the geographical communities in which they met, were often inspired by progressive ideologies that saw education as an agent of social change, or else by a more conservative philosophy that valued education for the social stability it fostered and education for education's sake.[24] The reading materials of each group reflected these ideologies.[25]

While these groups were often established by churches, universities and other institutions, they frequently evolved into semi-formal and self-directed bodies. Modelling themselves after the existing groups, members of a new group might appropriate and adapt features of established systems, norms, policies or practices to suit their own purposes. This process is typified by the semi-formal reading and study groups that grew out of two influential US and British cultural programmes. Like other groups that began under formal organizations, there is evidence that members of the Chautauqua Literary and Scientific Circles and the National Home Reading Union (NHRU) sometimes created their own reading lists and interpretative practices to fit their specific needs, while still maintaining the ideology of education and socialization through prescribed reading and dialogue.[26]

By the 1960s, formal study clubs had largely disappeared. The semi-formal groups that had branched off from institutions gave way to less formal groups that began with readers already loosely affiliated to one another, perhaps by geographic proximity or through a social network such as a self-help group or activist circle. The political and cultural complexities of these groups are especially evident in the oral histories of the private women's reading clubs that emerged in the 1960s and 1970s. These clubs followed the model of the Chautauqua and the NHRU reading circles in that the members often met in each other's homes, but differed from those groups in that their membership consisted mainly of women whose socio-economic backgrounds and educational experiences closely resembled one another, and who lived in the same neighbourhood and had reached a similar stage of life. Because they owed no allegiance to the philosophy of a parent institution, and because the gender composition of the group was often exclusively female, readers in these groups sometimes achieved an intellectual and social respite from domestic routines and responsibilities. This allowed them to discover and nurture and maybe even pursue new interests and activities, and to break the bonds of domestic drudgery.[27]

Book clubs moved into mainstream culture in the early 1990s through their popularization by American talk-show host Oprah Winfrey. Not only have they appeared in the story lines of prime-time television series in the US, such as *Bob and Margaret*, *The Chris Isaak Show* and *Ed*, but book clubs also appear as part of episodic plots and jokes in the UK series *The Savages*, and as the backdrop to an entire series in the British situation comedy *The Reading Group*. Nintendo even makes a video game targeted at young girls: *Smart Girls: Magical Book Clubs*. Novels such as *The Jane Austen Book Club*, *Reading Group* and *Angry Housewives Eating Bon Bons* feature book club members as central characters.[28] American comedian Kathy Griffen illustrates the popularity of Oprah's Book Club by cheekily titling her memoir *Official Book Club Selection: A Memoir by Kathy Griffen*.[29]

Reading Communities: Processes and Formations 7

The private book club model has been appropriated by different media production companies and networks. Most obvious is Harpo's 'Oprah's Book Club', but others, such as MSNBC's Today Show and ABC's Good Morning America in the US, have also attempted to promote reading through television.[30] Save for 'Oprah's Book Club', the websites for these network programmes offer readers information on recently published books but provide little opportunity for readers to engage directly with one another. However, like 'Oprah's Book Club', 'Richard and Judy's Book Club' in the UK is a good illustration of book and television convergence and the potential for building reader relationships.[31] In 2004, Richard Madeley and Judy Finnigan began a book club segment on their daytime television programme. 'Richard and Judy's Book Club' was aired each winter and summer on the popular UK magazine format afternoon television show. Joined by two celebrity guest reviewers, the hosts introduced selected books chosen from more than 600 submitted by UK publishers to the show's producer. At the end of the season, and in conjunction with the British Book Awards, the book club concluded with viewers choosing Richard and Judy's Best Read of the Year. Borrowing and adapting key elements from Oprah's Book Club, such as the in-studio book discussion and the opinions of 'real' face-to-face book clubs, the husband and wife team became hugely important actors in the contemporary literary print culture field.

While in many respects the present-day book club resembles the 'grassroots' literary community of the past, it is inevitably influenced by rapidly evolving mediated forms of popular culture. Contemporary readers engage in social practices that are unique to the digitized spaces of twenty-first century life. Online book groups, interactive fan-fiction[32] sites where fans re-write favourite fiction and share it with one another, online retailers and their customer-generated book reviews (such as Amazon.com), and book swapping (such as Bookcrossings.com) and review websites (such as LibraryThing.com and GoodReads.com) provide readers with many opportunities not only to connect with one another but also to exchange book recommendations. Readers who Tweet, to use contemporary parlance, can exchange book talk on several sites, such as Twitter.com/thebookclub and www.thebookstudio.com/twitterbookclub. These social networking sites, along with literary blogs or LitBlogs, as they are often termed by their writers and readers, have reconfigured traditional notions of cultural authority, making it possible for anyone to become a writer, and for anyone with an Internet connection and a desire to express his or her opinion to become a reviewer.[33] So while the world wide web provides a new and radical medium for the production and distribution of texts and thus acts as a disruptive force upon traditional processes of literary creation, production, distribution and reception, it also provides opportunities for many (though certainly not all) readers to connect with one another regardless of factors such as cultural or socio-economic background, gender, reading level or geography.

'The Big Read', a programme organized by the National Endowment for the Arts in the US, which, since 2006, has made over 800 grants to support community-wide reading projects, is another indication of the popularization of book clubs. On 20 December 2005, the National Endowment for the Arts (NEA) released a press statement announcing its new nationwide reading programme. The Big Read was the NEA's response to a national study that found that reading in the US was in drastic decline. Chairman Gioia says in the release:

> If cities nationally unite to adopt The Big Read, our community-wide reading program, together we can restore reading to its essential place in American culture. Call me naïve, but I can actually envision an America in which average people talk about *To Kill a Mockingbird* and *The Great Gatsby* with the same enthusiasm as they bring to *Lost* or *Desperate Housewives*.[34]

According to that same release, literary reading in the US is not only on the decline but reading for 'pleasure and enlightenment' is *in crisis*.[35] Modelled on successful One Book, One City programmes in which all residents of a city or region are encouraged to read the same book, the Big Read's aim is 'To restore reading to the center of American culture', and, by implication, to educate and civilize American citizens through shared reading of 'classic' books.

At the turn of the previous century, cultural authorities lamented the *rise* of novel reading. The NEA has turned this around 180 degrees, though it ignores non-fiction reading in its description of the dire situation of reading among the American public.[36] The *Reading at Risk* study does not report participation by non-fiction readers or those who might read online. Instead, the main message of the Big Read is that reading a certain type of literary fiction will encourage civic engagement.

Now in its fifth year, the Big Read programme and its partners fund more than 800 programmes across the US. Participants in these programmes are often provided with one of twenty-two books, many of which could be considered part of the traditional American canon, and some of which have also been the source of controversy.[37] For example, titles such as *Fahrenheit 451* (1953) and *The Great Gatsby* (1925) have – as late as the 1980s – been included on lists of banned books. Big Read participants also have access to a centrally produced reading guide and to reading events, such as panel discussions after a film-showing or traditional book group discussions, that sometimes, but not always, provide opportunities for alternative readings of the text.

The NEA website lists the geographical communities that sponsor Big Read programming (www.neabigread.org/communities.php) and hosts a blog where readers can learn about books and programming (www.arts.gov/bigreadblog). The website provides little evidence about the relationships that readers build with one another, but scholarly work has started on reading communities that are formed and facilitated through the Big Read.[38] How best might we critically analyse the relationships that develop between readers, and the factors that play into that process? In the chapters below, the contributors to *Reading Communities from Salons to Cyberspace* explore various manifestations of book clubs and while doing so illustrate an array of research techniques available to scholars interested in the experience of collective reading. The differing lenses reveal the rich history that informs contemporary reading practices.

Theorizing (reading) communities

Recent scholarship on contemporary book clubs critically analyses perhaps the most famous reading group in recent history: Oprah's Book Club.[39] This burgeoning area of study illustrates the diversity of contemporary manifestations of reading communities, and the findings of researchers sometimes question the benefits of shared reading as a practice and as a form of social interaction. Jenny Hartley and Sarah Turvey were two of the first scholars to pose general questions directly to book club members.[40] Hailing the rise in popularity and significance of the clubs as, in their phrase, 'the reading-group movement',[41] Hartley's *Reading Groups*, written for a non-scholarly audience and published in a trade paperback format, provides general information that forms a useful background for an understanding of the cultural, social and educational roles book clubs have played in the last thirty to forty years.

First, Hartley finds that book clubs are comprised primarily of middle-class, well-educated women predominantly over the age of 40. Not surprisingly, considering that social theorists have argued that education and work play a significant role in valuing books and reading,[42] most club members are highly educated. Second, readers report that the search for new knowledge is often a key reason for joining and belonging to a club.[43] They are looking for points of view that differ from their own, and these are made available to them through the varying interpretations and opinions members express when books are being discussed. Third, book clubs read primarily fiction.

Of course, by describing book clubs in this general manner we ignore complexities that are intrinsic to any human relationship, as well as to any relationship between a reader and his or her books. This collection joins a growing body of work that pays critical attention to the social aspects of reading and concentrates on the discussions that take place within groups, their reading lists, and the contexts in which the reading takes place. Several historical studies were discussed above. Other works include Patricia Gregory's comparative analysis of historical and contemporary book clubs in St Louis, Missouri.[44] She explores the social bonds that are formed over time when readers read together for many years, and argues that communal reading is a cultural process that can become a ritual for group members. Contemporary scholarship includes Michelle Winter Sisson's discussion of the educational potential of book clubs.[45] Sisson studies an African-American book club in the American South and concludes that the women read differently as individuals and as a community. Meanwhile, Kimberly Chabot Davis explores the reception strategies of white book club members who read African-American literature.[46] Jane Missner Barstow's 'Reading in Groups: Women's Clubs and College Literature Classes',[47] and Temma Berg's '"What do you Know?"; or, the Question of Reading in Groups and Academic Authority'[48] are comparative studies of reading groups within and outside the academy. While Missner Barstow privileges the level of literary interpretation outside the university classroom, Berg argues that variations in readers' reception are influenced by social position. Linda Griffin's critical ethnography of a romance reading group identified the self-awareness and self-improvement potential in that group,[49] and Norma González's study of a group that read Nancy Drew novels identified female family members and librarians as influential 'literary agents'.[50] Joan Bessman Taylor's work concentrates on the 'discussibility' of book club books.[51] Identifying the process and place between private and social reading as 'the grafted space', Jen Pecoskie presents an original contribution to the understanding of how social factors influence private processes, and vice versa, when readers read.[52] Similarly, Elizabeth Long's analysis is especially important to this collection because it questions the distinction between public and private reading practices while providing opportunities to critically assess the 'moral and ideological dimensions of social identity'.[53] Long persuasively argues that an individual's participation in a book club is based on a *shared* need that informs the individual's sense of identity and contributes to the group's solidarity.

Bringing together scholars who all study shared reading, but who come from varied academic backgrounds and disciplines – communication studies, history, literary studies, leisure studies and occupational therapy – this collection illustrates how a reading community can be conceptualized as emotional, psychological and/or social. As Anna S. Ivy argues in the introduction to Chapter 8, it is naive to generalize about book clubs because they take many forms and serve many purposes. A similar argument can be made about reading communities across centuries and cultures. Members of such communities might attain the emotional gratification that a sense of belonging can provide, or the security of being part of something larger than oneself, or the community might fulfil the individual's need for emotional connections with other people.[54] Community is constructed and maintained socially. The 'commune' is the key social construct that emerges when people build and share connections through a book, or a serial, or a readers' guide, or even a review. Using the term 'community' gets to the heart of the notion that social formations can shape themselves around a text. It helps us recognize the factors at play as community members search for meaning within a text, sort out power structures, and, ultimately, gain the knowledge that comes from exposure to, and discussion of, new and unfamiliar concepts. The reading communities discussed in this collection are diverse, and, coming from different backgrounds, the authors don't necessarily agree on what they mean by the word 'community'. However, while there is no consensus on a definition of 'community' in the collection, we each illustrate that a community is comprised of relationships and that the people involved in these relationships *feel* they have an affiliation with one another.[55] The chapters also cover a wide assortment of readers' relationships with texts in their various forms, and with those involved in the creation, marketing, distribution, collection and analysis of texts. These include readers' relationships with authors; readers' relationships with cultural and social institutions such as publishers, booksellers, mass media, universities, schools and libraries; and readers' relationships with each other, as mediated by texts.

Reading communities across time share certain signifiers: friendship, enlightenment, education. They have in common political and cultural conflicts, both internal and external. Robert Snape's analysis of late nineteenth-century National Home Reading Union (NHRU) groups in

Chapter 3 concludes that 'for many readers the social aspects of the circle meeting were its principal appeal, although for some the circle was valued primarily as a form of self-education or as a means of continuing education for young women who had left school'. In remote areas of Australia, Canada and South Africa, NHRU reading circles enabled 'socially and culturally isolated people to retain intellectual contact through reading'.

The letters that passed between the Bluestocking salon members, which are the focus of Betty Schellenberg's findings in Chapter 1, reveal a different approach to reading from those we see in other accounts of well-educated and socially privileged women. The circle acted as a means by which members were able to continue their education under their own auspices, in defiance of the norms of their time. Acting within a supportive and nurturing atmosphere, members were encouraged by one another not only to become more vocal critics of what they read, but also to seek publication of their own work. The intimate connection between writing and reading that evolved within the Bluestocking community suggests a reconsideration of the circle as simply a community of readers. Upon closer examination, as Schellenberg observes, the Bluestockings illustrate how 'hegemonic gender ideology might be experienced, negotiated, modified, even produced, by a particular group of women' in the eighteenth century. Not only did their reading responses influence how they thought about themselves, their responses to what they read and the critical conversations of that reading become in this case 'cumulative and constructive', leading to new knowledge for each of the participants. Ultimately, the influence of their responses extended well beyond the immediate circle of readers, a remarkable achievement considering the size of the print community during the mid-eighteenth century.

While Schellenberg's readers articulated a pattern of friendship that influenced their reading practices, those readers discussed by Linsey Howie in Chapter 7 described their reading groups – more effusively – as 'nurturing, supportive, accommodating, sharing, safe, accepting, comfortable, tolerant, respectful and non-threatening'. Meanwhile, my own contribution (Chapter 5) questions this utopian idealism of community. The differences that emerge between Howie's book club women and the reader community I studied suggest that the face-to-face environment, nurtured over time, allows for a normalizing process that does not always exist in groups who meet online. With cultural literacy comes agency in a book club, but it is an evolutionary process. The texts change as the readers' life situations change, and the book club setting provides them with an opportunity to introduce a personal element into the dialogue. Tangential discussion within the community need not be limited to personal issues, but can extend to topics of a political, historical or social nature. This is, of course, dependent on the *type* of reading community one belongs to. Whereas Howie's readers meet in each other's homes, the formal structure of 'Great Books' that Daniel Born discusses in Chapter 4 – where the text remains at the centre of analysis – may not allow for this kind of talk. In my study of a virtual YA (young adult) book club, only a few of the members mention personal issues and even fewer discuss politics.

'Space' assumes special significance in the study of reading communities. Where people meet to read or discuss a book influences our understanding of how knowledge is acquired and perhaps even determines the questions we can ask about the process. Quoting Jürgen Habermas, in Chapter 2 Jenny Hartley identifies the importance of the novel and of communal reading in our histories. The process of enlightenment, and the movement of reading from the personal into the public sphere, demanded a critical and public reflection, which was collectively shaped. Familial interactions, such as reading aloud to one another, moved easily into the semi-public sphere of circle members' homes. The movement of familial interactions and specifically that of reading aloud translates easily into the semi-public sphere of circle member's homes, but this intimacy results in a subordination by critics of the cultural importance of the reading circles, largely because the readers were women.

In Chapter 6, 'The Growth of Reading Groups as a Feminine Leisure Pursuit: Cultural Democracy or Dumbing Down?', Anna Kiernan directly confronts the critics of women's reading habits and tastes. She argues that it is specifically the domestic spaces wherein much of women's reading and participation in face-to-face, online or televised book club meetings takes place that critics find problematic. Inevitably it seems, cultural values related to assumptions about the locations of meetings are assigned to reading and the discussions that result from the experience of reading: low cultural status is assigned to book clubs that meet in a home or a pub, higher cultural status is endowed upon book discussions in the academy. Also, like Ivy, Kiernan is especially interested in the cultural tensions that ensue when books and television encounter one another.

In this collection, 'space' does not only signify the home or other meeting venue, but refers as well to the wider geography that the book, the text, can occupy. In Chapter 3, Robert Snape follows the movement not only of texts, but of an institutionalized reading programme that we can broadly interpret as a cultural text. From its origin in Great Britain to its various iterations in the colonies of Australia, Canada and South Africa, the NHRU promoted fixed ideologies and encouraged normative cultural practices. Snape demonstrates that the communities that formed around NHRU-distributed reading material and texts and the material left behind by members' friends and family, served to homogenize the actual and imagined communities that developed in the colonies.

The transnational character of reading communities is also addressed by co-authors Fuller, Squires and Rehberg Sedo in Chapter 9, 'Marionettes and Puppeteers? The Relationship between Book Club Readers and Publishers', where we follow the marketing efforts of publishing houses and the international communication networks of book club readers.

The relationship between social institutions and formal and informal reading communities becomes especially evident when studying the social and economic pressures that people faced in the eighteenth, nineteenth and early twentieth centuries. In 'Marionettes and Puppeteers', we are reminded that the educational reforms of the late nineteenth and early twentieth centuries played a central role in creating new readers and thus a new market for reading materials. In his chapter, Snape argues that 'while repressive legislation was deployed to regulate what ordinary people read in the early years of the nineteenth century, coercive measures were inappropriate in later decades as economic progress depended upon a literate population with ready access to printed materials'. Like the 'Great Books Program' that was the brainchild of Mortimer Adler and Robert Maynard Hutchins a century later, prescribed reading programmes were meant to provide lists of acceptable literature and instructions on how to read the books – and talk about them – correctly. Collaborations remained strong between state agencies such as the London authority and, until its demise, the NHRU. Interestingly, while the ideals of British nationhood were successfully conveyed across oceans with the Union, the priority of maintaining formal educational ties was not.

Crossing disciplinary boundaries in communal reading scholarship

In *Old Books & New Histories: an Orientation to Studies in Book & Print Culture,* Leslie Howsam provides a thorough and succinct synopsis of the contested historical and theoretical foundations of scholarly inquiry into book and print traditions.[56] She shows how the convergence of the core disciplines of history, bibliography and literary scholarship led to a new area of study known as 'Book History'. More recently, the increasingly interdisciplinary nature of fields such as cultural studies, communication studies, political science and sociology – to mention just a few – has influenced how scholars approach and regard terms such as 'history' and 'books'. *Reading Communities from Salons to Cyberspace* provides unique insights into the evolution of the study of book and print culture by guiding the reader through the span of time and across the varied geographies with which students of book history engage. The collection brings together scholarship that investigates and interrogates reading communities, and suggests divergent methods of enquiry that we can use to explore collective reading practices and formations. In assembling this collection, we are aware that crossing disciplinary boundaries is not always elegant and can be messy – even controversial – but we are cognizant too of the richness that different theoretical assumptions and methodological practices bring to our attempt to become better acquainted with one another as readers.

By interrogating reading communities from 1740 to 2009 we illustrate how methods of inquiry that have proven useful in creating a better understanding of the power, agency and experience of reading at the individual and collective levels have advanced in step with the technology, and yet remained consistent over time.[57] Readership studies have traditionally referred to readers' notes and marginalia, along with letters and diaries. But such studies have evolved in their approach and researchers in this area now also examine the (sometimes archived) content of listservs, blogs and websites, not to mention radio and television transcripts, in order to construct their analyses. These new technologies converge to create novel ways of experiencing reading and interpreting readers' responses to and interactions with literature.[58]

A collection that focuses on communities of readers that have existed over time and across geographies thus provides a unique opportunity to examine the diversity of forms that book culture can assume. We hope the reader comes away from this book with a better understanding of what has happened and what can happen when people engage with a single book or study the same genre of literature. The individual contributions included in these pages pay special attention to elements of Robert Darnton's oft-cited, and sometimes criticized, communication circuit model of book history.[59] Like Darnton's original model, the collection as a whole poses questions about how economic, social, ontological and political issues can influence readers. It illustrates Thomas R. Adams and Nicolas Barker's 'new model' of book history, which allows us to consider readers who may read individually, but who in the end are members of a wider social network that takes part in a form of shared reading.[60] Like Adams and Barker, we position the book as the unifying, central object of our investigations but our methods of analysis of what happens with the book are in constant dialogical collaboration across disciplines, eras and continents.

The chronologically arranged chapters in this volume illustrate the many ways in which books have been put to use, over time and within a variety of cultural contexts. The discussions take into account a great many factors – among them gender, economic and political climates, and the means by which knowledge is produced and spread – as they build an argument in support of the notion that all reading is rooted in the social. The work thus addresses through investigation of groups, gender, generation, religious beliefs and community membership Roger Chartier's call to understand the diversity in apprehension, handling and comprehension of books.[61] The chapters below examine not only the meanings that readers take from what they read, but also what it means to a society to have members who are literate. Analysis of reading communities bound together under one cover allows us to better consider the nexus of power across time and space, and helps us to identify the material and ideological struggles and structural inequalities in a given book or print culture. These cultures, of course, mirror the wider culture in which we live or have lived.

Schellenberg's 'Reading in an Epistolary Community in Eighteenth-Century England' suggests that it is not unwarranted to regard the correspondence between members of the Bluestocking salon as testimony of their responses to their reading, especially if we consider these writings in tandem with the perceptions recorded by readers outside the circle. Schellenberg analyses the content of letters and compares them to edited collections of correspondence, but the focus of her inquiry is not necessarily on individual reading selections and responses. Rather, she examines epistolary exchanges that seek to alter or re-shape responses by correspondents and the group to their reading. By widening the analysis to include not only the edited exchanges between the women, but also the letters themselves and outsider commentary, Schellenberg extends our current assumptions regarding Bluestocking reading and shows us how these women writers and readers simultaneously negotiated with and resisted the cultural community of which they were members.

Working with Pierre Bourdieu's theory of cultural fields, Jenny Hartley temporally recreates reading reception of Charles Dickens's serial *Little Dorrit*. Her experiment uncovers reading techniques with which we might not be familiar: 'double-reading', 'back-reading' and 'art of memory'. Taking into account the time that has elapsed since the book's original publication in serial form, 'Nineteenth Century Reading Groups in Britain and the Community of the Text: an Experiment with *Little Dorrit*' demonstrates how readers will respond to literary works in different ways depending on the format of publication. Hartley also looks at a modern parallel in the case of Stephen King's *The Green Mile*, and discusses the variety of assumptions that Dickens and King make about the literacy levels and reading practices of their readers.

Robert Snape's account of the nineteenth- and twentieth-century British-based prescribed reading programme, the NHRU, employs an analysis of association newsletters, magazines and reports, references to the NHRU that appear in memoirs, along with interviews with living members, to argue that when the programme travelled to the colonies, readers themselves determined the purpose and function of communal reading. While there are no organized NHRU archives and the organization's history is therefore somewhat obscure, Snape's contribution demonstrates how such available mixed methods enhance our understanding of the impact that communal reading has had. In 'Reading Across the Empire: the National Home Reading Union Abroad' we find a rich account of institutionalized reading programmes that tells us much about the transnational migration of social and cultural norms and the ideologies inherent in them.

Daniel Born's 'Utopian Civic-Mindedness: Robert Maynard Hutchins, Mortimer Adler, and the Great Books Enterprise' is a case study of the social and cultural assumptions and ideals underlying the foundation in 1948 of a substantial American bibliographic project called Syntopicon. Born asks us to consider how the idea of Great Books functions within the pedagogical traditions of higher education. Is 'commitment to the Great Books the enemy of progressive education ... or in fact a foundation *for* it?' he asks. As Born points out, while today the discussion of books among teacher and students is 'standard operating procedure in the best classes', when Mortimer Adler brought John Erskine's methods to the University of Chicago, where Robert Maynard Hutchins was president, it was, as a theory and practice, 'nothing short of revolutionary'. By presenting documentary evidence of Hutchins's ideological, professional and cultural accomplishments in the shape of letters, biographies and institutional documents, Born offers a history of twentieth-century education.

Mortimer Adler's 102 Ideas (Syntopicon) constituted an ideological platform promoted and perpetuated through formal and informal reading programmes that were supported by people with cultural and/or economic influence, both of which Adler possessed. It was also the starting point for the 'Great Books Program', whose ideological genesis, as Born observes, can be traced to the Syntopicon, an educational toolkit 'powerful enough to save the world from self-destruction'. Born situates the project within the larger social movements following the Second World War, demonstrating the liberal philosophy of the programme's co-founders, who saw a direct link between literature and democracy, and democracy and freedom.

Following upon Daniel Born's broad social enquiry, two chapters bring the collection into the twenty-first century. Anna Kiernan (Chapter 6) in 'The Growth of Reading Groups as a Feminine Leisure Pursuit: Cultural Democracy or Dumbing Down?' and I (in Chapter 5) both make use of social theory to help explain the way in which cultural authority works in popular media to determine what is viewed as worthy literary work. While both chapters analyse online book discussion, Kiernan bases her study on the UK talk show sensation 'Richard and Judy's Book Club' and to a degree, 'Oprah's Book Club', while I use as my starting point an ethnographic study that gathers evidence through participant observation, interviews and a poll of an online book club of Young Adult Literature enthusiasts. This cyber study demonstrates that discussions about books that take place in a virtual YA book club setting can shape cultural production when certain members, who possess real and symbolic power, express a preference for specific books.

In Chapter 7, Linsey Howie undertakes an investigation of individual reader behaviour and the familiar notion of contemporary book clubs in Australia. Using quantitative survey data coupled with personal interviews, Howie interrogates the relationship between the isolated individual reading experience and the social factors of group reading. Her contribution, 'Speaking Subjects: Developing Identities in Women's Reading Communities', draws on philosophy, sociology, psychoanalysis and feminist theory to help us understand the 'relational ways of being' and 'subjects in process' that members of women's book clubs in Australia experience.

In 'Leading Questions: Interpretative Guidelines in Contemporary Popular Reading Culture' (Chapter 8), Anna S. Ivy applies her skills as a literary critic to the language of reading guides produced by book publishers and television programme producers to determine how these documents influence reading practices and direct readers' responses. Do readers use the guides that are found online, in the books themselves, or on shelves in bookstores? Obviously, readers can use them however they want, but like the text itself, the guides are a stimulus for discussion. Ivy explores the ways in which texts – including televised book club discussions – and reader guides interact to generate new meanings, and suggests, as well, that television has created a new category of readers. This emerging faction of readers gives a new twist on a familiar conundrum – how to account for 'high-' and 'low-brow' reading tastes and practices.

Ivy's analysis of the questions posed by reading group guides also proposes a link between pedagogical ideals and philosophies and the expectations that can arise within certain disciplines of study. She concludes that 'there is no clear distinction between reading for pleasure and reading for intellectual engagement; rather, they are linked, the classroom functioning as a place wherein pleasure, as well as insight, can be taught'.

In a critique of the commodified relationship between publishers and book club readers, Fuller, Squires and Rehberg Sedo (Chapter 9) make use of interviews with publishers and a quantitative online survey to create the first study that examines the process of book distribution, marketing, consumption and reception in Canada, the US and the UK at the turn of the last century. Like Ivy's contribution, 'Marionettes and Puppeteers? The Relationship between Book Club Readers and Publishers' demonstrates the influence that book clubs exert in the contemporary publishing milieu. In the past 50 years the book publishing industry has undergone massive changes, and this has had a huge impact on the relationships that publishers enjoy with readers. Regardless of the kind of club or group that readers might belong to, their reading choices will be influenced by a wide variety of factors: from personal recommendations to mass media promotional campaigns that can propel a book to best-seller status. Because they function as a social communications network, primed to spread the word, book clubs represent a tempting new target market for publishers. Yet, to some extent, book clubs and their readers remain immune to the publishing industry's marketing efforts.

'Despite its richness, the history of the book is not *l'histoire totale*, and nor is all historical, literary and material-text scholarship reducible to the study of book and print culture', writes Leslie Howsam in her appeal for mutual respect across the disciplinary boundaries that compose book and print culture studies.[62] This collection, while maybe not '*l'histoire totale*' of reading communities, nonetheless presents cogent and lively discussions of a wide variety of communal reading practices, and in the process demonstrates that intellectual rewards accrue when we set aside obstructive disciplinary, theoretical and methodological assumptions. In reconstructing reading communities across time and space, we hope to make other readers knowable to you.

Notes

1. Leah Price, 'Reading: the State of the Discipline', *Book History* 7, 1 (2004): 310.
2. Cathy N. Davidson, 'Towards a History of Books and Readers', *American Quarterly* 40, 1 (1988): 15.
3. See in particular, Robert Darnton, *The Literary Underground of the Old Regime* (Cambridge, MA and London: Harvard University Press, 1982); Davidson, 'Towards a History of Books'; Davidson, *Reading in America: Literature and Social History* (Baltimore: Johns Hopkins University Press, 1989); Davidson, *Revolution and the Word: the Rise of the Novel in America,* expanded edn (New York: Oxford University Press, 2004); Michael T. Gilmore, *American Romanticism and the Marketplace* (Chicago: University of Chicago Press, 1985); William J. Gilmore-Lehne, *Reading Becomes a Necessity of Life: Material and Cultural Life in Rural New England, 1780–1835* (Knoxville: University of Tennessee Press, 1989); Ronald J. Zboray and Mary Saracino Zboray, *Everyday Ideas: Socioliterary Experience among Antebellum New Englanders* (Knoxville: University of Tennessee Press, 2006).
4. Madeleine Jeay, ed., *Les Évangiles des quenouilles*, cited in Alberto Manguel, *A History of Reading* (Harmondsworth: Penguin, 1996), 117. See also Kiernan, Chapter 6 below.
5. William St Clair, *The Reading Nation in the Romantic Period* (Cambridge: Cambridge University Press, 2004), 254; Stephen Colclough, *Consuming Texts: Readers and Reading Communities, 1695–1870* (Basingstoke and New York: Palgrave Macmillan, 2007).
6. Jennifer Phegley, *Educating the Proper Woman Reader: Victorian Family Literary Magazines and the Cultural Health of the Nation* (Columbus: Ohio State University Press, 2004).
7. Thomas Augst, 'Introduction: American Libraries and Agencies of Culture', in *The Library as an Agency of Culture*, ed. Thomas Augst and Wayne A. Wiegand (Lawrence, KS: American Studies, 2001), 5–22.
8. Kenneth M. Price and Susan Belasco Smith, 'Introduction', in *Periodical Literature in Nineteenth-Century America*, ed. Kenneth M. Price and Susan Belasco Smith (Charlottesville, VA: University Press of Virginia, 1995), 3–16; Joan D. Hedrick, *Harriet Beecher Stowe: a Life* (New York: Oxford University Press, 1994), 73–123; Barbara Sicherman, *Well-Read Lives: How Books Inspired a Generation of American Women* (Chapel Hill: University of North Carolina Press, 2010), 57–75; 79–108; 165–92.
9. Zboray and Saracino Zboray, *Everyday Ideas*, 129–31; Elizabeth McHenry, '"Dreaded Eloquence": the Origins and Rise of African American Literary Societies and Libraries', *Harvard Library Review* 6, 2 (1995): 32–56; Elizabeth McHenry, *Forgotten Readers: Recovering the Lost History of African American Literary Societies*, New Americanists (Durham, NC: Duke University Press, 2002).
10. General readership income is discussed in Jon P. Klancher, *The Making of English Reading Audiences, 1790–1832* (Madison: University of Wisconsin Press, 1987).

11. Anne Ruggles Gere, *Intimate Practices: Literacy and Cultural Work in U.S. Women's Clubs, 1880–1920* (Urbana and Chicago: University of Illinois Press, 1997), 5.
12. Barbara Sicherman, 'Sense and Sensibility: a Case Study of Women's Reading in Late-Victorian America', in *Reading in America*, ed. Cathy Davison (Baltimore: Johns Hopkins University Press, 1989), 209.
13. Karen Blair, *The Clubwoman as Feminist: True Womanhood Redefined, 1868–1914* (New York: Holmes & Meier).
14. Ibid.
15. Ruggles Gere, *Intimate Practices*; Christine Boyko-Head, 'Stay at Home Writers: the Women's Literary Club of St Catherine's', paper presented at 1999 Popular Culture Conference in San Diego, California.
16. Heather Murray, 'Great Works and Good Works: the Toronto Women's Literary Club 1877–1883', *Historical Studies in Education/Revue d'Histoire de l'Education* 11, 1 (1999): 75–95; *Come, Bright Improvement! The Literary Societies of Nineteenth-Century Ontario* (Toronto: University of Toronto Press, 2002).
17. Tahera Aftab, 'Reform Societies and Women's Education in Northern India in the Later 19th Century', *Journal of the Pakistan Historical Society*, 35, 2 (1987): 121–35; P.J. Prinsloo, 'Die Pietermaritzburgse Debat En Letterkundige Vereniging, 1908–1918', *Historia (South Africa)*, 40, 1 (1995): 75–95; Ericka Kim Verba, 'The Circulo de Lectura de Senoras (Ladies' Reading Circle) and the Club de Senoras (Ladies' Club) of Santiago, Chile: Middle- and Upper-Class Feminist Conversations (1915–1920)', *Journal of Women's History*, 7, 3 (1995): 6–33.
18. DeNel Rehberg Sedo, 'Badges of Wisdom, Spaces for Being: a Study of Contemporary Women's Book Clubs', PhD dissertation, Simon Fraser University, Burnaby, BC (2004).
19. Sicherman, 'Sense and Sensibility', 209.
20. Ellen Gruber Garvey, 'The Power of Recirculation: Scrapbooks and the Reception of Nineteenth-Century Books', in *New Directions in American Reception Study*, ed. Philip Goldstein and James L. Machor (Oxford and New York: Oxford University Press, 2008), 211–31; Sarah A. Wadsworth, 'Social Reading, Social Worth and the Social Function of Literacy in Louisa May Alcott's "May Flowers"', in *Reading Women Literary Figures and Cultural Icons from the Victorian Age to the Present*, ed. Jennifer Phegley and Janet Badia (Toronto: University of Toronto Press, 2006), 149–67. See also DeNel Rehberg Sedo, 'Case Study: Margaret McMicking and the Victoria Literary Society', in *History of the Book in Canada, Vol. II, 1840–1918*, ed. Yvan Lamonde, Patricia Lockhart Fleming and Fiona A. Black (Toronto: University of Toronto Press, 2005), 479–81, along with Robert Snape's chapter below on the National Home Reading Union, and Ruggles Gere's chronicle of various literary societies in the United States, *Intimate Practices*.
21. Benedict Anderson, *Imagined Communities: Reflections on the Origin and Spread of Nationalism*, revised edn (London: Verso, 1991).
22. McHenry, *Forgotten Readers*; Rehberg Sedo, 'Reading and Study Groups', in *History of the Book in Canada*, V. III, ed. Carole Gerson and Jacques Michon (Toronto: University of Toronto Press, 2006), 509–12.
23. Jack Quarter, 'James John Harpell: an Adult Education Pioneer', *Canadian Journal for the Study of Adult Education* 14, 1 (2000): 89–112.
24. Rosabel Fast, *The Impact of Sponsorship: the University of Manitoba's Rural Adult Education Program, 1936–1945* (Edmonton: University of Alberta, 1991).

25. Jean L Preer, 'Exploring the American Idea at the New York Public Library', in *The Library as an Agency of Culture*, ed. Thomas Augst and Wayne A. Wiegand (Lawrence, KS: American Studies, 2001), 135–54.
26. Murray, *Come, Bright Improvement!*; Snape, Chapter 3 below; John C. Scott, 'The Chautauqua Vision of Liberal Education', *History of Education* 34, 1 (January 2005): 41–59.
27. Rehberg Sedo, 'Badges'.
28. Karen Joy Fowler, *The Jane Austen Book Club* (New York: Putnam, 2004); Elizabeth Noble, *The Reading Group* (New York: Perennial, 2005); Lorna Landvik, *Angry Housewives Eating Bon Bons* (New York: Ballantine Books, 2003).
29. Kathy Griffin, *Official Book Club Selection: a Memoir According to Kathy Griffin* (New York: Ballantine Books, 2009).
30. See www.msnbc.msn.com/id/3041344/ and www.bcnews.go.com/GMA/Books (accessed 2 December 2009).
31. See Anna S. Ivy (Chapter 8) and Anna Kiernan (Chapter 6) below.
32. See, for example, Karen Hellenkson and Kristina Busse, eds, *Fan Fiction and Fan Communities in the Age of the Internet: New Essays* (Jefferson, NC: McFarland & Co., 2006).
33. For a critique of the changing cultural hierarchy terrain, see Sven Birkets's response to LitBlogs at www.boston.com/news/globe/ideas/articles/2007/07/29/lost_in_the_blogosphere/?page=full (accessed 31 July 2007).
34. National Endowment for the Arts, *NewsRoom*, at www:nea.gov/news/news05/BigReadAnnounce.html (accessed 10 October 2009).
35. On the eve of his departure, Chairman Gioia and the NEA released the latest NEA report, 'Reading on the Rise: a New Chapter in American Literacy', claiming that reading novels, short stories, poems, or plays in print or online has increased nearly 4 per cent in four years. The brochure can be accessed at: www.arts.gov/research/ReadingonRise.pdf (accessed 31 January 2009).
36. Catherine Sheldrick Ross, Lynne (E.F.) McKechnie and Paulette M. Rothbauer, *Reading Matters: What the Research Reveals about Reading, Libraries, and Community* (Westport, CT: Libraries Unlimited, 2005), 23. For a clever and entertaining analysis of the *Reading at Risk* and its follow up study, see Leah Price, 'You are What You Read', *New York Times Book Review*, 23 December 2007, www.nytimes.com/2007/12/23/books/review/Price-t.html?ref=review (accessed 4 October 2008).
37. The current list can be found at http://www.neabigread.org/ (accessed 23 December 2010).
38. See 'Searching for good news about American literary culture' at: www.beyondthebookproject.org/content_list.asp?itemtype=paper&section=0001000100060001&page=3 (accessed 3 January 2011).
39. R. Mark Hall, 'The "Oprahfication" of Literacy: Reading "Oprah's Book Club"', *College English* 65, 6 (2003): 646–67; Kimberly Chabot Davis, 'Oprah's Book Club and the Politics of Cross-Racial Empathy', *International Journal of Cultural Studies* 7, 4 (2004): 399–419; Cecilia Konchar Farr and Jaime Harker, eds, *The Oprah Affect: Critical Essays on Oprah's Book Club* (Albany, NY: State University of New York Press, 2008); Konchar Farr, *Reading Oprah: How Oprah's Book Club Changed the Way America Reads* (Albany: State University of New York Press, 2005).

40. Jenny Hartley, *Reading Groups* (Oxford: Oxford University Press, 2001).
41. Book clubs are commonly called reading groups in the UK.
42. Pierre Bourdieu, *Distinction: a Social Critique of the Judgment of Taste*, trans. Richard Nice (Cambridge, MA: Harvard University Press, 1984); Bourdieu, *The Field of Cultural Production* (New York: Polity Press, 1993); Tony Bennett, Michael Emmison and John Frow, *Accounting for Tastes* (Cambridge: Cambridge University Press, 1999).
43. Hartley, *Reading Groups*, 44–5.
44. Patricia Gregory, 'Women's Experience of Reading in St Louis Book Clubs', PhD dissertation, Saint Louis University, Saint Louis, MO (2000).
45. Michelle Diane Winter Sisson, 'The Role of Reading in the Lives of African American Women who are Members of a Book Club', PhD dissertation, University of Georgia, Athens (1996).
46. Kimberly Chabot Davis, 'White Book Clubs and African American Literature: the Promise and Limitations of Cross-Racial Empathy', in *LIT: Literature Interpretation Theory* 19, 2 (2008): 155–86.
47. Jane Missner Barstow, 'Reading in Groups: Women's Clubs and College Literature Classes', *Publishing Research Quarterly* (Winter, 2003): 3–17.
48. Temma Berg, '"What do you Know?"; or, the Question of Reading in Groups and Academic Authority', in *LIT: Literature Interpretation Theory* 19, 2 (2008): 123–54.
49. Linda Griffin, 'An Analysis of Meaning Creation through the Integration of Sociology and Literature: a Critical Ethnography of a Romance Reading Group', PhD dissertation, University of Houston, Texas (1999).
50. Norma Linda González, 'Nancy Drew: Girls' Literature, Women's Reading Groups, and the Transmission of Literacy', *Journal of Literacy Research* 29, 2 (1997): 221–51.
51. Joan Bessman Taylor, 'When Adults Talk in Circles: Book Groups and Contemporary Reading Practices', PhD dissertation, University of Illinois at Urbana-Champaign (2007); 'Readers' Advisory – Good for What?' *Reference & User Services Quarterly* 46, 4 (2007): 33; and 'Readers' Advisory – Good for What? Non-Appeal, Discussability, and Book Groups (Part 2)', *Reference & User Services Quarterly* 47, 1 (2007): 26.
52. Jen (J.L.) Pecoskie, 'The Solitary, Social, and "Grafted Spaces" of Pleasure Reading: Exploring Reading Practices from the Experiences of Adult, Self-Identified Lesbian, Gay, Bisexual, and Queer Readers and Book Club Members', PhD dissertation, University of Western Ontario (2009).
53. Elizabeth Long, *Book Clubs: Women and the Uses of Reading in Everyday Life* (Chicago: University of Chicago Press, 2003), 34.
54. David W. McMillan and David M. Chavis, 'Sense of Community: a Definition and Theory', *Journal of Community Psychology* 14 (1986): 6–23; David W. McMillan, 'Sense of Community', *Journal of Community Psychology* 24, 4 (1996): 315–25.
55. Because there are so many debates about how to define community, especially within the field of sociology, I have decided to employ a loose interpretation of a model outlined by McMillan and Chavis 'Sense of Community'.
56. Leslie Howsam, *Old Books & New Histories: an Orientation to Studies in Book & Print Culture* (Toronto: University of Toronto Press, 2006).
57. Judith Walkowitz cited in Howsam, *Old Books & New Histories*, 12.

58. See James L. Machor, *Readers in History: Nineteenth-Century American Literature and the Contexts of Response* (Baltimore: Johns Hopkins University Press, 1993) and James L. Machor and Philip Goldstein *Reception Study: From Literary Theory to Cultural Studies* (New York: Routledge, 2001) for theorizing a new historicism in reading reception studies.
59. Robert Darnton, 'What is the History of Books?', in *The Kiss of Lamourette: Reflections in Cultural History* (New York: Norton, 1990). For a useful overview of Darnton's model and the concerns it has raised, see Howsam, *Old Books & New Histories*, especially 29–48.
60. Thomas R. Adams and Nicolas Barker, 'A New Model for the Study of the Book', in *A Potencie of Life: Books in Society*, ed. Nicolas Barker (London: British Library, 1993), 12.
61. Roger Chartier, *The Order of Books: Readers, Authors, and Libraries in Europe between the Fourteenth and Eighteenth Centuries*, trans. Lydia G. Cochrane (Stanford: Stanford University Press, 1994).
62. Howsam, *Old Books & New Histories*, 26.

1
Reading in an Epistolary Community in Eighteenth-Century England

Betty A. Schellenberg

The particular scene of reading examined in this first chapter is that of the Bluestocking network of the second half of the eighteenth century in Britain; more broadly, the study of this reading group invites consideration of sociable reading as mediated across physical absence, the dialogic creation of reader identities, and the negotiation of cultural norms – issues central to the study of collaborative reading across temporal and geographical boundaries. The principal Bluestocking hostesses, Elizabeth Montagu (1718–1800), Elizabeth Vesey (1715?–91), and Frances Boscawen (1719–1805), established their gatherings in London in the 1750s; this movement attained the height of its popularity and cultural power in the 1770s, but continued with a second generation of hostesses and groups into the 1780s and 1790s. Characterized by a focus on rational conversation in explicit opposition to 'superficial' amusements such as card playing, the Bluestocking circles brought together wealthy and professional-class women (and men) of intellectual tastes, Anglican religious practice, and broadly conservative social views. As prominent women of their time, the Bluestockings have been the subject of renewed recent attention for their political, social, and literary influence; among others, Gary Kelly and Harriet Guest have argued for their significance as feminists, a significance that has often been overlooked because of their social conservatism.[1]

Topics of discussion at Bluestocking gatherings certainly included the latest publications, whether in poetry, history, or religious controversy. Established authors such as Montagu's sister Sarah Robinson Scott (1721–95), a novelist and historian, and the classicist and poet Elizabeth Carter (1717–1806), whose translation of the works of the Greek Stoic Epictetus and of Algarotti's guide to Newton's philosophy led her contemporary John Duncombe to describe her as the joy of Plato and the admiration of Newton,[2] were members of the group; aspiring and needy authors such as Sarah Fielding, a young Edmund Burke, and the poet Ann Yearsley were among those it patronized. Clearly, this was a reading community. This chapter will focus on the collective reading of Montagu, Scott, Carter, and Catherine Talbot (1721–70), examining their practical exchanges of knowledge about books, their dialogic development of readerly identities and of critical judgements, the range of their reading, and their responses to the novel and to women novelists in particular. I begin, however, with a brief discussion of theoretical and methodological issues.

Women readers as writers and agents of culture

Establishing a fuller picture of this community's reading promises to test the premises of the period's own extensive discussion of women as readers, a discussion which tended, inconsistently, to idealize the woman who devoted her leisure time to reading as a form of improvement and harmless pleasure, and to express anxiety about the possibility that women's reading would seduce them away from the fulfilment of their private domestic duties. In other words, as women formed an increasingly visible proportion of the reading public, there was considerable anxiety over the positive or negative effects of their reading on their fulfilment of an increasingly defined domestic social role.[3] Lawrence Klein has observed that 'even when theory was against them, women of the eighteenth century had [conscious] public dimensions to their lives'; the spaces created by social reading in the eighteenth century, whether in relatively 'public' domestic settings such as salons, or in more restricted family circles, or even in the virtual dimension of the familiar letter, can be theorized as one means by which women participated as agents in the creation of a public sphere of letters.[4] Speaking of women as writers about reading, Terry Lovell has noted that 'writing is a social practice ... There are many positions within society and culture from which writing is not only possible, but sometimes, enjoined, and some of the most significant of these are occupied by women.'[5] The Bluestocking community of women, then, offers an ideal site for an examination of how a hegemonic gender ideology might be experienced, negotiated, modified, even produced, by a particular group of women through their conversation – and their writing.

Indeed, any attempt to determine more fully how reading functioned in the Bluestocking salons of eighteenth-century England raises the methodological problem that our primary record of Bluestocking reading, the voluminous manuscript correspondences between Elizabeth Montagu and other Bluestockings such as Elizabeth Carter, Elizabeth Vesey, and Sarah Scott, records their reading and responses when they are not physically together in London. Accounts of the gatherings of group members when together are limited to generalized descriptions of the guests and the atmosphere, whether to distant members or to the general public. This relative absence of a firsthand record can, however, be reformulated as an opportunity to examine the role of reading in epistolary communities of women. Such a project is eminently feasible given the fact that the demands of family roles, business responsibilities, ill health, and limited means led to constant physical displacement and lengthy periods of isolation in country houses or provincial towns. The geographical mobility of these women's lives was countered by more enabling material conditions of the period, including the rapid improvement of both roads and the postal system in the eighteenth century, the simultaneous development of efficient distribution methods for print materials, and the growth of provincial bookselling and of libraries. Thus the necessity of frequent separation, together with the expansion of opportunities for exchange of reading materials and accounts of reading combined to create remarkably stable epistolary communities built around shared reading – in the case of the sisters Elizabeth Robinson Montagu and Sarah Robinson Scott, across a span of fifty-five years, from their first separation as women of about twenty to the death of Scott in 1795 at the age of 77.[6]

Although the chain of the Robinson sisters' correspondence is relatively complete, a second methodological issue arises from the fact that most of the other records are available only in the selective and silently edited versions prepared by early nineteenth-century editors, who were generally family members concerned with preserving – indeed, correcting or enhancing – the reputations of their illustrious forebears in the reactionary aftermath of the French Revolution. The effect of this spirit on the edited letters' accounts of reading is to leave us with a picture of women who seldom concerned themselves with writing that belonged to suspect genres such as the romance or novel. Fortunately, a comparison of the manuscript and print versions of the Montagu correspondence, edited by her nephew and heir Matthew Montagu, sheds light on these editorial principles. The editor describes himself as guided by 'the wish of producing nothing which may cast a less favourable light upon [Montagu's] disposition', and as 'strik[ing] out many insignificant passages relating to private concerns, and many anecdotes and observations of a personal nature' (2.314).[7] As a result, much of Montagu's informal, allusive, and cumulative conversation with her sister, a conversation that contains many of her references to women's writing, is submerged or omitted altogether. With Montagu Pennington, Carter's nephew and Montagu's godson, similarly promising 'not ... to publish any thing which his respected relation would have thought improper',[8] the Montagu Collection becomes an invaluable manuscript resource.

This chapter will therefore focus particularly upon manuscript records of Montagu and Scott's discussions of their reading, supplemented, in the knowledge of those editorial principles, by the published correspondences between the sisters, between Talbot and Carter, and between Montagu and Carter. Although each body of correspondence forms a continuous dialogue between two individuals, frequent cross-references stitch these dialogues to one another. For example, Scott first met Carter through Montagu, benefiting from her connections with London booksellers and sending regular greetings through Montagu to her, although they themselves never established a particular closeness; Talbot later writes to Carter that she 'love[s] Mrs. Montagu for the justice she does to your merit' (2.270), and Carter wishes the dying Talbot had invited Scott to visit when too ill to go to her (3.163–4). Between them, these four women represent influential segments of the author-supporting and book-reading publics of the time: the well-connected, if not always personally wealthy, metropolitan-based woman with the leisure, education, and tastes to support socially worthy writing projects, and the well-educated professional with his or her own writing and publishing experience.[9] I will focus, not on the individual reading choices and responses of these women, but rather on the ways in which their epistolary exchanges worked to modify individual positions and shape group responses to genres, modes, individual authors, and categories of authors. It was this collectivity, after all, which lent so much power to the group that Charles Burney, rightly or wrongly, would urge his very successful author-daughter Frances to suppress a stage comedy that might be seen as attacking them.[10]

Collective reading and the construction of a readerly identity

Even in its unedited manuscript state, the letter itself, as the medium of exchange for this epistolary community, must of course not be assumed to open a transparent window into the writers' 'true' thoughts and responses. Indeed, the familiar letter in the eighteenth century was a well-established and highly theorized genre; both prominent authors such as Pope, who arranged to have his edited letters published, and educated readers from social levels as humble as that of the servant, who read epistolary novels like *Pamela* with enthusiasm and created a market for letter-writing manuals for themselves, were conscious of the unique capacity of the familiar letter to fashion a desirable self-portrait for a reading audience while revealing a private self that might exceed the constraints of form. If the embodied interactions of the salons were not without their formal structures (Montagu's gatherings were noted for their large, fixed circles, whereas Vesey's were characterized by a deliberately disrupted seating arrangement), the disembodied communication of the letter was also required to work within the forms of genre and language. In the Bluestocking letters, shared reading becomes the foundation not only of self-characterization, but also and simultaneously the common material from which a frame of reference and a culture of reading and response can be constructed collectively. Over time in the correspondence studied here, oppositional self-characterizations are interwoven with a dialectical approach to criticism that allows the writers to experiment in the process of working towards congruent final views.

At the level of the reading materials that enabled this epistolary community's reading, the women worked collectively to alert each other to new books, to find and obtain copies of them, and to exchange materials. Montagu facilitated much of her sister's reading, which for many years was limited by the interdependent factors of her straitened circumstances and her residence in country towns; repeated exchanges show Montagu looking out in London for books that might be of professional use to Scott, whether a recent French novel that might be translated, an up-to-date French dictionary, or source texts for one of her historical biographies.[11] Similarly, Talbot in London might send Carter a list of the season's new books (1.146). Books and shorter works are sent back and forth constantly, in packages of country produce and forgotten clothing. At times, conversation was stymied by a book's going astray or by the unavailability of postal franks and the prohibitive cost of postage for one of the correspondents. In their later years, considerations of both cost and convenience led the very wealthy Montagu and the relatively poor Scott each to take advantage of the burgeoning number of circulating libraries and more selective subscription libraries as a strategy for gaining access to both light entertainment and more serious material while avoiding the costs of purchasing books. Since, in Montagu's terms, 'the fee simple of a novel is hardly worth the expence of the purchase', 'a Leasehold is certainly the best tenure for a Novel', according to Scott, who continues, 'at Norwich they lett them out for a penny per day at numberless circulating Libraries. At the great Library there are scarcely any Novels, & the subscription is a formal affair, but taking them all together one gets a pretty sufficient supply both of sense & nonsense' (14 Oct. [1790] mo6205; 24 Oct. [1790] mo5467).[12]

Catherine Talbot's letters provide the most detailed glimpse of physical scenes of reading. The highly sociable nature of her life as a member of the household of Thomas Secker, Bishop of London and later Archbishop of Canterbury, suggests how reading functioned in a physically embodied community: her reading is sorted according to the genre appropriate to morning walks, her mother's dressing, mixed company 'en famille' after dinner (the manuscript of the first volumes of Richardson's *Sir Charles Grandison* is read in this way [2.65]), and long stretches of retirement in the country (she saves what she calls 'the second history of *Tom Jones*' for this purpose [1.320]). At the same time, description of such embodied reading often functions to reveal its limitations in comparison to the exchange by letter between two sophisticated readers of compatible intellects and tastes. Talbot writes to Carter,

> Is it possible you should not have seen that admirable copy of verses [that is, Isaac Hawkins Browne's *The Fire-side*] yet? If I can get one in time I will send it you, for though you should have got it before, you are certainly more worthy of having such a thing twice over, than some fine folks I shewed it to yesterday, were of hearing it once. It is really quite provoking to see wit thrown away upon people who discover their total want of taste by such ill placed marks of approbation, as one sees are thrown in, out of mere civility. Yet this is a sort of people that deserve toleration, for after all if they are easy and good humoured, they vary one's thoughts with such sort of chit chat as saves us from growing too wise.
>
> (1.153)

Montagu is less charitable, frequently complaining of the neighbouring country squires who only read 'for their particular entertainment, Quarles's Emblems, the Pilgrim's Progress, Æsop's Fables, and, to furnish them with a little ready wit, Joe Miller's Jests' (to Mrs Donnellan, 1.157–8). That Montagu is engaged in self-characterization by means of this characterization of her neighbours is shown by the context of this complaint: she is expressing her impatient desire to lay hands on the French scholar Anne Dacier's translation of Homer in this intellectual wilderness.

Often, however, the oppositional characterizations are part of the dialectic of the correspondence itself, providing each writer with a safe opportunity to try out a range of readerly personae. Thus, although the correspondence reveals important character differences and points of tension between the sisters, I would argue that much of the oppositional self-characterization in which Montagu and Scott engage is part of a collaborative and constructive composition process.[13] Montagu seems particularly adept at trying on personae, downplaying her critique of Bishop Gastrell's *Moral Proof of the Certainty of a Future State*, for example, with an exaggeratedly modest contrast between the learned and worldly bishop and 'I, a simple reader, a young and ignorant damsel, God wot' (2.122), or pronouncing sententiously to the poet Gilbert West, when yet a young woman herself, 'I believe it is of great consequence to young people to read none but the very best authors, which will not be the case of the women while French trumpery is so much the fashion among them' (2.39). At the same time, her most persistent stance, used with both Scott and Carter, is that of the frivolous, empty-headed society lady, at one point in London reading the 'mushrooms of the day' while Scott in Bath reads the classics (3.291), but also schooling the intellectual Carter in urban sociability, according to the latter: 'I yesterday knocked at three doors, but not at home was the answer, and I was too prudent to attempt any more visits, even under the temptation of becoming as illustriously fashionable as you so gaily flattered me I should be, and wearing off the scandal of my Greek, by rapping at people's doors when I was half asleep' (2.360).

Like their self-characterizations, the women's readerly, critical conversation is cumulative and constructive, with judgements picked up, elaborated, and sharpened in the process. Scott and Carter appear to have functioned as the more intellectually critical poles of the correspondences they were involved in. While Montagu tends to be very swayed by what she is reading, and increasingly reads through her friendships and political persuasions, Scott keeps a critical distance. As young readers, when Montagu is very taken with Mme de Maintenon's memoirs (4.17–20), Scott responds that she cannot accept her treachery, concluding, 'She will never be my Heroine' (2 Sept. [1756] mo5264). Much later, when both are very anxious about unfolding events in France and their potential for inciting unrest in England, Elizabeth enthuses about 'Mr. Burkes admirable, excellent, incomparable pamphlet' (15 Nov. [1790] mo6207), but Scott replies coolly that she has read excerpts of it, including 'such a rhapsody about the Queen of France as must have given a little shock to the delicacy of Mrs Burkes conjugal sensibility', and adds that strong sales of the pamphlet after its qualities became well known would be 'more flattering, as appearing the consequence of approbation', than those already generated as 'the fruits of expectations' (10 Nov. [1790] mo5468).

Collective critical authority

Whatever the relative position-taking, however, as the producers of a collaborative critical discourse, these correspondents together exercise considerable critical authority against a context of potentially condemnatory contemporaries. In this context, the confidence with which Montagu, Scott, Carter, and Talbot evaluate the works they recommend to each other, read, and send back and forth is remarkable. This critical authority may arise in part because of the women's cultural positions – Montagu a leader of the Bluestocking circle and author of Shakespeare criticism, Scott an author extensively published in both history and fiction, Carter the premier woman of letters in mid-eighteenth-century England, and Talbot well-known in coterie circles as an astute critic and a writer of occasional pieces. However, this picture differs significantly from that of another well-educated and socially well-connected woman, Anna Margaretta Larpent, as John Brewer has represented the reading noted in her private journals. Brewer traces, in Larpent's record of her own spiritual and intellectual state and her supervision of her sons' educations, a fragile and unstable readerly identity which was so overdetermined by prescriptions for women's reading as to silence the intellectual female reader of history and politics, while dictating that this same woman maintain a suspicious distance from fictional reading materials interpellating a feminized, passively consuming reader.[14]

I suggest, then, that the crucial difference lies in the manner in which these four women mutually authorize their reading and their critical authority as readers; Lovell's observation that 'writing is a social practice' which 'always comes from particular places, and ... is addressed to particular readers' is relevant here.[15] In a key exchange early in their friendship, Talbot complains of 'the persecutions I have most unjustly undergone sure le chapitre du bel esprit' as an explanation for her reluctance to speak openly of her reading and intellectual acquaintance, but admits that 'I would venture upon this utmost peril, would my kind stars but happily allow me to be near you, we would then together laugh over all these ridiculous notions, both of my own and other peoples.' Carter replies firmly,

> I can by no means approve the frights and terrors you seem to be under sur le sujet du bel esprit, nor do I think there is any deference due either to the ignorance of trifling heads, or the perverseness of worthless hearts, which will always find something or other to exercise their folly or ill-nature about ... [I] have always found that endeavouring to

acquire a tolerable degree of common sense has amply repaid me for anything I may have suffered in the article of learning or wit, and thus have born with great tranquility the scandal of absurdities I never committed, and of nonsense that I never wrote.

(1.185, 187)

Talbot in turn tirelessly urges Carter to publish, whether her poetry or the translation of *Epictetus* from the Greek.

Similarly, when it comes to their own aspirations as intellectuals and writers, there can be no doubt of Montagu and Scott's mutual encouragement and advocacy. Very early in her letters, Montagu laments the loss of the writings of Sappho and Cornelia as cause of concern for both herself and her sister (12 Nov. 1739 mo5525). Much later, they gleefully criticize and parody the stylistic faults of a political pamphlet published by their brother Matthew, and preen themselves on one reader's 'wishing Mr Robinson had submitted his work to the correction of his Sisters'; a considerable proportion of their satisfaction clearly comes from this challenge to their brother's 'poor opinion of female capacity' ([1774] mo5967). The epistolary community functions as a discriminating but internally loyal readership, encouraging each individual member to take up the role of critic and, often, to seek a wider audience through publication.[16]

As these examples have already suggested, the critical and authorial skills of these Bluestocking women were founded upon a very wide range of reading. Betty Rizzo has said of Scott that she 'read all the new publications, both English and French',[17] a generalization borne out by the references in the sisters' correspondence to a very broad range of material. In a report of her reading written at age twenty-three, Scott lists 'the history of Florence & Lord Bacons Essays & the old Plays; Christianity not founded on argument Randolph's answer to it, Fontaines Tales; some of Mr. Harris on arts and happiness & some of David Simple's life I am now reading an account of the government of Venice Montaignes Essays & some more of Fontaines Tales' ([5 June 1744] mo5187). In later years, this wide spectrum of history, theology, moral philosophy, essays, and fiction is supplemented by such reading as contemporary exploration accounts, political pamphlets, Celtic poetry, and the 1785 translation of the *Bhagvad Geeta*, which Montagu praises as a work that 'gives the genuine doctrines of that peculiar race [the Brahmans]', and reflects 'the purest principles of the Stoicks, & the Religious & moral opinions of the Epicureans' ([9 Dec. 1785] mo6122). On a less metaphysical note, Scott records the increasing engagement of a provincial such as herself in public affairs through the newspapers: 'I believe the dearth of events to engage ones mind in the Country makes ones head run more on public transactions than when one is immersed in the dissipations of society; & while the body is confin'd to a narrow home ones thoughts ramble from Army to Army with great velocity & strong interests' (13 May [1792] mo5485). Almost the only generic distaste of both sisters seems to be for writings in natural philosophy or science.[18]

Carter's and Talbot's correspondence is characterized by reference to a similarly wide range of publications; if anything, the reach is broader, with the inclusion of materials in Italian and in the classical languages at the top of the generic hierarchy, and at the other extreme, the discussion of current periodicals, indicating an inside knowledge of the London publishing world. They know, assist, and attempt to advise Samuel Johnson, as the anonymous author-editor of the *Rambler* papers, discuss the processes behind the compiling of Dodsley's miscellanies and the *Gentleman's Magazine*, to which Carter was an early contributor, and contribute to the development of Samuel Richardson's hero Sir Charles Grandison. Although there were differences between Carter and Talbot's reading materials and tastes (most notably, Carter read in the classical languages and could interpret these texts and evaluate translations of them for Talbot; Talbot, on the other hand, resisted Carter's distrust of all satire and parody), they worked consciously to establish common ground in their reading responses, perhaps all the more so because they did not have the bond of kinship and long coexistence to take for granted. Thus, early in their friendship, Carter writes that she has left her walking companions behind 'like *Christian* climbing up the hill *difficulty*, till at length they quite sink into the *slough of despond*. (Have you ever read "Pilgrim's Progress?")' (1.58).

The sheer breadth of these reading tastes clearly serves as a corrective to the extensive public discourse of the time lamenting the enthralment of women by fiction. But the relation between this public discourse and the Bluestocking correspondence is more than one of simple opposition. For one thing, these women appear to share their culture's early resistance to the fictionality of fiction. Montagu early regrets that truth no longer 'dares show her head ... into publick but in an allegorical habit, or veiling her Speech with some fictitious gloss' (12 Nov. 1739 mo5525). Her insertion in this statement – 'notwithstanding a silly story told by Duck & some others of equal credit in ye land of fiction' – reflects the status implications of this anti-fiction position: Stephen Duck, 'the Thresher poet', had in this decade been enabled through the patronage of Queen Caroline and many others to rise above his original station as a farm labourer. Thus the Bluestockings align themselves with contemporary strictures placed upon fiction – when the readers are younger, less educated, less intelligent, or of a lower class than they. As an author of prose fiction herself, Scott clearly feels that the genre is both inferior to the histories she prides herself on writing and the necessary form by which to appeal to an inferior class of reader; thus her 1762 Utopian novel *A Description of Millenium Hall* is dismissed as 'a thing like that [which] takes so very little time in writing that I can not say but my time was sufficiently paid for; it was not a month's work, therefore it brought me in about a guinea a day; more than I cou'd gain by a better thing' ([Jan. 31 1763] mo5300), yet she avows that 'shou'd it bring into any person's mind and inclination the means of doing one benevolent action, I shall be very happy' ([Nov. 1762] mo5299).

As noted above, although early editions of the correspondence support this stance by portraying the Bluestockings as ideal readers devoting only a little time to the most approved novels, the unedited manuscripts show them reading and discussing a wide range of novels and other fictions. In the remainder of this chapter, I will trace three distinct, though interwoven, stances of this epistolary community towards fiction, revealing a complex process of negotiation and resistance in relation to the broader cultural community of which they formed a part.[19]

Negotiating fiction

First, the correspondence shows a practice of reading narrative fiction critically, bringing to bear the same criteria for a work's moral, informational, and literary qualities as are invoked for materials of all genres; the model is definitely not one of absorbed self-abandonment, whether it be the work of an authoritative author or a minor scribbler. Not only is *The Adventures of David Simple* (Sarah Fielding's first novel) the only contemporary fiction listed in Scott's early account of her eclectic reading, quoted above, but it is read only in part, rather than as a narrative to be pursued from beginning to end. Apparently suggesting that Montagu write critical remarks on Richardson's *Sir Charles Grandison*, Scott admits, 'tho' to me all after the third volume appears exceeding dull yet I make no doubt but you cou'd enliven the subject' (19 Feb. [1754] mo5239). Carter in turn writes of Henry Fielding's *Joseph Andrews*, after thanking Talbot for recommending it and praising its 'surprizing variety of nature, wit, morality, and good sense', as well as its 'spirit of benevolence', that 'it must surely be a marvellous wrongheadedness and perplexity of understanding that can make any one consider this complete satire as a very immoral thing, and of the most dangerous tendency, and yet I have met with some people who treat it in the most outrageous manner' (1.23–4). Indeed, Talbot and Carter thought well, in varying degrees, of Fielding's *Joseph Andrews*, *Tom Jones*, and *Amelia*, and felt free to criticize aspects of *Clarissa* and *Sir Charles Grandison*; these were no mindless daughters of Richardson. Nor, in later years, did Carter object to Gothic novels such as Radcliffe's *Sicilian Romance* and Walpole's *Castle of Otranto*. As with their non-fiction reading, these correspondents discriminate between degrees of originality, craft, and moral weight: Talbot writes of Charlotte Lennox's *The Female Quixote* that 'I have begun a book which promises some laughing amusement, "The Female Quixote"; the few chapters I read to my mother last night while we were undressing were whimsical enough and not at all low' (2.68–9), and of Frances Brooke's *History of Lady Julia Mandeville* that it 'has faults and excellencies enough to raise it above this denomination [that is, of nonsense]', but more ephemeral minor novels such as Eliza Haywood's *Jemmy and Jessamy*, the unattributed *Betty Barnes*, and Edward Kimber's *Maria* are referred to as what one is 'reduced to studying' when one lacks better materials, or as 'silly harmless story book[s] ... which [serve] to entertain myself at minutes when I am fit for nothing else' (2.108–9; 3.93).

Second, Brewer's claim that Larpent's confident critical judgement in discussing fiction is based on the authority of her own experience holds true for the Robinson sisters as well. Whether the author of the fiction be male or female, a central standard of judgement is what they see as a realistic reflection of women's lives, whether or not the text represents an improving moral picture. Thus when Montagu writes to Scott, 'I recommend to yr perusal the Adventures of Peregrine Pickle, Lady Vanes story is well told' ([1751] mo 5722), or 'I am impatient for the second volume [of Mrs Pilkington's memoirs] which she promises shall be more entertaining than the first' (3.98), the response is feminocentric. Sarah Fielding's *Cleopatra and Octavia* is likely to be absurd because 'how should a virtuous maiden who has lived in single blessedness guess at all the arts of a Wanton Cleopatra?' ([1757] mo5765), and Richardson's account in *Sir Charles Grandison* of Clementina's love-induced insanity is no better, according to Scott: 'No man I think ever knew so well how to cook up a madness; his third volume contains so amiable a madness, that was I a man I shoud go into bedlam, to seek for an object for my love' ([1754] mo5246). Conversely, they appreciate the capacity of fiction to capture social realities such as snobbery, enjoying the irony of a 'fine Ladies Criticism' of Tom Jones and Sophia for socializing after their marriage with the lower-born Mrs Miller (Feb. 1748/49 mo5710).

A third component of these Bluestockings' stance toward fiction is a mediated version of the period's commonly expressed fear of its effects on the reader. As I have shown, these women are preoccupied with the effects of fiction on the young, the less-educated, and the lower class, readers distinctly 'other' to the Bluestockings. Commentary of this nature thereby defines the writers' own community as an exception to the contemporary profile of the passive reader-consumer. In her early twenties, Scott refuses to loan 'the Arcadia or any romance' to a young friend lest it 'deprav[e] her taste' for her lover, a country squire (May 1744 mo 5184). Fifty years later, in 1794, she recommends to Montagu 'a Novel call'd Woman as she shou'd be, written by a Mrs Parsons; & tho' a Novel it will do no harm to your young Reader Mrs Ann Brown' (10 Mar. [1794] mo5501). While Montagu and Scott enjoy Pilkington's 'saucy' memoirs (3.98), Montagu comments to Carter that *The Histories of Some of the Penitents in the Magdalen House* (1759) are useful for 'all the girls in England', who insist on reading novels, as a pious antidote to sin (4.216–17). Talbot, similarly, writes to Carter: 'if you had rather aspire to the character of an author [than a reader], pray write me some plain books that shall be just on a level with the capacity of my farmers and spinners, and weavers, and teach them useful sentiments in an amusing lively way. Seriously I think something in this way much wanting' (1.88).

In Larpent's similar case, Brewer notes 'Anna's desire, even while reading novels, to avoid being condemned as a particular sort of reader'.[20] These writers were more confident, I believe, that they were exempt from this class of consuming reader, 'destined to eternal emptiness', as Montagu puts it in her 1760 dialogue between Plutarch and the Bookseller;[21] this exemption is for them a given of their education and social position, and eventually, their age. Thus they appear to see no contradiction between their own selective use of circulating libraries, noted above, and a typical disapproval of such libraries: 'Formerly the best Books were usefull only as they banish'd ignorance, but now they are necessary to drive out what is more pernicious *error*. All people read in this age, & the circulating Libraries make the girls Gallante and the young men Freethinkers' ([9 Dec. 1785] mo6122).

Despite their sense of distinctness from the general reading public, the women's reading shifts along with the generic balance of publication over the century, moving increasingly away from translations of the classics towards fiction, for example. Thus, their accounts reflect what Brean Hammond has called the 'novelization' of eighteenth-century

English culture, the 'underlying process of cultural change' which demanded that stories be 'relevant, realistic, narrative, and domestic'.[22] This novelization is visible in the growing importance of realist prose fiction in their references, particularly regarding specifically female culture and concerns. In the early letters, fables, Shakespeare's plays, and Pope's *Epistle to a Lady* and *Rape of the Lock* serve as points of reference: Scott describes herself coming home from the public rooms at Bath 'as much swell'd with mirth as the toad in the fable was with envy' (11 Oct. 1743 mo5173); Montagu characterizes 'that sort [of Woman] who Shakespear says, are fit to suckle fools and chronical small beer' as 'hav[ing] the best health' (3 Jan. 1750 mo5716); and Scott teases the young Montagu in 1741 about dreams of 'a youth more glittering than a birthnight Beau, who even in Slumber made your cheek to glow' (Feb. 1740/41 mo5168). In her published writings of the 1760s, Montagu values Shakespeare's histories over his tragedies, but stories of 'domestic merit' over histories of 'illustrious persons', both on the criterion of their speaking to the audience's everyday experience.[23] Accordingly, over the decades of the correspondences, descriptions of women's experiences in fiction seem to take on this mimetic role. Books are now referred to in terms of favourite characters: Talbot signs off on a letter with 'Now, had I not better (it is after supper) be reading Bell Fermor to my mother, than so ill filling this sheet to you' (3.183), a reference to Brooke's *History of Emily Montague* which she obviously assumes Carter will understand. In 1779, Montagu explains that she has written in a soothing style to a friend 'who has the art of ingeniously tormenting herself', alluding to Jane Collier's 1753 *Essay on the Art of Ingeniously Tormenting*, which elaborates in the form of short narratives on the sufferings of both victimized and self-victimizing women (7 May [1779] mo6058). Such casual allusions indicate that novelistic, realist habits of reading have penetrated these women's patterns of thought to a depth more fundamental than that of mere generic classification.

Ultimately, there is some evidence that the sisters' ability to control the threat of fiction by means of these dissociations of themselves as intellectuals and patrons from the inferior reader whose responses are beyond her rational control is under stress by the end of the century. In one of the most telling comments in the correspondence, the elderly Scott reports to Montagu in 1795 that she will never again read a novel of 'horrors' because Ann Radcliffe's *Mysteries of Udolpho*, 'which no doubt is well written', has been 'too much for my weak nerves; I shall endeavour to keep my imagination in sunshine. I am not equal to anything affecting' (18 Feb. [1795] mo5519). Thus the dangerous habits of reading that Scott has always located in someone else, and especially with the young women whose educations she and her sister have supervised at various points in their lives, suddenly become a threat from within.

Bluestocking readers and the female author

Intersecting with the issue of women's relation to fiction is the matter of responding to the woman author. As I have noted, each of these women was herself an author, and Montagu Pennington famously notes of his aunt in his introduction to her correspondence with Talbot that 'she had a decided bias in favour of female writers, and always read their works with a mind prepared to be pleased'.[24] Carter and Talbot indeed take an interest in such works as 'Mrs Squire's scheme of the Longitude' (1.35) and Mme de Chatelet's philosophy (1.219) for the sake of their female authors. Similarly, both Carter and Scott express admiration for Catharine Macaulay's histories (Carter to Montagu, 2.309–10; 30 Nov. [1763] mo5307), despite their dislike of her republicanism and, later, of her public flamboyance. While the general approach seems to be one of enlarged tolerance, as the above-cited reference to Lady Vane's scandalous memoirs illustrates, when the correspondents take a particular interest in the progress and impact of a woman writer's career, as they do in the cases of the two prominent mid-century novelists Sarah Fielding and Charlotte Lennox, they take complex positions that cannot be reduced simply to impersonal questions of intellectual or aesthetic value. By the time Talbot writes in 1753 of the *Familiar Letters between the Principal Characters in David Simple* as her amusement while travelling in a coach, Fielding is known to Carter, whom Talbot 'think[s] ... happy in her acquaintance' (1.131). Even though the two women complain repeatedly about Fielding's excessively refined moral sensibility, especially in her most experimental work, *The Cry* (1754), such complaints inevitably resolve into affirmations like 'But is she not in general a most excellent writer?' and 'On the whole, Mrs Fielding is a favourite with us all' (2.182, 188).

By contrast, Talbot and Carter apparently find both Lennox's poetry and her fiction highly readable, but constantly undermine such admissions with generalizations about the author's dangerous moral tendencies as they perceive them. They disapprove of Lennox's early poem 'The Art of Coquetry', which first appeared in the *Gentleman's Magazine*, for advocating female artfulness:

> For the edification of some of my young friends, we read one of [Lennox's poems] on the art of coquetry, at which they were much

scandalized. The poetry is uncommonly correct, but the doctrine indeed by no means to be admired. It is intolerably provoking to see people who really appear to have a genius, apply it to such idle unprofitable purposes.

(Carter to Talbot, 1.367)

Yet they make the poem a point of reference for years afterward, as in Carter's 1757 'In walking about the rooms we were joined by one of the most celebrated beauties in the assembly, the study of whose life, as far as can be judged by appearances, has been Mrs Lenox's sort of coquetry' (2.260). Lennox's greatest fictional success, her *Female Quixote*, was enjoyed by Talbot, as we have seen. Yet the suggestion of grudging praise here ('whimsical enough and not at all low') becomes explicit when in 1758, despite Lennox's intervening well-known and well-received translations of French political memoirs (the sort of works Talbot loved to read, we recall), her new novel *Henrietta* was unanimously dismissed by these correspondents. In Talbot's words, despite the fact that it 'has been useful to us here [in the country] ... there are many things in it that I dislike, and that tally with my opinion of the writer' (2.271).

Talbot and Carter's categorization of *Henrietta* and its author illustrates how communal reading might work to standardize and reinforce judgements, with powerful implications in the relatively small literary world of the mid-eighteenth century, where for all the ostensible anonymity of many publications, a separation of the published product and the private writer was impossible. It also provides us, by inference, with a glimpse of how the community's readings and its patronage might be interdependent. In the case of the impoverished but genteel Fielding, Carter and Talbot promoted her as a friend of Richardson and later a recipient of Montagu's charitable support. Montagu, while criticizing the story of Cleopatra as an unpromising choice of subject for the unmarried Fielding, takes a patron's pride in its publishing success, confessing that 'The pages that gave me most pleasure were those that contain'd the names of the subscribers' ([1757] mo 5765). Certainly Montagu and her correspondents agreed in disapproving of the patronized lower orders when they became 'ungrateful' and presumptuous, as in the case of Montagu's protégé the shoemaker-poet James Woodhouse, or Hannah More's milkmaid-poet Ann Yearsley.

A full understanding of the influence of the Bluestockings' reading, among its own members individually and collectively, and on the larger community of English readers in the second half of the eighteenth century, remains elusive – if tantalizingly hinted at – in the correspondence. Two questions I have not treated here are the extent of variations between individual correspondents, and the role of male readers in the exchanges (the responses of some are recorded by the women, but others – Lord Bath, Lord Lyttelton and Gilbert West, for example – are also part of the manuscript record). Nevertheless, this body of correspondence provides an invaluable record of an epistolary community of women's responses to their reading over the period 1740 to 1795, so crucial to the feminization of reading audiences, to the development of the novel as a genre strongly associated with women, and to the expansion of women's professional writing. The responses represent a range of individual stances influenced by age and social status as well as gender, but also reveal the formative role of a reading community in establishing positions reflective of, yet distinct from, the broader cultural and social milieu. In their discussions of their reading, these Bluestocking women can be seen as working through and elaborating on a communal critical theory and practice, despite, or perhaps because of, the disembodied nature of so much of their community's life.

Of course, the close kinship or friendship of the women involved in this particular correspondence was a continuous fabric woven of physical meetings and periods of absence that strove to bridge distance through the embedding of circumstantial details about states of health, the settings in which the writing was taking place, and the sociable or solitary scene of reading. The written materials upon which this chapter is based do not present the whole picture. However, it is plausible to suppose that the actual salon conversations of these women reflected the reading tastes and critical views worked out in their epistolary conversations. The salons were at the height of their reputation and influence in the 1770s and 1780s, when the body of letters had already been in formation over a period of between twenty and forty years, depending on the correspondents. At the same time, in those latter years the first generation of Bluestockings, including three of the four women discussed here (Talbot had died in 1770), had grown older and more socially conservative, and the society around them had become characterized by more rigidly divided gender roles, and by a narrowing association of women writers with the novel and related educational genres. To understand the full import of the eighteenth-century English salon as the site of a reading community, then, it is paradoxically necessary to look at the virtual community they constructed through letters.

Notes

1. Gary Kelly, 'Bluestocking Feminism and Writing in Context', in *Bluestocking Feminism: Writings of the Bluestocking Circle, 1738–1785*, 6 vols, gen. ed. Gary Kelly (London: Pickering and Chatto, 1999), 1.ix–liv; Harriet Guest, *Small Change: Women, Learning, Patriotism, 1750–1810* (Chicago: University of Chicago Press, 2000), especially 13–17.
2. John Duncombe, *The Feminiad* (London: Cooper, 1754), 23.
3. Jan Fergus's important study of *Provincial Readers in Eighteenth-Century England* (Oxford: Oxford University Press, 2006) has demonstrated empirically that many of these eighteenth-century assumptions about women's reading, particularly the view that women were the principal readers of novels, are inaccurate.
4. For discussions of the importance of social reading in eighteenth-century English culture, see Patricia Howell Michaelson, *Speaking Volumes: Reading and Speech in the Age of Johnson* (Stanford: Stanford University Press, 2002), and Naomi Tadmor, '"In the Even my Wife Read to Me": Women, Reading and Household Life in the Eighteenth Century', in *The Practice and Representation of Reading in England*, ed. James Raven, Helen Small and Naomi Tadmor (Cambridge: Cambridge University Press, 1996), 162–74.
5. Terry Lovell, 'Subjective Powers? Consumption, the Reading Public, and Domestic Woman in Early Eighteenth-Century England', in *The Consumption of Culture 1600–1800: Image, Object, Text*, ed. Ann Bermingham and John Brewer (New York: Routledge, 1997), 37.
6. I will refer to Elizabeth Robinson Montagu by the surname 'Montagu' and Sarah Robinson Scott by 'Scott' throughout, even where my reference is to the time before their marriages.
7. Matthew Montagu, ed., *The Letters of Mrs. Elizabeth Montagu*, 4 vols (London: Cadell and Davies, 1809–13), 1.8; 2.314. For this and the other two published letter collections used in this essay (*A Series of Letters between Mrs. Elizabeth Carter and Miss Catherine Talbot, from the Year 1741 to 1770, to which are added, Letters from Mrs. Elizabeth Carter to Mrs. Vesey, between the Years 1763 and 1787*, ed. Montagu Pennington, 4 vols (London: Rivington, 1809), and *Letters from Mrs. Elizabeth Carter, to Mrs. Montagu, Between the Years 1755 and 1800*, ed. Montagu Pennington, 3 vols (London: Rivington, 1817)), I will provide parenthetical references indicating volume and page numbers. Manuscript letters from the Montagu Collection will be referenced in the text in parentheses indicating manuscript number and date; original spelling and punctuation are left unchanged and conjectural dating is indicated by square brackets. All manuscript letters quoted are from this collection and are reproduced by permission of the Huntington Library, San Marino, CA.
8. Pennington, *A Series of Letters*, 1.iii.
9. Elizabeth Eger's *Bluestockings: Women of Reason from Enlightenment to Romanticism* (Basingstoke and New York: Palgrave Macmillan, 2010), ch. 2, details the influence of the Bluestockings as patrons, while Fergus's *Provincial Readers* presents a careful and convincingly documented case for the predominance of the aristocratic, gentry, and professional classes in mid-eighteenth-century book consumption.

10. See Lars E. Troide and Stewart J. Cooke, eds, *The Early Journals and Letters of Fanny Burney*, Vol. 3 (Montreal and Kingston: McGill-Queen's University Press, 1994), 347 n.74 for a summary of the likely reasons for suppression. For a media-centred approach to the cultural power of the Bluestocking women's conversational and scribal practices see my chapter, 'Bluestocking Women and the Negotiation of Oral, Manuscript, and Print Cultures', in *The History of British Women's Writing, 1750–1830*, ed. Jacqueline M. Labbe (Basingstoke: Palgrave Macmillan, 2010), 63–83.
11. See, for example, Montagu to Scott [10 Jan. 1754] mo5738 and [29 Aug.1759] mo5777.
12. Despite Scott's characterization here, Fergus's detailed study of provincial reading records has provided evidence that actual borrowing and reading patterns were more complicated than these associations suggest.
13. For a detailed study of this dialogic process in the sisters' correspondence, see Nicole Pohl and Betty A Schellenberg, 'Sarah Scott, Elizabeth Montagu, and The Familiar Letter in Dialogue' (forthcoming in festschrift for Betty Rizzo, ed. Temma Berg and Sonia Kane).
14. John Brewer, 'Reconstructing the Reader: Prescriptions, Texts, and Strategies in Anna Larpent's Reading', in *The Practice and Representation of Reading in England*, ed. James Raven, Helen Small and Naomi Tadmor (Cambridge: Cambridge University Press, 1996), 226–45.
15. Lovell, 'Subjective Powers?', 37.
16. See, for example, Scott to Montagu ([28 Nov. 1761] mo5287).
17. Betty Rizzo, Introduction to *The History of Sir George Ellison* (Lexington: University Press of Kentucky, 1996), xix.
18. See, for example, Scott on 'Mr. Martin's Monthly Magazine' ([Jan. 1755] mo5248) and Montagu on 'Mr. de Lucs work' ([Oct. 1780] mo6086).
19. I have discussed these stances in the context of a study of the Bluestockings as theorists of the novel in 'The Bluestockings and the Genealogy of the Modern Novel', *University of Toronto Quarterly* 79, 4 (2010): 1023–34.
20. Brewer, 'Reconstructing the Reader', 233.
21. Elizabeth Montagu, 'Dialogue III', in *Women Critics, 1660–1820: an Anthology*, ed. by the Folger Collective on Early Women Critics (Bloomington and Indianapolis: Indiana University Press, 1995), 102.
22. Brean S. Hammond, *Professional Imaginative Writing in England, 1670–1740: 'Hackney for Bread'* (Oxford: Clarendon, 1997), 8.
23. Montagu, from *Essay on the Writings and Genius of Shakespear* and 'Dialogue III', *Women Critics*, 103–4, 101.
24. Montagu Pennington, *Memoirs of the Life of Mrs. Elizabeth Carter, with a New Edition of Her Poems* (London: Rivington, 1808), 1.448.

2
Nineteenth-Century Reading Groups in Britain and the Community of the Text: an Experiment with *Little Dorrit*

Jenny Hartley

What was it like to be in a reading group in Britain in the middle of the nineteenth century? Late twentieth and early twenty-first-century historians of nineteenth-century reading in Britain are adding considerably to our knowledge of reading throughout the century. William St Clair has produced a quantified history of reading for the romantic period; Kate Flint and Jonathan Rose have investigated reading practices among women and the working classes.[1] At the same time, other studies have emphasized and demonstrated the importance of reading as a collective phenomenon. This chapter takes a qualitative rather than a quantitative approach. It shadows, by way of a real-time experiment, the experience of those first readers enjoying a mid-nineteenth-century serialized novel in a communal setting. In doing so, it explores the implications of such a reading both for our understanding of the novel's first readers, and for our own appreciation of the novel.

By the beginning of the nineteenth century reading groups were a well-established part of the British literary scene. Peter Clark has made the case for a 'major provincial expansion' of book clubs in the last decades of the eighteenth century.[2] Evidence from Clark and R.J. Morris suggests that membership of these clubs was mainly male,[3] although according to Amanda Vickery, 'female club life' was also 'in full flower in the provincial north by 1820'.[4] These book clubs contributed to the growth of the bourgeois public sphere identified by Jürgen Habermas:

> The privatized individuals coming together to form a public also reflected critically and in public on what they had read, thus contributing to the process of enlightenment which they together promoted. Two years after *Pamela* appeared on the literary scene the first

public library was founded; book clubs, reading circles and subscription libraries shot up.[5]

If enlightenment was a spur to the nascent book club world – although book club members were not invariably liberal, as William St Clair reminds us[6] – so was friendship. A book club which started in Stockton in the north of England in 1776 records their genesis as a 'friendly Society or Monthly Clubb [sic] for the Promoting, easy and chearful, but liberal Conversation; mutual Entertainment and literary Improvement'. A few months later they decided to become a book club, with each member contributing twelve and a half pence a quarter to buy books.[7]

By the mid-nineteenth century reading groups and clubs, which often started as distribution networks, had proliferated and sometimes diversified. Specialist societies sprang up for reading and appreciating the works of particular authors such as Shakespeare, Browning, and Ruskin. Specialist audiences were also identified. Elizabeth Fry read to groups in prison; matrons read to emigrants on board ship to Australia. At the same time, informal groups of family and friends were flourishing, with new journals assuming a collective readership in the family circle. Friendship networks distributed and discussed books: Jemima Clough's brother Arthur sent boxes of books from Oxford to be circulated round her friends; at the same time Jemima was organizing a weekly reading group for women in her area. More formally, as the century ended, Societies for Mutual Culture and the National Home Reading Union, together with the reading rooms in Working Men and Women's Clubs, all testify to the educational benefits seen to accrue from reading together.

Thus education, enlightenment, and friendship were all to be promoted by the reading group in the nineteenth century. But it was not without its critics, then as indeed today. This hostility amassed along two axes, one political and the other cultural. One concerns aspiring up, the other levelling down. Cultural critics of the book group see it as the enemy of true culture and enlightenment. The book circle stands for all that is philistine, pretentious, undiscriminating, and snobbish. Its members prefer gossip and laying down the law to reading. Hollingford Book Society, in Elizabeth Gaskell's *Wives and Daughters* (1866), is

> the centre of news and gossip, the club, as it were, of the little town. Everybody who pretended to gentility in the place belonged to it. It was a test of gentility, indeed, rather than of education or a love of literature. No shopkeeper would have thought of offering himself as

a member, however great his general intelligence and love of reading; while it boasted on the list of subscribers most of the county families in the neighbourhood, some of whom subscribed to the Hollingford Book Society as a sort of duty belonging to their station, without often using their privilege of reading the books.[8]

Where Gaskell anatomizes social evil, Elizabeth Barrett Browning accentuates intellectual shortcoming. Aurora Leigh's narrow-minded 'cage-bird' aunt belongs to 'The book club' which 'guarded from your modern trick | Of shaking dangerous questions from the crease.'[9] The animosity continued unabated into the twentieth century with Queenie Leavis's attack on the Book Society in *Fiction and the Reading Public* (1932). She uses the phrase 'levelling down',[10] and this case against reading groups can still be found today. At the heart of this hostility is one literary genre, the novel. Reading groups have always read novels – the Dalton Book Club in Cumbria, which opened its doors in 1764 and is still flourishing two and a half centuries later, read novels from its earliest days[11] – but they have always had a problem with them. Alice Ainsworth, a member of a book circle in Bolton in the early nineteenth century, commented: 'We do not tolerate the common novels of the day.'[12] 'Common', 'middle-brow', and always popular, the novel has besmirched its readers with the bad press which it has attracted to itself.

Frequently slandered by their mutual association, the trinity of women, book clubs, and the novel found a stout defender in the novelist Wilkie Collins. Writing for Dickens's magazine *Household Words* in 1856, he tackles the hypocrisy of contemporary attitudes to the novel and book clubs at some length.[13] He starts by saying how he, his wife, daughters, and nieces, a pointedly all-female circle apart from him, have just created a 'Disreputable Society' as a breakaway group from their Book Club, which has instituted a ban on fiction. Collins claims that hypocrisy about the novel has permeated the book trade itself.

> Look, for example at the Prospectus of any librarian. The principal part of his trade of book-lending consists in the distributing of novels and he is uniformly ashamed to own that simple fact. Sometimes, he is afraid to print the word Novel at all in his lists, and smuggles in his contraband fiction under the head of Miscellaneous Literature. Sometimes, after freely offering all histories, all biographies, all voyages, all travels, he owns self-reproachfully to the fact of having novels too, but deprecatingly adds – Only the best! As if no other branch of the great tree of literature ever produced tasteless and worthless

fruit! In all cases, he puts novels last on his public list of the books he distributes, though they stand first on his private list of the books he gains by. Why is he guilty of all these sins against candour? Because he is afraid of the dull people.

By 'dull people', Collins means 'people of all degrees of rank and education, who never want to be amused. I don't know how long it is since these dreary members of the population first hit on the cunning idea of calling themselves Respectable; but I do know that, ever since that time, this great nation has been afraid of them – afraid in religious, in political, and in social matters.'

Collins's reference to the 'political' dimension articulates a secondary cause for the hostility. The role of the book club in the spread of democracy did not go unnoticed; hence its detractors. Collins's outlaw group, with its predominantly female membership, poses a potential threat. Jennifer Phegley argues that Victorian family literary magazines 'empowered' women in encouraging them to 'participate in a wide public debate that affected the intellectual lives of women for years to come'.[14] Likewise, Ann Thompson suggests that the women's clubs who read Shakespeare together in this period 'constitute a kind of pre-history of modern feminist criticism'.[15] It was, however, the novel which led the field in its potential for damage. Patrick Brantlinger's book about the perceived threat of mass literacy cites parliamentary discussions in 1849, in which '"the fear" was expressed that public libraries "would be filled with novels of the worst description of literature"'.[16] When Collins chooses a novel for his 'respectable' club to read, the other members object violently. High feelings are also documented in real as opposed to fictional groups. At the end of the nineteenth century the minutes of the Bristol Friendly Reading Society record a heated meeting as members attempt to guard the sanctity of the Victorian home:

> Dr Waterman brought back to meeting Oscar Wilde's *Salome* with illustrations by Aubrey Beardsley. After warmly denouncing both poem and illustrations as obscene he cast the book on the floor and set his foot on it. In this condemnation he was heartily supported by the Revd. Henry Oliver. Though others deprecated the severe treatment of the book it was withdrawn from circulation.[17]

As the Bristol Society records also show, however, by the mid-nineteenth century collective reading was a standard and often much appreciated practice, a recognized part of the social climate and calendar. One of the more familiar examples from the period is the anecdote about the charwoman in Forster's *Life of Charles Dickens*: 'It turned out that she lodged at a snuff-shop kept by a person named Douglas, where there were several other lodgers; and that on the first Monday of every month there was a Tea, and the landlord read the month's number of *Dombey*, those only of the lodgers who subscribed to the tea partaking of that luxury, but all having the benefit of the reading.'[18] This struck a chord. A few years ago I was teaching *Little Dorrit* (1855–57) on an undergraduate course that takes its nineteenth-century novels at the rate of one huge novel every two weeks. Weary but game, we finally reached the climactic revelations of Book two, Chapter thirty. Here, after more than seven hundred pages, Mrs Clennam admits under duress that she is 'not Arthur's mother'.[19] But stunning though Dickens clearly means this moment to be – the way towards it is elaborately paved – for us it fell rather flat, and I myself had unaccountably forgotten it. Was this Dickens misfiring, or were we missing something? The revelation, together with information about Arthur's real mother, comes in the last monthly number. I started to wonder what it would have been like to find out not after a month and a half or even a week and a half, but after a year and a half, as Dickens's original readers had, over the eighteen months between 1 December 1855 and 1 June 1857. (*Little Dorrit* was originally published in nineteen monthly numbers of three or four chapters, with six chapters for the last double number.)

I decided to try an experiment: a reading group which would meet once a month to read *Little Dorrit* in the real time of those nineteen monthly numbers. I found ten volunteers through an advertisement in our local community newsletter. A few came and went over the 18 months, and we settled down to eight regular members. All reading groups have rules, and I had two. First, we should start at the same time of year as the original readers, because seasonality might be important.[20] Second, there should be no reading ahead. A few had already read *Little Dorrit*, but most had not, and there was to be no hinting or giving away the plot. This could be difficult, given the perversity of some of our editions. The cast list printed at the front of the 1907 Chapman and Hall edition identifies 'Arthur, adopted son of Mrs Clennam': so much for that climactic revelation.

The experiment now finished, what sort of readers did our group become? Does it help us to understand those original readers of *Little Dorrit*, who needed to know exactly what a little dorrit was? This is Dickens's only novel to be named after a woman, so it would not have been an obvious guess, and the *Athenaeum* opens its lengthy review on publication day for the first part: 'Let us say at once, that Little Dorrit is not a broom, not a village, not a ship, – as has been variously surmised at various tea-tables, – where the book in the green cover is as eagerly expected as the news of the last battle, – but a live flesh and blood little girl.'[21] The *Athenaeum* calls *Little Dorrit* a 'book'; other contemporary reviews refer to a 'periodical', a 'serial', a 'tale', a 'novel', 'one of Dickens's monthly number books', and 'one of his shilling numbers'.[22] These definitions will all variously affect reception and illustrate Robert L. Patten's point that 'privileging the volume edition over the periodical issue distorts the nature of the fiction and the history of the book'.[23] In this small exercise in reading reception practice, and following Pierre Bourdieu's dictum that 'the meaning of a work (artistic, literary, philosophical, etc.) changes automatically with each change in the field within which it is situated for the spectator or reader',[24] I have attempted to embed the text as far as possible in the field of Dickens's first readers, those with whom he himself felt a special bond. I have focused on the text as a collective monthly reading experience, drawing on the evidence of our experiment, and accounts of contemporary readers.

Critics have speculated about Dickens's first readers. Richard Altick suggests that 'in the interval between instalments, many readers must have passed the time by re-reading the latest one. They thereby noticed touches they missed the first headlong time through.'[25] Altick says 'must have', and I can say yes, we did; and that over the eighteen months the group developed distinctive modes and attitudes of reading. In terms of attitude, Hughes and Lund's characterization of the nineteenth-century audience in *The Victorian Serial* would serve well for us:

> The serial publishing format encouraged a kind of kind of loyalty from its readers that could also transcend the absence of a story's characters in the intervals between parts. Readers who persisted, becoming 'loyal fans,' lived on intimate terms with characters, taking them inside homes and even minds, sharing their acquaintance with others outside the pages, and so extending a kind of intimacy also associated with home.[26]

That this should happen for us was not surprising: we already appreciated the comforts of serialization from television and radio. I was pleased that eighteen months of *Little Dorrit* could engage and sustain our affections; I was more intrigued by what would happen to our reading habits.

Richard Altick was right about re-reading. Quite early on some group members adopted the practice of racing through the new number at the beginning of the month. They then re-read it more slowly. This double reading had a two-fold effect. Intricacies of plot and motivation became more important than they usually are for my students. We asked each other who would have posted Rigaud as missing, or why was Pancks so keen to research the Dorrit family fortunes? This may sound as though we were trying to catch Dickens out, but it felt more like peering under the bonnet to inspect the workings of the engine. The second effect was the attentiveness dividend. These were not literature graduates, but they became closer readers than I was trained to be, as we saw from the instances of the mermaid, the letter, and the box.

In Part Seven (Book I, Chapter 23, p. 267) Clennam mentally alludes to his childhood sweetheart Flora, now middle-aged and stout, as a 'mermaid', with no explanation. To understand the allusion we had to back-read three months to Part Four, where Flora is described as grafting her eighteen-year-old persona on to her present self 'thus making a moral mermaid of herself' (p. 156). Picking up such a throw-away reference felt like responding to a deliberate and playful challenge. This was a little in-joke to reward the wide-awake. The letter initially looked more plot-significant. In the penultimate number (Book II, Chapter 28), Rigaud admits that he has sold information about the Gowans to Miss Wade. Pet Meagles (now Gowan) is, he says, 'charming but imprudent. For it was not well of the fair Gowana to make mysteries of letters from old lovers, in her bedchamber on the mountain, that her husband might not see them' (p. 718). Pet's old lovers: what was this? By a process of collective retrieval we worked back to Switzerland in Part Eleven (Book II, Chapter 1), where Little Dorrit gives Pet an innocuous 'little note' of introduction from Arthur Clennam. Pet asks Little Dorrit to 'take it back again ... then my husband is sure not to see it. He might see it and speak of it, otherwise, by some accident' (pp. 429–30). They then hear someone outside (Rigaud). But this set-up leads nowhere, even seven months later. It might exacerbate the discord between the Gowans, but we are not shown this directly. Its interest lies rather in what it reveals about Dickens's working methods: how he sows seeds, some of which grow hugely, some a bit, some not at all, but which readers trained to attentiveness in reading detail across time will be able to pick up.

My third instance is more central to the plot, or rather that strange non-plot which is the unique characteristic of this novel. The first instalment ends with some hurried business involving a box, 'an iron box some two feet square' stealthily removed from Mrs Clennam's house by Jeremiah Flintwinch's Double (Book I, Chapter 4, p. 54). This looks like what Alfred Hitchcock called a MacGuffin: the secret something which propels a story, what people want or want to stop others getting.[27] Flintwinch's locked box would be a perfect MacGuffin, strategically placed right at the end of the first number. But it disappears for the next eighteen months, not to reappear or even to be mentioned until near the end of the last number. Little Dorrit has relayed Mrs Clennam's revelations about Arthur's real mother to Mr Meagles, who then dashes round France in fruitless pursuit of the 'original papers' (p. 768). Back in England, he visits Arthur, now imprisoned for debt in the Marshalsea. At this point, only fifteen pages before the end, Tattycoram bursts in 'with an iron box some two feet square'. This box was one of the starting points for my experiment in reading in real time. Would we remember it, and did we care about it? For once Dickens does give us some help: 'Such a box had Affery Flintwinch seen in the first of her dreams, going out of the old house in the dead of the night, under Double's arm' (p. 772). But the box is never opened for us, and its contents are never read. We hear only of the single sheet of paper which Little Dorrit asks Arthur to burn, folded and unread, in the closing moments of the novel. By this time none of our reading group cared about box or papers; we were more concerned about Fanny missing her sister's wedding. On first reading, the locked box looked like a non-activated MacGuffin; later it was to provide clues to the novel's latent text, which this kind of reading can tease to the front.

Was the close reading we were evolving – double-reading, back-reading to pick up clues, and collective retrieval – what Dickens's first readers did too? We found ourselves drawn to that first reading experience, those readers we were keeping time with. What did they do with their monthly numbers; did they hold on to them or pass them round? The evidence of a book club in Cornwall in the 1840s shows that by February 1845 parts of *Martin Chuzzlewit* (1843–44) had travelled more than a hundred miles and changed hands more than thirty times.[28] Book club members were allowed only three or four days with each number before having to pass it on. Not for them the luxury of back-reading. Nor does Dickens give much help to the memory-challenged, by way of cliff-hanging suspense endings, or recapping and synopses: he just expects a high degree of attention and an efficient memory. We modern readers have little training in the 'art of memory', and it was instructive that in this sphere the older members of our group out-performed the younger.

The focus on the 1855–57 readers and on what they had in their hands brought a new dimension to the meaning of the embedded text. We located a set of the original parts and saw that each monthly instalment had twelve or so pages of advertisements at the beginning and another six or so at the end, labelled 'Little Dorrit Advertiser'. The first advertisement in the first number recalls the wartime context for the first months of *Little Dorrit*'s publication. 'Edmiston's Crimean Outfit' is offered at eighteen pounds and eighteen shillings. The outfits were adaptable and the copywriters inventive: with the coming of peace in the spring of 1856 Edmiston could offer their 'Pocket Siphonia or Waterproof Overcoat' to 'Sportsmen, Tourists and Travellers'; there were also yachting trousers, fishing and shooting boots, and in September 1856 a new line, 'Inflated Hoops for Ladies' Dresses'. These original numbers provide physical evidence for *Little Dorrit* embedded as a product among other products, and as one with permeable borders. It takes its place in the world of ingenious Victorian artefacts such as 'The Caspiato, or Folding Bonnet' (jokes about it appeared at the time in *Punch*). Advertisements for new and established magazines such as *The National Magazine*, *Cassell's Family Paper*, *The Train*, and *The Leader*, and the coloured inserts and fold-ins, all testify to thriving times for the publishing industry. And as the experiment went on, we felt the need to embed the book in its contemporary fields of production. Trips, visits, and walks took us into Little Dorrit's London; and Dickens's biography took on an importance which it could not have had for his contemporary readers, ignorant as they were of his childhood prison trauma.

When I started this experiment I assumed that the modern parallels would be with Stephen King's late twentieth-century adventures in serial publishing. In the Introduction, the Foreword, and the Afterword to the one-volume edition of *The Green Mile* (1996, originally in six parts), King constantly refers to Dickens as his model, but the differences in serialization methodology are instructive. King expects a less attentive reader than Dickens did, one who may be in literal terms more literate (not all of Dickens's first audience could read) but who has a less sophisticated grasp of language and who is less educated in habits of memory. King evolves skilful devices for recapping, and goes unashamedly for the cliff-hanger. The suggestion in the Foreword, 'why not read this aloud, with a friend?' takes us back to those original nineteenth-century readers, but also to our twenty-first-century group. Quite early on, reading aloud a few pages seemed the natural and soon the necessary thing to do – something I had not anticipated – and sometimes to powerful effect. There had, for example, been some scoffing about the sentimentality in the scene at the end of Book One, when Clennam tells William Dorrit of his changed fortunes. When read aloud, the scene became genuinely moving.

King also seeks to forge connections with his readers as Dickens had done, inviting us in his Foreword and Afterword to *The Green Mile* to write in with comments and ideas. But perhaps a closer match to Dickens in terms of relationship between serial author and audience would be Oprah Winfrey, particularly with *O, The Oprah Magazine*. Her name and initial feature constantly throughout the magazine, a device which echoes the 'Conducted by Charles Dickens' banner at the top of every page of *Household Words*. The intimacy with her audience which Oprah has made her hallmark resembles 'that particular relation' which Dickens valued so highly, describing it to Forster in 1858 as '(personally affectionate and like no other man's) which subsists between me and the public'.[29] The Preface to *Little Dorrit* fell into its right place when we saw where it was placed originally, at the very end of the last number. Here it works as farewell and sign off, leading out of rather than into the relationship he has enjoyed with his readers over the last eighteen months: 'Deeply sensible of the affection and confidence that have grown up between us, I add ... May we meet again!'

The sociability of Dickens's metaphor of meeting is apt for what was happening between the text and its first readers and reviewers. For both of these audiences, the text has its own community or collective aspect. Reviewers welcomed *Little Dorrit* on its first appearance as a social rather than literary phenomenon 'which for the next year and a half will form a topic of conversation in many circles scarcely less interesting than that of the war itself'.[30] Corroboration of this would come from readers such as Elizabeth Gaskell passing on to her daughters what she had just read of the first number over the shoulder of a fellow-passenger on the bus:

> Oh *Polly*! He was such a slow reader, *you*'ll sympathize, Meta won't, my impatience at his *never* getting to the bottom of the page ... *We* only read the first two chapters ... heroine's name Pet Meagles, had a little dead twin sister, the remembrance of whom is always pricking her relations up to virtue, & who, I suspect, is 'little Dorrit.'[31]

Other readers, however, were inclined to back away: 'We are almost frightened lest we should have been too confiding and unquestioning followers.'[32] This protest against seduction resents Dickens for getting too close, and illustrates the book's mixed reception by contemporary reviewers.

Early in the publication of *Little Dorrit* a rift appeared. At the top end of the market the monthly or quarterly reviews dedicated themselves to disliking the book for political reasons. Dickens was deliberately courting such opposition with his satire on the Barnacles, and referred to the first Circumlocution Office chapter as 'a scarifier'.[33] Further down the market are 'the critics selected', according to a *Blackwood's* reviewer, 'from the most ill-judging of his readers', and dismissed by the *New Quarterly* as 'Mr Dickens's sworn band of followers in the weekly press'.[34] The weeklies and the 'heavies' agreed that *Little Dorrit* was Dickens off the boil, but for different reasons. The heavies hated the Circumlocution Office and Dickens's attacks on the upper and merchant classes; the weeklies relished the Circumlocution Office but deplored the lack of plot. There is also a marked difference in the kinds of relationship which the weeklies and the heavies think they are having with Dickens. While weeklies such as *Bell's Weekly Messenger* offer progress reports on every number, the weightier reviews hand down definitive judgements; the analogous distinction would be the regular check-up with your family doctor compared with the momentous appointment with the consultant. In what reads like a conversation with Dickens, *Bell's Weekly Messenger* remarks 'we much prefer the latter half of this number to the former', or 'by far the best number for several months'. It advises him to profit by reading the work of Charles Lever, then also appearing in serial form.[35] This sort of commentary, although not working-class, bears out Jonathan Rose's observation that 'when Victorian workers read things that contradicted their own experience, they were quite willing to talk back to the author'.[36]

And the author might talk back again to them. Dickens's responsiveness to his readers is legendary. His change of direction with Miss Mowcher in *David Copperfield* is well known, and in December 1856 he wrote to invite the Duke of Devonshire to a performance of *The Frozen Deep*, adding 'NB I put Flora into the current No on purpose that this might catch you, softened towards me and at a disadvantage' – the duke had previously told Dickens how 'amused and excited' he was by her.[37] But such examples are unusual. More characteristic of Dickens's dealings with his readers is the warm reciprocal milieu into which the novel settles, embedded on its appearance into a flux of interest and business. This process had started with Dickens's earliest serials and starts early in a serial's life: an advertisement for 'The Little Dorrit Polka' appears in the fifth number of the novel. 'Little Dorrit, A Ballad Sung by Mrs Caulfield' was also apparently composed well before the novel finished its run, and had to rely on reasonable but wrong guesses about the plot.[38] Mrs Caulfield sang, presumably with much feeling, about the twenty years that have passed 'Since first that ancient prisoner had felt oppression's power', but 'Perhaps within a wealthy home some guilty one may mourn', so 'Cheer up Little Dorrit!' 'Little Dorrit's Vigil' confined itself more sensibly but less dramatically to the tableau of Little Dorrit and her father: 'She guarded him till morning broke.' Other *Little Dorrit* songs included 'Floating Away' (Clennam's roses on the river at Twickenham), and 'My Dear Old Home'. Pianists could enjoy the 'Little Dorrit Serenade', and there was more dancing to be had with a 'Little Dorrit Schottische' and a 'Little Dorrit Quadrille'.

'Breaking up a pleasant family circle' is the simile the *New Quarterly Review* uses to describe the 'completion of a periodical by Charles Dickens'.[39] For some a reality, for others a welcome simulacrum, this circle could play, sing, and dance along with *Little Dorrit* as it was coming out, and collaborate, as it were, in its appearances. In this way a Dickens novel is an interactive text, attaining diverse virtual realities in the process of production. On one occasion collaboration actually preceded composition. Frederick Fox Cooper's adaptation of *Little Dorrit* was based on the first half of the book, and ran for nearly three weeks in November 1856, when the book was only just over half-way through publication. The editors of Dickens's *Letters* suggest that he borrowed from this version, perhaps unconsciously, in the way he wraps up the plot in the closing scenes of the whole novel.[40] Cooper's denouement involves Flintwinch's Double, and his version was pirated in turn by the abridged Penny Pictorial Series, a playbill for which gives the part of Little Dorrit as played by Miss Ternan.[41] Which Miss Ternan we do not know, and the playbill may be a 'star-studded cast' hoax, but nonetheless it is suggestive that the name of Ternan appears next to Little Dorrit's at this time. Dickens, avid theatre-goer that he was, would probably have seen it.

Our real-time group-reading of *Little Dorrit* took us, then, to some surprising places and stimulated us to embed it in a range of contexts. What resonance, if any, did this have in evoking new interpretations of the novel? I would argue that it accentuated aspects and perspectives often neglected by literary criticism. The most obvious effect was to foreground the material text itself as a focus for investigation: both, as we have seen, in its original format, and then also in its first materialization as manuscript and number plans. At first sight the manuscript appears so heavily worked on that there seems to be no sentence without alterations or deletions.[42] Comparison with the manuscript of *Oliver Twist* shows that Dickens did not always compose in this way. *Little Dorrit* begins to look like an overwritten, superimposed text, with another text behind it. This is, after all, a book about the buried, the imprisoned, what lies beneath the surface, a novel of many secrets, including the misunderstood 'secrets of my own breast', as Arthur Clennam finally confesses to Little Dorrit (p. 726). A novel of and about repression, *Little Dorrit* presents a striking image for the act of repression itself in the description of Clennam's solitary thought processes: 'As though a criminal should be chained in a stationary boat on a deep clear river, condemned, whatever countless leagues of water flowed past him, always to see the body of the fellow creature he had drowned lying at the bottom' (p. 649).

The number plans and manuscript suggest that Dickens had problems or at least second thoughts with Miss Wade in particular, a character who has intrigued many critics. Miss Wade belongs to the book's antispirit party. If you can persuade someone, presumably you can also 'missuade' them,[43] and this is what she does with Tattycoram, persuading her to leave the Meagles and live under her blighting protection. She is described by Dickens as both 'reserved' and 'unsubduable' (pp. 35, 36), a strange and fissile combination. The number plans (reproduced in the Penguin Classics edition) often raise her as a possibility, to be followed by 'no' or 'not yet' (pp. 796, 798, 802, 820); perhaps Dickens once had other plans for her. In manuscript she is frequently cut and reworked. In the first number Dickens has, unusually for him, to start a page afresh because he wants to alter so much about her.[44] At this point she looks as though she will be important, if marginal: Dickens puts into her mouth the keynote speech about 'all the people who are coming to meet us from many strange places and by many strange roads' (p. 37).

Miss Wade is an enigma, as is Arthur's biological mother, the invisible character who first provoked my experiment in reading. Mrs Clennam's biased account in the last number refers to 'a graceless orphan, training to be a singing girl' (p. 744), but the denouement is so muffled that the Penguin Classics edition feels obliged to offer an explanatory Appendix. The box which arrived and exited in the first number (in a short chapter which the manuscript shows to be a late addition) is the box containing this woman's papers. Flintwinch later describes how 'she had been always writing, incessantly writing – mostly letters of confession' (p. 747). Like Dickens, an incessant writer, but unlike him, her writing is, as far as we know, never read. She has no relationship with any character, certainly not with the reader; we are not even told her name. That Dickens, who can produce adequate denouement when he wants to, should withhold her as a writer unnamed and unread, is suggestive.

Little Dorrit is a novel in two books. The second part seems to start again with an apparently new cast of characters in a new setting (Switzerland), who have to be mapped on to the old cast in the earlier prison setting. A member of our reading group described the effect as a haunting, and haunting is one of the book's leitmotifs. Affery Flintwinch hears the story of Arthur's mother and mistakenly assumes that the woman is still 'kept here, secretly'. When told that the woman is dead, '"so much the worse," said Affery, with a shiver, "for she haunts the house then. Who else rustles about it, making signals by dropping dust so softly?"' (p. 794). These 'signals' presage the fall of the house of Clennam, brought down in part by the injustice done to the silenced and imprisoned woman. It seemed both paradoxical and fitting that our close, protracted reading of the text should lead us finally towards this enigmatically unreadable figure.

In conclusion, this exercise in embedded reading can, I suggest, illuminate and collocate some diverse reception practices. The novel can be seen as permeable: what goes on inside it relates to what goes on outside it. To paraphrase Emily Dickinson, the novel selects its own society; or rather, it generates it. *Little Dorrit* creates a community within itself – the society of its characters – and, in parallel and by analogy, around itself in those reading circles on first publication. Susan Belasco Smith's work on *Uncle Tom's Cabin* (1851–52) emphasizes the importance of serialization, as 'a mode of literary production that creates within the text of the novel a web of relationships and experiences and exchanges, the false starts, distractions, and breaks that occur within the family circle'.[45] Stowe, in Smith's view, envisioned her readers as a friendship group which clearly included herself. So did Dickens, as evidenced in *Little Dorrit*'s prefatorial farewell. Our experiment afforded us the privilege of joining this circle as belated fellow-travellers, reaping the benefits of knowledge, insight, and indeed, pleasure.

Notes

1. William St Clair, *The Reading Nation in the Romantic Period* (Cambridge: Cambridge University Press, 2004); Kate Flint, *The Woman Reader, 1837–1914* (Oxford: Oxford University Press, 1993); Jonathan Rose, *The Intellectual Life of the British Working Classes* (New Haven: Yale University Press, 2001). Part of this chapter was originally published in *Publishing History*, 52, 2002. Permission to reproduce it has been generously given by ProQuest Information and Learning (formerly Chadwyck-Healey Ltd), Cambridge.
2. Peter Clark, *British Clubs and Societies 1580–1800: the Origins of an Associational World* (Oxford: Oxford University Press, 2000), 109.
3. R.J. Morris, 'Clubs, Societies and Associations', in F.M.L. Thompson, ed., *The Cambridge Social History of Britain 1750–1950* (Cambridge: Cambridge University Press, 1990), 3, 395–443.
4. Amanda Vickery, *The Gentleman's Daughter: Women's Lives in Georgian England* (New Haven and London: Yale University Press, 1998), 258.

5. Jürgen Habermas, *The Structural Transformation of the Public Sphere: an Inquiry into a Category of Bourgeois Society*, trans. Thomas Burger (Cambridge, MA: MIT Press 1989), 51.
6. See William St Clair, *The Reading Nation*, 259. St Clair gives the figures for 'Collective reading institutions' and 'Reading societies' in the early 1820s in Tables 13.2 and 13.3.
7. Minute books of the Stockton Book Club in my possession.
8. Elizabeth Gaskell, *Wives and Daughters* (1866: Oxford: Oxford University Press, 1987), 521–2.
9. Elizabeth Barrett Browning, *Aurora Leigh* (London 1857), I, 302–3.
10. Q.D. Leavis, *Fiction and the Reading Public* (London: Chatto & Windus, 1932), 185.
11. See Ernest H. Boddy, 'The Dalton Book Club: a Brief History', *Library History*, 9 (1992): 97–105, and records of the club held by the secretary, to whom I am grateful.
12. Vickery, *The Gentleman's Daughter*, 258.
13. Wilkie Collins, 'A Petition to the Novel-Writers', *My Miscellanies* (London: S. Low, 1863), 172–89.
14. Jennifer Phegley, *Educating the Proper Woman Reader: Victorian Family Literary Magazines and the Cultural Health of the Nation* (Columbus: Ohio State University Press, 2004), 2, 30.
15. Ann Thompson, 'A Club of Our Own: Women's Play Readings in the Nineteenth Century', *Borrowers and Lenders: the Journal of Shakespeare and Appropriation* 2, 2 (2006): 15.
16. Patrick Brantlinger, *The Reading Lesson: the Threat of Mass Literacy in Nineteenth-Century British Fiction* (Indiana: Indiana University Press, 1998), 20.
17. Unpublished records of the Bristol Friendly Reading Society, in the keeping of the society secretary.
18. John Forster, *The Life of Charles Dickens* (1872–74; London 1927), i.454.
19. Charles Dickens, *Little Dorrit* (1855–57), ed. Stephen Wall and Helen Small (Harmondsworth: Penguin, 1998), 739. All subsequent references are to this edition.
20. For example, the novel opens on 'a fierce August day' in Marseilles. Contemporary readers appreciated the tour-de-force: 'Chapter One makes the reader perspire by its torrid fervour even in this foggy December weather', *Weekly Dispatch*, 9 December 1855.
21. *The Athenaeum*, 1 December 1855.
22. See *The Illustrated London News, The Sun* and *Charles Dickens, The Critical Heritage*, ed. Philip Collins (London 1971), 350–73.
23. Robert L. Patten, 'Dickens as Serial Author: a Case of Multiple Identities', in *Nineteenth Century Media and the Construction of Identities*, ed. Laurel Brake, Bill Bell, and David Finkelstein (Basingstoke: Palgrave Macmillan, 2000), 137.
24. Pierre Bourdieu, *The Field of Cultural Production* (Oxford: Polity, 1993), 31–2.
25. Richard D. Altick, 'Varieties of Readers' Response: the Case of Dombey and Son', *Yearbook of English Studies*, 10 (1980): 79.
26. Linda K. Hughes and Michael Lund, *The Victorian Serial* (Charlottesville: University Press of Virginia, 1991), 16.
27. See John Russell Taylor, *Hitch: the Life and Times of Alfred Hitchcock* (London: Pantheon Books, 1978), 129.

28. M.J. Swanton, 'A Dividing Book Club of the 1840s: Wadebridge, Cornwall', *Library History*, 9, 3 and 4 (1992): 106–21.
29. John Forster, *The Life of Charles Dickens*, ii. 205.
30. *The Athenaeum*, 1 December 1855.
31. *The Letters of Mrs Gaskell*, ed. J.A.V. Chapple and Arthur Pollard (Manchester: Manchester University Press, 1966), 373.
32. John Cordy Jeaffreson, *Novels and Novelists from Elizabeth to Victoria* (London: Hurst and Blackett, 1858), reprinted in *Dickens, The Critical Heritage*, 381.
33. Quoted in C.P. Snow, 'Dickens and the Public Service', in *Dickens 1970, Centenary Essays*, ed. Michael Slater (London: Chapman & Hall, 1970), 127.
34. *Blackwood's Magazine*, April 1857, reprinted in *Dickens, The Critical Heritage*, 359, and *New Quarterly Review* 23, 1857 (Dickens House Museum).
35. *Bell's Weekly Messenger*, 5 April 1856.
36. Jonathan Rose, 'How Historians Study Reader Response: or, What did Jo Think of *Bleak House?*', in *Literature in the Marketplace*, ed. John O. Jordan and Robert L. Patten (Cambridge: Cambridge University Press, 2003), 208.
37. *The Letters of Charles Dickens*, Pilgrim Edition, Vol. 8, ed. Graham Storey and Kathleen Tillotson (Oxford: Clarendon Press, 1995), 228, 129n.
38. All the music referred to here is in the collection of the Dickens House Museum, London. I am grateful to the curators for their assistance.
39. *New Quarterly Review*, 23, 1857 (Dickens House Museum).
40. *The Letters of Charles Dickens*, Vol. 8, 232n, 290n.
41. Malcolm Morley, '*Little Dorrit*, On and Off', *The Dickensian*, 49–50 (1954), 136–40.
42. The manuscript (MS) of *Little Dorrit* is in the Victoria and Albert Museum, London. I am indebted to Andrew Russell, the curator of the Forster collection, for his help and knowledge.
43. Dickens's puns on his characters' names dates back as least as far as *Oliver Twist* (1837–9), where Charley Bates is cheekily and repetitively referred to as Master Bates.
44. MS of *Little Dorrit*, Vol I, Part One, p. 18; Penguin Classics edn., 36: paragraph begins 'The shadow in which she sat'.
45. Susan Belasco Smith, 'Serialization and the Nature of Uncle Tom's Cabin', in *Periodical Literature in Nineteenth Century America*, eds. Kenneth M Price and Susan Belasco Smith (Charlottesville: University of Virginia Press, 1995), 71.

3
Reading Across the Empire: the National Home Reading Union Abroad

Robert Snape

The National Home Reading Union

The National Home Reading Union[1] was established in Great Britain in 1889 by John Brown Paton, a prominent Congregationalist minister, to improve popular reading through the formation of local reading circles. It aimed, through its prescriptive lists, 'to guide readers of all ages in the choice of books', 'to unite them as members in a reading guild' and 'to group them where possible in circles for mutual help and interest'.[2] Readers who were unable to find a local circle could join as individual members and follow the set courses of reading as they wished, although the Union's preference was that readers should combine in circles whenever possible.

The Union was modelled upon the North American Chautauqua Literary and Scientific Reading Circle, which was formed in 1878.[3] This evolved from the annual Chautauqua summer camp meeting and aimed to maintain its educational provision through a winter programme of prescribed reading in local circles and discussion groups. While originating in England, the Union quickly developed a presence in British colonies and dominions and in other countries. Though never gaining a large membership, the National Home Reading Union remains important to an understanding of why popular reading remained a cause of cultural concern in the late nineteenth and early twentieth centuries and of how reading groups formed around shared cultural and social identities. It is of particular interest in that its adoption in distant parts of the British Empire represented a process through which national social reading practices were dispersed beyond Great Britain and invokes questions concerning the relationships between reading, nationality and place. This chapter addresses these questions; first however, it outlines the rationale for the Union, which, being devised in response to patterns of reading in Great Britain, was not originally intended to become international in scope.

The Union was launched at a summer assembly in Blackpool, a popular seaside resort in the north-west of England, in the hope of recruiting working-class readers en masse, but was unsuccessful in gaining the hoped-for mass appeal.[4] The summer assembly was followed by a winter season of reading. Each circle chose which of the prescribed courses of reading it wished to follow and met regularly, usually fortnightly or monthly, to work under the guidance of a voluntary leader who directed the meeting and served as a link between the circle and the Union's headquarters. Initially three courses were offered: a general course, a young people's course and an artisan's course, though the latter was discontinued after only one year and was replaced by a special course of more advanced texts for the educated reader.

Systematic reading was of the utmost importance and circles were advised to ensure that all members read the same book in order to maximize the effectiveness of the group discussions. Readers who completed a number of courses of reading over a substantial period of time were issued with a certificate signed by Princess Louise, the Union's patron. The lists below provide some indication of the type of recommended reading:

General and young people's lists in 1891–92[5]
J. Thorold Rogers, *The British Citizen*
A. Mongredien, *History of the Free Trade Movement in England*
M. Creighton, *The Age of Elizabeth*
Lord Macaulay, *Lord Clive and, Warren Hastings*
L. Stephen, *Samuel Johnson*
T. Huxley, *Introductory Primer*
J. Stuart, *A Chapter of Science*
E. Butler, *Pond Life*
E. Parkes, *On Personal Care of Health*
F. Burnaby, *A Ride to Khiva*
Herodotus, *Egypt* and *Scythia*
C. Dickens, *Barnaby Rudge*
S.T. Coleridge, *Poems*

Young people's course 1891–92
N. Hawthorne, *Tanglewood Tales*
W. Scott, *The Talisman*

C. Dickens, *Christmas Carol*
W. Scott, *Marmion*
H. Longfellow, *Narrative Poems*
C. Yonge, *Historical Ballads*
L. Creighton, *England a Continental Power*
S.R. Gardiner, *Illustrated English History pt 1*
S. Smiles, *Life of Livingstone*
C. Yonge, *A Book of Golden Deeds*
A. Geikie, *Geology*
A. Geikie, *Physical Geography*
J. Wright, *Little Asker*
J.G. Wood, *Common Objects of the Microscope*
W. Tegetmeier, *The Handbook of Household Management and Cookery*
J.T. Burgess, *English Wild Flowers*
E. Parkes, *On Personal Care of Health*

The special courses offered more advanced and technical reading. Examples of these courses and their prescribed books in 1903–04 are as follows:[6]

Folklore: the past in the present
J.G. Frazer, *The Golden Bough*
M.R. Cox, *Introduction to Folklore*
L. Gomme, *Ethnology in Folklore*

The making of modern Italy
Bolton King, *Mazzini* (Special NHRU edition 2/6)
R.M. Johnston, *The Roman Theocracy and the Roman Republic*

Free trade
A.C. Bowley, *National Progress in Wealth and Trade since 1882*
C.F. Bastable, *Commerce of Nations*
J.P. Sheldon, *The Future of British Agriculture*
Rider Haggard, *Rural England*

Political and religious life in the seventeenth century
S.R. Gardiner, *The First Two Stuarts and the Puritan Revolution – 1603–1660*
J.R. Seeley, *The Growth of British Policy*
J. Milton, *Aeropagitica*
Lord Macaulay, *History of England*
H.D. Traill, *Lord Strafford*

Novels and essays
G. Eliot, *Scenes of Clerical Life*
W. Hazlitt, *Winterslow*

Open air course
Mrs Brightwen, *Glimpses into Plant Life* (NHRU edition 1/6)
H. Thoreau, *Walden*
W. Wordsworth, *Poems*
E.S. Armitage, *Introduction to English Antiquities*
O. Goldsmith, *The Deserted Village*

Colonization of America in the seventeenth century
J. Smith, *Description of New England*
Rufus Choate, *The Romance of New England*
Cotton Mather, *Lives of Bradford and Winthrop*
F. Goodwin, *The Pilgrim Fathers*
S. G. Fisher, *The True History of the American Revolution*
N. Hawthorne, *The Scarlet Letter*
M. Johnston, *The Old Dominion*

Circles met in church halls, technical schools and public libraries, though most meetings were held in members' houses. In the Union's early years some circles were formed in factories, meeting in lunch-breaks to discuss books,[7] while others were founded by philanthropically-inspired individuals to introduce working people to books and literature.[8] Few working-class circles survived for long, a likely reason being that, as the public library pioneer Thomas Greenwood noted, home conditions were not conducive to serious reading.[9] Although there are isolated examples of working-class readers attempting to form their own circles, records suggest that most circles depended on the support of middle-class philanthropy, typically the intervention of a clergyman or middle-class woman. However, even these struggled to survive, not least because the advanced level of the prescribed reading was usually too difficult for relatively uneducated readers.

Many successful circles originated within existing social formations in which reading formed a natural part of cultural life, a typical example being those formed by church groups, which often managed to survive for several years within the educational and social programmes organized by nonconformist churches.[10] Public libraries too operated circles, though a suspicion amongst librarians that the Union was trespassing upon their professional territory prevented this form of partnership from developing widely.[11] The most successful and durable circles were those formed by women as domestic circles that met in the afternoons in members' houses where they integrated easily into the social calendar. The popularity of these female home-based circles reflected the social context of Victorian and Edwardian reading. The need to regulate domestic reading, especially that of young women, was widely understood and advice manuals and reading groups were a valuable means to this end. Reading aloud was a popular family pastime and was readily absorbed within circle practice. Additionally, only middle-class houses were sufficiently spacious to accommodate comfortably the dozen or so members of a Union circle. For many readers the social aspects of the circle meeting were its principal appeal, although some valued circles as a form of self-education or a means of continuing education for young women who had left school. This was particularly important for middle-class girls who, unlike working-class girls, did not enter employment but remained at home until old enough to marry.[12] Reading circles not only encouraged such young women to continue to read the 'right' kind of books but also developed their social and conversational skills. Union circles were also valued by older women for the intellectual engagement that they offered.[13]

Although it did not acquire the status of a mass movement, the Union's impact extended beyond its membership. Its prescribed reading lists were recognized as authoritative and some public libraries displayed these to assist their borrowers. Some 13,052 readers had joined the Union by 1906, and by 1912 the estimated number was approximately 70,000, though this included children from several London schools. Paton's death in 1911 heralded the start of a gradual decline in which the Union, lacking his inspirational leadership, lurched through a series of financial difficulties. The Union never recovered from the crisis of cultural confidence that followed the First World War, and rival forms of popular education, notably the Workers' Education Association and the BBC, evolved to replace much of the work that the Union had set out to undertake. Throughout the 1920s its level of activity declined and in 1930 it declared itself defunct.

Circles beyond the British Isles

Although established to address a specific concern about popular reading in Great Britain, the National Home Reading Union quickly acquired an international dimension. At the launch of the Union in

Blackpool, Paton[14] reported letters of support from Australia, India, South Africa, California, New York, Turkey and Russia, while according to Churton Collins[15] circles were established in the Channel Islands, Germany, India, St Petersburg and Japan, with some about to be formed amongst the English in China. By 1897 the Union had spread further, recording centres in Havre, Oporto, Stockholm, Barbados, Bombay, Gold Coast Colony, New Zealand and Cape Town, and with corresponding members – those studying through correspondence rather than circle meetings – in Jamaica, India, Cape Town, Adelaide and Montreal.[16] By 1906 there were also corresponding members in West Africa and Canada. While the progress of the Union in India was eventually constrained through the difficulties members experienced in obtaining the prescribed books, it flourished in Australia, South Africa and Canada.

Methodological considerations

Records of Union circles are rare and elusive, the primary source of evidence being the Union's magazines. These were published monthly throughout the annual reading season from autumn to early summer.

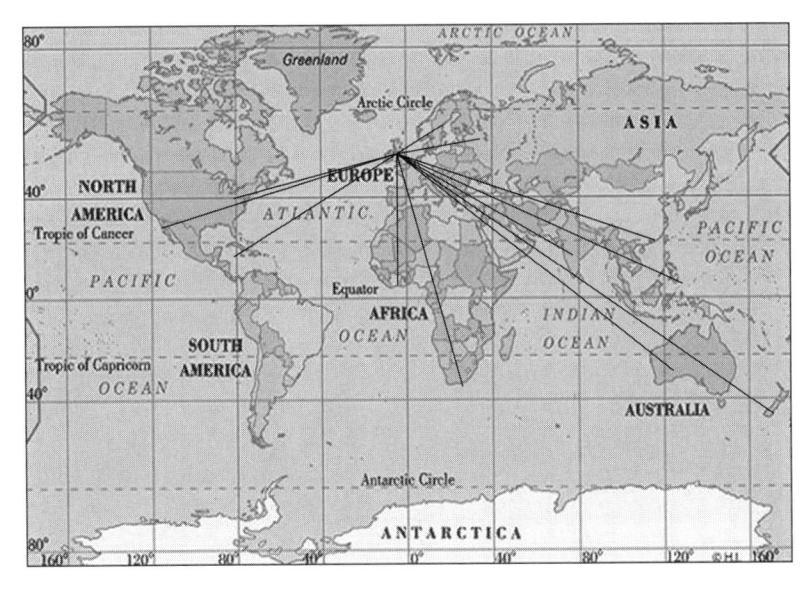

Figure 3.1 An indicative map of the geographical spread of National Home Reading Union activity in the 1890s

They included essays on topics related to the reading courses, official announcements, reports of the annual summer assembly and, on an ad hoc basis, reports from individual circles. The Union also published annual reports, again not all of which have survived. Occasionally the magazines included reports from circles in countries beyond Great Britain, though offering only a glimpse of Union activity in other countries. Moreover, because such reports were usually submitted by successful circles, they say little about those which struggled or ceased to function. As there is little consistency in style or content, it is difficult to obtain an accurate impression of the average size or longevity of circles, especially those which may have existed for only a short period. This necessarily means that interpretative reconstructions of Union activity based on fragmented sources available in England remain incomplete and tentative. Nevertheless, there is sufficient evidence to construct an outline picture of the geographical range and socio-cultural composition of Union circles beyond Great Britain, and of the ways in which both the Union and its readers conceptualized the function and significance of these.

The Union was founded as a missionary undertaking to improve levels of reading and literary knowledge amongst working-class people in Great Britain, but when transplanted to other countries this rationale became less meaningful as circles formed in different social and cultural contexts, as is evident in the reports from circles in Australia, South Africa and Canada published in the Union's magazines. A letter from a colonist, reprinted in Paton's biography,[17] gives some insight into the nature of the changed social and cultural environment of the Union abroad:

> The loneliest reader, buried in the bush, will be kept in touch with the reading life of thousands of companions, through his monthly magazine ... One of the privations which educated colonists often feel most is the absence of intellectual conversation for their children to hear. Yet there must be few colonial townships, if any, without men and women of intelligence and cultivation who can talk well, if anything occurs to draw them out and draw them together ... It is hoped that the Union will also provide a pleasant link with friends and relatives in the dear old country. Young cousins on opposite sides of the world, following the same course of reading, would find they had topics in common when they sat down to the difficult task of corresponding with relatives whom they had never seen. We need to draw closer together, individually and nationally.

Drawing primarily on reports available in libraries and archives in England of circles in Australia, South Africa and Canada, the remainder of this chapter explores the ways in which the changed social and cultural environment of the Union gave meaning to reading practice beyond Great Britain.[18]

Australia

There were registered Union members in Australia as early as 1890 although it seems likely that these had joined on an individual basis. In 1906 Alex Hill, Master of Downing College and a senior official of the Union, undertook a university extension lecture tour of Australia, following which a branch was formed in Western Australia and 76 members enrolled. This was interpreted by the Union as a display of admirable spirit in which 'our colony has answered the call of the mother country, speaking through the voice of one of her old universities'.[19] Little is currently known about the size and longevity of this branch but another was formed in 1909 by Miss Henderson, formerly Principal of Clyde who had learned of the Union while attending an educational conference in England organized through the League of the Empire.[20] This organization was a forerunner of the League for the Exchange of Commonwealth Teachers, whose support the Union had been anxious to obtain. As had been the case in Britain, the development of the Union in Australia owed much to the voluntary efforts of women, a fact the Union acknowledged in describing the indefatigable Mrs D. Avery, the secretary of the Australian Branch in 1923, as 'the right kind of woman to hold such a post, that calls for energy and alertness'.[21] Circles also existed in Kew, Malvern, South Yarra and in remote rural locations where Mrs Avery's efforts to recruit volunteers elicited a number of responses from 'interested women'. While some circles were formed primarily as social gatherings, the missionary ethos that had originally characterized the Union remained evident in her campaign to promote the Union 'in those quarters where lack of literary knowledge is a lack that might be beneficially remedied'.[22] One such group was the city typists, who, being thought unlikely to have an intimate knowledge of the major literary or philosophical writers, might benefit from circle membership. A similar attempt to recruit business 'girls' resulted in the establishment in Melbourne of a circle for young women 'with few means of satisfying their higher tastes'.[23] The Melbourne branch, which was simultaneously the headquarters of the Union in Australia, flourished throughout the 1920s, a period in which the Union was in decline in Great Britain, suggesting that even before the Union became defunct, its Australian operations were virtually independent of the parent organization. This may be due in part to the fact that, in remote rural regions, the Union fulfilled a different function to that in Great Britain by enabling geographically and culturally isolated people to retain intellectual contact through reading. A member in Great Britain, for instance, sent books and notes of circle discussions to a nephew on an Australian ranch while another reader sent copies of the Union magazine to a solitary relation for 'a bit of intellectual interest'.[24] These books and magazines were shared between many readers, thus extending the Union's reach and deploying reading as a means to incorporate remote communities, a function it continues to fulfil in modern Australia.[25]

In addition to the National Home Reading Circles described above there were also indigenous reading organizations. The Brisbane Literary Circle, which was established in 1888, could later have become a National Home Reading Union circle but opted instead to imitate the example of Chautauqua as this was felt to be more suitable for new countries such as America and Australia; this did not prevent it, however, from adopting a focus on British culture.[26] In 1892 it became affiliated to the newly founded Australasian Home Reading Union, a break-away movement from the Australasian Association for the Advancement of Science. This reading union aimed to encourage the habit of reading amongst non-readers. Like the National Home Reading Union, it prepared lists of recommended reading on specific topics, encouraged the formation of local circles with voluntary leaders, published a magazine, *The Australasian Home Reader*, and insisted upon systematic reading to facilitate discussion at meetings. By 1893 it had 76 circles and 1407 members, its rapid growth being due in part to the incorporation within it of existing literary circles. Table 3.1 shows the geographical spread of the Australasian Home Reading Union and the distribution of its membership.

While the courses bore many similarities to those offered by the National Home Reading Union, there was a greater emphasis on the natural sciences, with five specific courses on chemistry, physics, geology and mineralogy, biology and physiology and hygiene.

Like the National Union, the Australasian Home Reading Union owed much to the voluntary input of women, particularly Susannah Maybanke Wolstenholme, founder of the Women's Federal League, who became its general secretary. Though affirmatively Australasian in its identity and management, the Union retained imperial associations, offering courses on the history of the British Empire, Shakespere (sic) and

Table 3.1 Geographical spread of the Australasian Home Reading Union and distribution of its membership

Colony	Number of circles	Members
New South Wales	31	538
Tasmania	17	204
Victoria	14	231
New Zealand	6	274
South Australia	7	119
Queensland	1	41
Total	76	1407

English literature and enjoying the patronage of the Countess of Jersey, wife of the Governor of New South Wales, as president.[27] Its rejection of an invitation to affiliate with the National Home Reading Union represented a shift towards autonomy in the promotion of social reading groups in Australia while remaining within the mainstream of British literary and scientific culture. However, its predominantly middle-class membership militated against its ability to engage working-class people and by 1913 it had ceased to exist.[28]

South Africa

The Union established a presence in South Africa through the Hilton College at Maritzburg, a public school founded in 1872 by Englishmen. By 1897 a local centre had been established that had gained 121 members by 1900.[29] By 1905 it was firmly established, with circles in Cape Colony, Grahamstown, Natal, Orange River Colony, Healdtown, Fort Beaufort, Johannesburg, Port Elizabeth, Wynberg, Knysna, Umtata in Tembuland and Libode in Western Pondoland. In addition, some circles operated on the Union model without becoming affiliated to it. The Cape Colony Literature Committee, for example, reported 33 honorary members and 13 circles registered with the Union in 1905 but noted that this was not an accurate representation of the number of active reading circles in South Africa. Most of these circles appear to have been formed by and for women readers except for the Knysna circle whose decision to include men attracted the accolade of being a 'wise plan'.[30] The habit of circle membership was frequently handed down from mother to daughter. A female reader from Queenstown wrote to the magazine requesting a book-list for her ten-year-old daughter, noting 'As a child I was a member and derived both pleasure and profit from the reading courses, and I have always looked forward to the time when my children would be old enough to join'[31]; in another instance a reader reported that her circle included a mother and her daughters who had recently left school.[32] The list for 1922–23 included the Song of Solomon, Keats's poetry, and books on Sir John Millais, astronomy, India, Greek drama and philosophy and London in fiction. The middle-class predominance that characterized the Union in England was replicated in South African circles, as the practice of accommodating around 20 members in domestic houses must have necessitated a reasonably large drawing room.[33] The Union was still active in South Africa in 1929–30, the point at which it closed in Britain through lack of interest.

As in Australia, circles served both to consolidate social bonds and to nurture a sense of expatriate collectivism, the latter function being acknowledged by the Union:

> In connection with the Cape section of the NHRU, one should add that many of the letters from teachers and residents on farms, or in remote corners of the Colony, are of intense interest, and the reading circles are fast becoming bonds of union between town and country ... the NHRU is really a University Extension movement on an immense scale, and may thus become a valuable factor in promoting that closer union of the Empire which we all desire.[34]

The nurturing of imperial consciousness was an inherent function of the Union in several colonies and dominions and it was aided in this by various women's cultural organizations. This was effected in South Africa through the support of the Guild of Loyal Women of South Africa[35] which, through its literature committee organized an essay competition for its members in the winter of 1904–05.[36]

There was also a South African Home Reading Union. This was formed in 1902 and differed from the National Home Reading Union in being for female readers only. By 1908 it had 330 members distributed across ten circles. However, it stood in contradistinction to the National Home Reading Union principally through its wider national appeal. It attempted to appeal to both British and Boer readers by, for example, issuing reading lists of books in English and Dutch, and thus differed from the Union in not being restricted to a British and imperial outlook but guided by a new sense of a South African community.[37]

Canada

As Heather Murray[38] has shown, there was a vibrant culture of social reading in Canada prior to the arrival of the National Home Reading

Union, largely because the Chautauqua system had, through its proximity to Canada, been widely adopted in the form of summer assemblies, or 'independent Chautauquas', particularly in the Ontario region. There were also several Chautauqua branches and circles in Canada. The prior existence of the Chautauqua system in Canada raises the question of why there should have been a perceived need for the National Home Reading Union. A clue is found in a contemporary comment, noted by Murray, that some readers, being uneasy with the 'foreign' origins of the Chautauqua system, preferred to ally themselves with the Union. This suggests that the Union's association with mainstream British literary culture and Britain itself was important to readers' self-identity. A further reason may be that some British emigrants already had connections to the Union; as Elizabeth Haldane recorded, several members of her Home Reading Union circle emigrated to Canada and 'took their books with them',[39] and it is not unreasonable to speculate that Union magazines, containing guidance notes to the prescribed books, might have been packed along with them.

Serendipity too could be important; an early reference to Union activity in Canada describes how the chance discovery of a Union magazine inspired the establishment of a circle in Ottawa in 1895 by two English women, Mrs Dale Harris and Mrs J.B. Tyrell.[40] Other circles were established in Peterborough, Norwood and Petriola.[41] Canadian circles also existed at Elmshurst and Kingston, Ontario, and by 1901, 249 Canadian readers had enrolled as members of the Union.[42] Again, the expansion of the Union in Canada owed much to middle-class women and was to a large extent coordinated through the National Council of Women of Canada. The Council's federated framework comprised representatives of diverse women's clubs, temperance unions, historical associations and educational unions, and reading circles fitted naturally into this pattern. The Earl of Aberdeen, at whose London home the Union had been founded, was the patron of the Council and Lady Aberdeen an Advisory President to its Executive Committee. The Union was thus represented on the Council, which in 1899 recorded the inauguration of the Home Reading Union 'to promote habits of good and systematic reading'.[43] Lady Aberdeen's support of the Union was consistent with her active involvement in the promotion of reading; she had previously established the Aberdeen Association for the Distribution of Good Literature to Settlers in the West following a visit to the Prairies in 1890. By 1898 this had 15 local branches, collecting and shipping books and magazines to isolated readers, leading the Montreal Herald to comment that Lady Aberdeen was 'particularly interested in the intellectual development of women' and had contributed much to the improvement of the social conditions of Canadian women of all social classes.[44] Unlike the situation in Britain, where the national leadership of the Union lay predominantly in male hands, the role of the National Council of Women and of Lady Aberdeen in its development in Canada reflects the role of socially-elite women in promoting cultural activity and as nation-builders.[45]

Canadian circles displayed many similarities to those that flourished in England as part of middle-class social life. One, for example, met fortnightly in a member's house, combining social association and informal education by not only reading the listed books but also by acquiring and studying supporting illustrative material, after which tea and cake were served. Its members believed the circle educationally superior to a local Book Lovers' Library, which charged five cents a week for the loan of novels because membership of the Union enabled readers to obtain a certificate upon completion of the prescribed course of reading.[46] Royal patronage provided a further spur for readers as at least one member of this circle intended to undertake the four-year reading course necessary to obtain the special certificate signed by Princess Louise, an ambition which further links Union membership to cultural and national identity. Writing in 1929 of the Ottawa branch, its secretary, Mrs. G.C. Wright, recorded that it had thirty-three years of continuous work and retained four original members, a longevity that few British circles could emulate.[47] Other branches had been formed in Ottawa by the turn of the century, again aided by Lady Aberdeen, who was at the time resident at Rideau Hall. The Ottawa branch appears initially to have modelled itself upon the majority of circles in Britain in its aim of helping members to acquire a greater understanding and appreciation of English literature. However, by the 1920s its scope had broadened; the 1927–28 season, for example, was devoted to citizenship and contemporary social and political issues. The reading aloud of plays was a popular feature of the seasonal programme, and had led to a 'marked improvement in the reading aloud of the branch'. The available evidence suggests that most Canadian Union circles were domestic and were mainly for women with few, if any, being established in factories or schools as was the case in Britain. This reflects not only the differing social and cultural environment but also the precedent set by Canadian Chautuaqua circles which were themselves predominantly home-based and female in composition.[48]

When the National Home Reading Union ceased to operate in 1930, colonial reading circles found themselves without a coordinating parent organization, though for some time prior to its closure the support that the Union had been able to offer to circles outside Great Britain was negligible. Indifference to the Union in Britain contrasted sharply with the enthusiastic support it enjoyed in South Africa and Canada. After the Wynberg Union Branch in South Africa wrote to the Ottawa Branch of their 'unanimous desire to try to carry on the work by ourselves' the Ottawa readers decided to form a Canadian Home Reading Union, renaming their circle the Dale Harris Branch in recognition of the founder of the first Canadian circle. The Ottawa branch invited the Toronto branch to join them in the new Canadian Union, with the organization once again being supported by Lady Aberdeen as its patron.[49] This marked the beginning of an enduring programme of organized social reading in Canada. Further branches joined and by 1939 the Canadian Union had six affiliated branches; this had risen to 12 by 1949, 25 by 1959 and 32 by 1969. Their geographical distribution in 1969 was as follows: Ontario 17, Quebec 10, Prince Edward Island one, and British Columbia one. The three other circles that made up the total were not actually based in Canada, being in New Hampshire, Belgium and Holland; the latter was formed by a Mrs John Read of Ottawa who lived for a time at The Hague where her husband was a judge at the International Court, again showing the importance of migratory patterns to the development of the Union. These circles retained some aspects of the National Home Reading Union ethos, notably its principles of self-help education, while necessarily having themselves to undertake organization and management tasks that had previously been undertaken centrally by the Union.[50] Though the Canadian Home Reading Union drew its inspiration from the National Home Reading Union, it did not replicate the modus operandi of its British prototype. Whereas the British model was one of central management and the improvement of working-class reading, the Canadian model was more democratic in its management – with its Central Committee including representatives of affiliated groups[51] – and less dedicated to social and educational reform.

The National Home Reading Union's Canadian legacy

The Canadian Home Reading Union nurtured a culture of local reading communities, some of which were still operating at the turn of this century. In the main these were women's circles, meeting in members' houses and creating opportunities for socialization and intellectual activity. The Kente Group in Kingston, Ontario, one of the first circles in the Canadian Home Reading Union, was formed by daughters of the members of Ontario's John Buchan Branch and comprised mainly young mothers. Ruth Stanley, a member of the Kente circle in the 1950s and 1960s, recalled that:

> The size of our group was perhaps 12 or 15. We met in each others' homes which precluded too large a club. We met once or twice a month, although not in summer. The members were all women. The group was added to as we brought in kindred spirits. A few were army wives who were often posted away after 2 or 3 years. This brought in new ideas and personalities. No one remembers any leader of our group. We chose a 'theme' for the coming year's reading and each member chose her own subject more or less to relate to that theme. When a member read her paper she would bring along an armful of books she had consulted. There was no attempt for us to read the same books like a book club. Believe me, the subjects were very diverse. I remember one on the Rothschilds, one on Josiah Wedgwood, one on Gold and one on the phallic symbol in art. We had fascinating question periods and, of course, we had wonderful refreshments.[52]

The Kente Group still existed in the early years of the twenty-first century, its eleven members preparing and delivering one paper a year; the theme for 2002 was Russian literature. The longevity of the group owed much to its social function, but this in itself was underpinned by its intellectual appeal. Reading provided a catalyst around which friendships, informal education and intellectual stimulation were nourished, and, according to Isabel Trumpour, also a member of the Kente group, offered intellectual engagement that tea and a social event in themselves could not. The importance of the voluntary effort of women in Canada mirrors that in both Australia and South Africa. In part this was a reflection of the essentially domestic context of the Union; it was after all women who were best situated to benefit from the social aspects of group reading during the daytime. However, for women seeking to contribute to social and cultural life more generally the Union also provided opportunities to obtain positions of power and responsibility and to work alongside representatives of colonial government.

Conclusion

While the mode of operation of the National Home Reading Union in British colonies and dominions reflected that in Britain to some extent, the context in which it operated was fundamentally different. The various geographical and socio-cultural environments of imperial nations changed its function and its circles acquired different meanings, particularly in terms of the ways in which circle membership contributed to the self-identity of readers. The relationships between reading and identity have been explored by Alberto Manguel,[53] who describes reading as a badge or a sign of alliance and by Francis Mulhern, who notes that the act of reading is concerned not only with what is read but with the identity of readers and 'as whom' they read.[54] How, then, might membership of a National Home Reading Union circle in a colony or dominion have formed the identity of readers, and what was understood to be 'national' about the National Home Reading Union?

As stated above, it was a declared aim of the Union to unite readers within a 'great reading guild'. The Union considered itself to be more than an aggregate of individual readers, claiming that:

> If the Union is a real Union, we are all part of a great living thing, and it takes all the members to work it. We want to know more about each other, what books are liked the best, where the difficulties lie, how the magazines can be made of more use and touch our lives more, and everything that can make us all feel that we are workers together. We must get this kind of corporate feeling, growing up through knowledge of each other and the remembrance that we are fellow-members of a great organisation or we shall fall short of the ideal of the N.H.R.U.[55]

The distinction drawn by Paul Jordan-Smith and Laurel Horton[56] between a group as a gathering of people organized for a single event and a community as a stable and integrated network is useful in setting local reading practice within a wider cultural context. If the individual reading circle was the group, the Union represented the community to which the group consciously felt itself to belong. Community is a term with several layered meanings, and the National Home Reading Union constituted a core around which a number of interconnected actual and imagined communities formed.[57] National Home Reading Union circles brought together people through a shared interest in books and reading. At one level this was a reading community in the sense of the Union as a national and international organization. At another level, the Union's colonial circles formed a framework within which a national identity was maintained across the colonies and dominions of the British Empire in both real and imagined ways. Unlike some examples of imperial leisure practice, such as sport,[58] which actively engaged colonized peoples in British pursuits, the National Home Reading Union did not seek to bring indigenous people within its social and cultural space but, by excluding native populations, enabled its members to retain an identity as members of a national imperial community in distinction to the 'other' of the colonized.[59] Union circles thus enabled their readers, through the normative and everyday practice of shared reading, to retain contact with family and friends in Great Britain. These layers of community were closely intertwined and the Union subtly conflated them; it had, it maintained:

> sought to extend its work to the Dominions, and to do what it could towards influencing the pursuit of reading as a social function, with the stimulus and guidance which our organisation provides, amongst our kinsmen overseas. This is as is should be. Nothing is useless which helps, in however small a degree, to link the nations of our Empire together in their intellectual, no less than their civic and social life.[60]

In furtherance of the pursuit of an imperial consciousness the Union wanted the support of governmental secretaries of education, describing how its reading circles would not only alleviate the intellectual isolation of readers in remote parts of the world but would also promote a sense of cultural communion throughout the Empire.[61] Communal reading thus assisted the formation and maintenance of a cultural community that extended across the British Empire, leading the Union to comment in 1912 that it hoped gradually to 'create a Reading Guild for the whole nation and the English-speaking Empire through which the heritage of English literature may be brought within the reach of all classes'.[62]

In this statement, distinctions between nation and Empire are dissolved within a unified cultural heritage, reflecting Ernest Renan's[63] idea of the nation as a 'large scale solidarity' of a shared cultural tradition. Literature, as a bearer of this cultural tradition, was an important means of preserving a national cultural heritage throughout the Empire, through organizations such as the Victoria League and the Guild of Loyal Women of South Africa, which both had dedicated literature committees, and through the operation of a reading union by the Girls' Friendly Society, which was based in England and had colonial branches.[64]

John Tomlinson has argued that national identity is an imagined identity, lived through representation.[65] Through its performative and spatial dimensions the National Home Reading Union nurtured such an imagined identity. While not founded with overtly imperialistic aims, it nevertheless helped to sustain the sense of a national culture throughout the Empire. As normative assumptions about the Empire in the late Victorian and Edwardian era become more fully appreciated,[66] the role of seemingly neutral organizations in the promotion of an imperial consciousness has become more fully recognized. For example, while public libraries were not introduced specifically in order to underpin imperial expansion, it was nevertheless taken for granted that they were a small but important part of the machinery of Empire. Speaking at the opening of the Edmonton (London) public library, for instance, Mrs Humphry Ward spoke of its 'great indispensable work of pushing forward and spreading the British Empire' while Lord Rosebery, at the opening of the Shepherd's Bush library, alluded to the need for education to maintain the British Empire. In a further example, at Newton Abbot, Lord Elrington urged the study of history to understand why empires declined: such an understanding would, he felt, stimulate patriotism in the ultimate interests of the British Empire.[67] Similar normative assumptions can, it is suggested, be ascribed to the National Home Reading Union. There was in fact a contemporary belief, widely attributed to Edward Wakefield, a nineteenth-century British politician and sometime director of the New Zealand Colonization Company, that successful colonization depended on the 'replication of the structures' of the founding society.[68] In recreating a 'real' community of readers the National Home Reading Union simultaneously nurtured an imagined community that supported a sense of national/imperial identity in countries throughout the Empire.

The review of colonial and post-colonial National Home Reading Union circles offered in this chapter does not claim, and is not intended to be, comprehensive or conclusive. A great deal of further research is required to locate and interrogate archives and personal memoirs of reading unions in countries throughout the former British Empire. However, it does suggest that social reading groups were important to the formation and maintenance of the self-identity of their members. It also hints at the possibility of subtle and progressive changes in the nature of this identity as the political relationships between these countries and Great Britain changed with the decline of the Empire. Further investigation of social reading circles – those of the National Home Reading Union and also those of the other reading unions to which brief reference has been made – has the potential to make an important contribution to the discourse of colonial and post-colonial cultural history.

Notes

1. Robert Snape, 'The National Home Reading Union', *Journal of Victorian Culture* 7, 1 (Spring 2002): 86–110.
2. *National Home Reading Union Magazine* 15, 3 (December 1903): 55.
3. J.G. Fitch, 'The Chautauqua Reading Circle', *Nineteenth Century* 24 (October 1888): 487–500; Theodore Morrison, *Chautauqua: a Centre for Education, Religion and the Arts* (Chicago: University of Chicago Press 1974).
4. Robert Snape, 'An English Chautauqua: the National Home Reading Union and the Development of Rational Holidays in Late Victorian Britain', *Journal of Tourism History* 2, 3 (2010): 213–34.
5. National Home Reading Union, *General Report*, 1891–92.
6. *National Home Reading Union Magazine*, 1903–04.
7. National Home Reading Union, *Notes, Reports and Announcements*, 1894.
8. *National Home Reading Union Magazine* 18, 1 (September 1906).
9. Thomas Greenwood, 'The Great Fiction Question', in *Library Year Book* (London: Cassell 1897): 107–16.
10. *National Home Reading Union Magazine* 4, 1 (October 1893).
11. Robert Snape, *Leisure and the Rise of the Public Library* (London: Library Association Publishing, 1995), 122–3.
12. Kate Flint, *The Woman Reader 1873–1914* (Oxford: Oxford University Press, 1993), 71–117.
13. Snape, 'The National Home Reading Union', 86–110.
14. 'The National Home Reading Union: Inaugural Meeting at Blackpool', *Leeds Mercury*, 17 July 1889, 7; see also National Home Reading Union, *Annual Report*, 1889–90.
15. John Churton Collins, 'The National Home Reading Union, and its Prospects', *Contemporary Review* (August 1890): 193–211; George Radford, *The Faculty of Reading: the Coming of Age of the National Home Reading Union* (Cambridge: Cambridge University Press, 1910).
16. National Home Reading Union, *Annual Report*, 1896–97.
17. John Lewis Paton, *John Brown Paton: a Biography* (London: Hodder and Stoughton), 291–3.
18. There is no national archive of the National Home Reading Union. Good, but incomplete collections of NHRU publications upon which the research for this chapter was based were consulted in the Manchester Public Library and the British Library (London).
19. *National Home Reading Union Magazine* 18 (3 November 1906): 59.
20. National Home Reading Union, *Annual Report*, 1908–1909.
21. *National Home Reading Union Magazine* 34 (5 February 1923): 131.
22. *National Home Reading Union Magazine* 35 (5 February 1924).
23. *National Home Reading Union Magazine* 35 (3 December 1923): 68.
24. *National Home Reading Union Magazine* 32 (7 April 1921): 272.
25. Jenny Hartley, *Reading Groups* (Oxford: Oxford University Press, 2002).
26. Leanne Day, 'Brisbane Literary Circle: the Quest for Universal Culture', *Journal of Australian Studies* 63 (1999): 92.
27. *Australasian Home Reader* 2, 1 (February 1893).
28. Martyn Lyons, 'Reading Models and Reading Communities', in *A History of the Book in Australia 1891–1945: a National Culture in a Colonised Market*,

ed. Martin Lyons and John Arnold (Queensland: University of Queensland Press, 2001), 370–88.
29. National Home Reading Union, *Annual Report*, 1900–01.
30. National Home Reading Union, *Young People's Magazine* 16 (5 February 1905): 82.
31. Ibid.
32. *National Home Reading Union Magazine* 18 (6 February 1907).
33. *National Home Reading Union Magazine* 17 (6 February 1906): 2.
34. *National Home Reading Union Magazine* 33 (3 December 1921): 6.
35. *National Home Reading Union Magazine* 34 (4 January 1923): 96.
36. *National Home Reading Union Magazine* 34 (5 February 1923).
37. Archie L. Dick, '"To Make the People of South Africa Proud of their Membership of the Great British Empire": Home Reading Unions in South Africa, 1900–1914', *Libraries and Culture* 40,1 (2005): 1–24.
38. Heather Murray, *Come, Bright Improvement! The Literary Societies of Nineteenth-Century Ontario* (Toronto: University of Toronto Press, 2002), 75–96.
39. Elizabeth Haldane, *From One Century to Another: the Reminiscences of Elizabeth S. Haldane* (London: Maclehose, 1937), 119.
40. National Home Reading Union, *The Reader* 14 (10, 1929): 389.
41. *Canadian Home Reading Union Magazine* (July 1968).
42. National Home Reading Union, *Annual Report*, 1900–01.
43. National Council of Women of Canada, *Handbook*, 1899.
44. Doris French, *Ishbel and Empire: a Biography of Lady Aberdeen* (Toronto: Dundurn Press, 1988), 253–4.
45. A.M. Austin, *Woman, Her Character, Culture and Calling a Full Discussion of Woman's Work in the Home, the School, the Church and the Social Circle, with an Account of Her Successful Labors in Moral and Social Reform* (Ottawa: Canadian Institute for Historical Microreproductions, 1980).
46. *National Home Reading Union Magazine* 15 (3 December 1903): 75.
47. National Home Reading Union, *The Reader*, 1929.
48. Murray, *Come, Bright Improvement!*, 89–90.
49. *Canadian Home Reading Union Magazine* (July 1968).
50. Correspondence from Mrs Trumpour, January 2003. I am deeply indebted to Mrs Ruth Stanley, Mrs Isabel Trumpour and Mrs Gibson who very kindly shared with me their experiences as members of Home Reading Union circles in Canada, and who provided much of the data on which the latter part of the chapter is based. Any errors of transcription, and certainly all hypothetical propositions, remain my own responsibility.
51. *Canadian Home Reading Union Magazine* (July 1968).
52. Correspondence from Mrs Stanley (January 2003).
53. Alberto Manguel, *A History of Reading* (London: HarperCollins, 1996), 214.
54. Francis Mulhern, 'English Reading', in *Nation and Narration*, ed. Homi K. Bhabha (London: Routledge, 1990), 250–64.
55. National Home Reading Union, *General Readers' Magazine* 4, 5 (February 1893).
56. Paul Jordan-Smith and Laurel Horton, 'Communities of Practice: Traditional Music and Dance', *Western Folklore* 60, 2, 3 (2001): 103–9.
57. Benedict Anderson, *Imagined Communities: Reflections on the Origin and Spread of Nationalism*, revised edn (London: Verso 1991), 37–46.

58. Derek Birley, *Land of Sport and Glory: Sport and British Society 1887–1910* (Manchester: Manchester University Press, 1995), 153–72; Roger Hutchinson, *Empire Games: the British Invention of Twentieth-Century Sport* (Edinburgh: Macmillan, 1996).
59. A good example of the ways in which the imposition of this distinction was effected through the control of leisure space is seen in Dr Vereswami's exclusion from the European Club in George Orwell's *Burmese Days*.
60. 'The NHRU in Australia', *National Home Reading Union Magazine* 35 (3 December 1923): 68.
61. Paton, *John Brown Paton*.
62. National Home Reading Union, *Annual Report*, 1912.
63. Ernest Renan, 'What is a Nation?', in *Nation and Narration*, ed. Homi K. Bhabha (London: Routledge, 1990), 8–22.
64. Julia Bush, *Edwardian Ladies and Imperial Power* (London: Leicester University Press, 2000), 131–4.
65. John Tomlinson, *Cultural Imperialism* (London: Pinter, 1991), 68–101.
66. See, for example, John M. Mackenzie, *Propaganda and Empire: the Manipulation of British Public Opinion 1880–1960* (Manchester: Manchester University Press, 1984) and John Springhall, *Youth, Empire and Society: British Youth Movements 1883–1940* (London: Croom Helm, 1977).
67. John Passmore Edwards, *A Few Footprints* (London, 1905).
68. A. James Hammerton, 'Gender and Migration', in *Gender and Empire*, ed. P. Levine, (Oxford: Oxford University Press, 2004), 156–80.

4
Utopian Civic-Mindedness: Robert Maynard Hutchins, Mortimer Adler, and the Great Books Enterprise

Daniel Born

Birth of an idea

In January 1948 *Life* magazine published a group photograph of scholars at the University of Chicago posing in an attitude of high seriousness.[1] Like an elite sports team, they stood or sat cross-legged behind 102 card catalogue drawers, each of which was marked with an upright cardboard flag bearing the name of a Great Idea. The photo celebrated the making of the Syntopicon. This massive index of Western thought, which in conception had grown godlike out of the head of Mortimer Adler, was intended to help readers navigate their way through the Great Books.

The Syntopicon enterprise had also required some assistance from mere mortals, diligent University of Chicago graduate students, and the article told part of their story: 'The exhausted-looking people grouped about the books and files above have just finished a monumental intellectual task. They have spent five years and nearly a million dollars making an index of every important idea of Western civilization.'[2] The effort was originally budgeted for $60,000, but monumental tasks usually require monumental cash outlays.

Robert Maynard Hutchins, Adler's pal and president of the university, was good at making broad gestures and sponsoring big projects. He was the man who had eliminated the university's varsity football program, and then several years later approved of the federal government's request to locate its Manhattan Project under the empty Stagg Field stadium – the site of the world's first controlled nuclear chain reaction.[3] Though I don't want to suggest that these two decisions were linked in any way, the sequence of events is sweet with irony. Hutchins always aspired to play on the biggest field of all – and his decision to help give

Figure 4.1 'The 102 Great Ideas'. Photo celebrating the making of the Syntopicon
Source: Photographer: George Skadding/Time & Life Pictures/Getty Images.

the world the atomic bomb put him and his university in the history books forever.

It is not entirely surprising that the Syntopicon project modelled itself on the great scientific achievements of the time – a sort of Manhattan Project for the humanities, if you will. In another early article and photo spread on the Syntopicon, a clean-cut young man weighs stacks of index cards, sorted by topic, on a laboratory scale, as if they are precious metal, and if there is ever a hall of fame for photo captions, this one will surely enter on the first round of voting: 'Discussions of love by great authors outweigh sin and eternity'.[4] Adler probably should have also developed a method to measure the longevity or half-lives of these ideas, but his staunch convictions about the eternal timelessness of Thought prevented him from doing so. Conversely, some ideas that we might deem very heavy elements, such as Sex and Equality, didn't weigh enough on Adler's scale to even get into the big table of 102 Ideas.[5]

The same article ('There Are Only 102 Great Ideas') announced that the Syntopicon 'will be a kit of educational tools which Chancellor Robert M. Hutchins feels may be powerful enough to save the world from self-destruction'.[6] How are we to interpret Hutchins here? As a cynical marketing mogul, or as the earnest spokesman for humanity's most redemptive potential? Probably both. The man was a university president, but who was he to say no to the power of love, the heaviest element of all? In this moment, Hutchins's utopian vision reached heights that would perhaps be matched only four years later on 15 April 1952, at the Waldorf Astoria Hotel in New York, when the actual Great Books of the Western World set, published by Britannica, was rolled out at a lavish banquet attended by prominent educators, business tycoons, and social luminaries. There Hutchins declared: 'Great Books of the Western World is an act of piety. Here are the sources of our being. Here is our heritage ... Here is the faith of the West, for here before everybody willing to look at it is that dialogue by way of which Western man has believed that he can approach the truth.'[7]

He continued, in the same speech, to say that this dialogue 'can be conducted only by free men. It is the essential reason for their freedom.'[8] The civics lesson is pretty straightforward, but the soaring rhetoric should also be read in the grain of Hutchins's utopian proclivities: these included association with the movement for world government (which put him strongly at odds with the dominant mindset of American triumphalism following the war), and then in the 1960s, at the peak of the Cold War and the struggle in Vietnam, a series of peace conferences stimulated by Hutchins's reception of Pope John XXIII's 'Peace on Earth' encyclical. It is worth recalling that Hutchins was a wayward preacher's son who, in the words of one biographer, perhaps sought substitutes for his lost religious faith.[9] This quasi-spiritual and aggressively liberal element of Hutchins's thinking is worth another look, I think, and one of the purposes of this chapter is to reconsider that element in hopes of reframing a crucial question: is commitment to the Great Books the enemy of progressive education (the scholarly consensus that has largely followed Dewey), or in fact a foundation *for* it? There is no doubt, at least, what Hutchins thought on that score.

But image in the modern era usually overshadows content – or *intent*. The main publicity picture for the Syntopicon, showing those hardworking scholars, helped to ensure that the reference tool itself would be consigned to ridicule and the dustbin of history. A young man named Marshall McLuhan, having glimpsed the photo shoot in *Life*, wrote with scathing insight in his first book, *The Mechanical Bride* (1951):

> The services of Dr. Hutchins and Professor Adler to education are justly celebrated. They have by their enthusiasm put education in

the news. It is therefore ironic that the present Life feature ... should have so mortician-like an air – as though Professor Adler and his associates had come to bury and not to praise Plato and other great men.

The 'great ideas' whose headstones are alphabetically displayed above the coffin-like filing boxes have been extracted from the great books in order to provide an index tool for manipulating the books themselves. By means of this index the books are made ready for *immediate use*. May we not ask how this approach to the content and conditions of human thought differs from any other merely verbal and mechanized education in our time?[10]

'Headstones' is pretty accurate. Another inspiration of local Chicago origins can also be glimpsed: this is a diorama in the style of the Field Museum stuffed-mammal exhibits, with the alpha male standing front left, strategically placed directly behind his first two ideas: Angel and Animal. Adler's facial expression illustrates both ideas at once. A background fresco completes the overall effect of adventures in taxidermy.[11] The devastating impression left by the picture is that the ideas promoted within the Syntopicon as being in perennial conversation with one another across time and culture have been put six feet under. Dwight Macdonald, following in the spirit of McLuhan, wrote in the *New Yorker* a year after *The Mechanical Bride* that,

> The Syntopicon ... was constructed by a task force commanded by Dr. Adler, who also contributes 1,150 pages of extremely dry essays on the Great Ideas, of which, according to his census, there are exactly a hundred and two. It also contains 163,000 page references to the Great Books plus an Inventory of Terms (which includes 1,690 ideas found to be respectable but not Great), plus a Bibliography of Additional Readings (2,603 books that didn't make the grade), plus an eighty-page essay by Dr. Adler on 'The Principles and Methods of Syntopical Construction' ... If these facts and figures have an oppressive, leaden ring, so does this enterprise.[12]

The dialogue about Great Books: Socratic and Talmudic method

Fortunately, Adler and Hutchins were as preoccupied with actual teaching and learning as they were with building an intellectual system based, in Hutchins's words, on 'first principles'.[13] The upshot of their more pragmatic aims was a dogged emphasis on close reading and the practice of Socratic, text-based dialogue – which they promoted first in the undergraduate seminar rooms of the University of Chicago, beginning in the 1930s, and later in the book salon movement that they launched nationwide in 1947 through the Great Books Foundation. This effort, at least for American intellectual life since the post-World War II period, has paid far greater dividends than any of the syntopical follies documented by McLuhan, Macdonald, and others. Most important was Adler and Hutchins's advocacy of a seminar method that featured dialogue – not the teacher's monologue. The style was Socratic in so far as the instructor's task was to ask questions rather than give answers. Yet in rigorously insisting that the conversation be grounded in the written text, it can more appropriately be thought of as Talmudic,[14] a method closely aligned to the close reading efforts of the New Critics who emerged in the academy during the 1920s and 1930s.

This method, or pedagogy, was singularly well suited to the Great Books reading groups that, with Adler and Hutchins's extraordinary powers of persuasion and personal charismatic leadership, were popping up in libraries, church basements, and living rooms everywhere around the country from the late 1940s. Central to this movement was the idea that ordinary laypeople who are willing to spend time with the great texts of the Western tradition can indeed enter into what Adler and Hutchins called 'The Great Conversation' – a conversation with the greatest writers and thinkers of the ages who continue to speak to contemporary readers.

The book salon movement of the Great Books Foundation peaked in the postwar boom of the 1950s, and in 1962 the Great Books Foundation added its Junior Great Books Program for grades kindergarten through 12th grade, in order to generate revenues to keep the nonprofit educational organization afloat. Junior Great Books became a primary vehicle for promoting Socratic teaching at every grade level, and the Foundation began to offer teaching workshops in the method to thousands of teachers annually. The principles of Shared Inquiry™, as they evolved after the 1960s, derive from the original vision of Adler and Hutchins, which mounts a Socratic challenge to traditional classroom lecture practice. Those principles suggest the uniqueness of the Great Books movement not only in terms of a commitment to lasting works of writing but also to radical pedagogy. To grasp what exactly is going on in the Great Books classroom or informal book discussion group as Adler and Hutchins envisioned, consider these principles of Shared Inquiry, as the practice is described in current Foundation literature:

1. **Read the selection carefully before participating in the discussion.** This ensures that all participants are equally prepared to talk about the ideas in the work and helps prevent talk that would distract the group from its purpose.
2. **Support your ideas with evidence from the text.** This keeps the discussion focused on understanding the selection and enables the group to weight textual support for different answers and to choose intelligently among them.
3. **Discuss the ideas in the selection and try to understand them fully before exploring issues that go beyond the selection.** Reflection on the ideas in the text and the evidence to support them makes the exploration of related issues more productive.
4. **Listen to other participants and respond to them directly.** Shared Inquiry is about the give and take of ideas and the willingness to listen to others and talk with them respectfully. Directing your comments and questions to other group members, not always the leader, will make the discussion livelier and more dynamic.
5. **Expect the leader to only ask questions.** Effective leaders help participants develop their own ideas, with everyone gaining a new understanding in the process. When participants hang back and wait for the leader to suggest answers, discussion tends to falter.

Many of the book groups begun by Adler's initial efforts on behalf of the Foundation still exist, and more than 800 book groups in the US and abroad still affiliate with the Great Books Foundation. They generally follow this particular style of reading and discourse, and participants attest to the rigour, as well as the pleasure that infuses the method. One might also make the case that the Great Books reading group movement that swept the country in the late 1940s and 1950s anticipated a more recent phenomenon that took hold in the 1990s. In what might be taken as the symbolic passing of the torch from Mortimer Adler to Oprah Winfrey, a number of the Penguin classics chosen by Oprah for her Book Club have carried on their covers the seal with the words, 'Recommended for Discussion by the Great Books Foundation'.

What we take now as standard operating procedure in the best classes is the notion that students and teacher actually talk with one another, making the task of textual interpretation a collective and dynamic one. But this method was nothing short of revolutionary when Adler went to Columbia early in the twentieth century and took John Erskine's General

Honors course.[15] Adler describes how he and Mark Van Doren, emulating Erskine, eventually conducted their section of General Honors there:

> In the first few years, we divided responsibility for the books to be discussed according to the fields in which they fell. After that, we both adopted Erskine's policy of proceeding like debonair amateurs, assured that even if the book under consideration was difficult for one of us, we at least should be able to read it better than our students and, in the light of that better reading, ask good questions to sustain a two-hour discussion ... The dance we did ... was designed to draw the students onto the floor and get them into the act, and we counted it a successful session only when a large number of them took part.[16]

Students in his seminars regarded Adler with affection and fear. His questions and follow-up questions poured forth relentlessly, requiring participants to define the terms set by the text, and to arrive at coherent interpretation that they could explain to themselves and others. Milton Mayer calls Adler the 'Talmudic terrier',[17] but uses the phrase to describe the style rather than theory of the educator. The dialogical teaching method that Adler tirelessly advocated has already outlasted his Thomist-inflected attempts at intellectual system-building. For Adler, the authority of the text, as far as setting the agenda for discussion went, was supreme. And in the Talmudic spirit, this is not a grovelling of a supplicant before authority; rather, it is so much respect for the text that you dare to wrestle with it the way Jacob wrestled with a mysterious stranger by the Jabbok River.

Hutchins and Adler would replicate Erskine's method at the University of Chicago, where they co-taught a section of the general education curriculum. This soon made them, in the very early 1930s, academic news; their Great Books seminar was enough of a novelty both in substance and method that celebrities on transcontinental train trips began to stop off in Chicago to take a look. Among these were Hollywood stars Lillian Gish and Orson Welles, and Eugene Meyer, publisher of the *Washington Post* (and father of Katherine Graham, a student enrolled in the seminar).[18] The most famous visitor of all was Gertrude Stein. At a dinner party one evening after Adler and Hutchins's seminar, she began to grill the men as to what they thought they were doing. They said they were teaching the Great Books.

Stein asked what those were. Adler went downstairs and rummaged through his briefcase and brought the list of books back to the table. Stein looked at the list and began to rant about the mistake of teaching books in translation. The men insisted that the ideas were the thing, and that great writers survived even in bad translations. Then Adler went on the attack. He began to interrogate Stein. Voices rose. Stein finally ran out of patience, and ran around the table toward Adler, whom she cuffed on the side of the head with what Adler described as 'a resounding thwack'. In his telling of the episode, Adler conveys how honoured he was by the punishment: not everyone could claim the privilege of getting 'bitch-slapped' by the queen bee of American modernism. Yet there is a kind of self-aggrandizing tone in his recollection of the words she spoke after the blow: 'I am not going to argue any further with you, young man. I can see that you are the kind of young man who is accustomed to winning arguments.' The evening ended when a butler came in to announce, 'The police are here.' The doyenne of the Parisian salon had ordered a tour of the city in a police squad car, and two captains were out front waiting to pick her up. Adler concludes: 'The way I felt about her at that moment, I wished they had done it earlier and taken her for a ride Chicago-style.'[19]

Adler's bombastic voice here is good for a laugh, but his verbal aggressiveness created genuine problems at the University of Chicago for President Hutchins – who was himself no verbal wallflower. Friends and enemies alike perceived the two men as part of a single creative entity, and any consideration of their Great Books Program must necessarily acknowledge their partnership and co-authorship. To speak of one necessarily requires speaking about the other; there can be no Siegfried without Roy, no Butch Cassidy without the Sundance Kid. And yet one significant difference was that Adler lacked the diplomatic and comic gifts that Hutchins most certainly possessed.

Hutchins's various biographers chalk it up to his good looks, wit, and charm. One story that looms large in the Hutchins legend is his confrontation with the drugstore mogul Charles Walgreen. When Walgreen brought charges that certain faculty were teaching his niece communism – a claim that the Chicago *Tribune* was more than happy to publicize – Hutchins appeared at the public hearing, organized by the state of Illinois, with trustee Laird Bell. *Time* magazine reported that on their way to the appointment, Bell told Hutchins that he would pay him '$25 for every wisecrack he didn't make'.[20] Hutchins went to the proverbial mat to defend his faculty's freedom of expression, and the case against the university disintegrated completely when details of the course were brought to light: the syllabus that included Marx also featured Herbert Hoover's *American Individualism*.[21] Hutchins knew how to exploit his day of triumph: always the gentleman, he invited Walgreen to lunch shortly after the hearings. At that meeting, the businessman pledged more than a half million dollars toward a new program, the Charles L. Walgreen Foundation for the Study of American Institutions.[22] In the process of deflecting charges against his institution for fomenting un-American ideas, Hutchins had also recruited a significant new booster for the university.

But if Hutchins was able to wield the fundraiser's Midas touch, he was perceived by many of his faculty as the enemy – with Adler frequently acting as the divisive wedge in between, who at times acted as an educational reformer and at other times as more of a marketing mogul, what to our eyes might seem like a sort of Don King of humanities education. If higher education today has made a fetish out of academic departments, Adler made a fetish out of trying to destroy them. And if the university department system perennially crowds the space in which general education can function, Adler attempted to turn general education into the 800-pound gorilla on campus at the University of Chicago. To understand why he sought this goal, we do well to survey briefly his youthful academic career at Columbia University, where there are hints of what would develop into his explosive years at the University of Chicago.

Young man Adler: academic resentments as spur to action

In his autobiography, Adler showcases his aggressive tendencies toward professors, beginning with his primary target while still an undergraduate at Columbia: members of the philosophy department. Adler provides exquisite detail of the barrage of questions and criticism he directed at them. The model of education in this account seems based on verbal antagonism of a kind that Adler thought would win him points. Dewey was his principal antagonist.

Adler must have come across to Dewey and his cohorts as a kind of maniacal attack dog. Badgering them during their lectures was one of the methods Adler used; other strategies included writing multiple-page single-space memos objecting to their arguments and requesting replies in writing, or delivering frontal assaults on their works at academic conferences.[23]

The fact is that Adler was about to be rejected by the admissions committee of the graduate program in philosophy at Columbia. And that rejection indelibly shaped his career. He had something to prove, and would spend the rest of his life proving it. He describes the chair of the philosophy department this way:

> ... Professor Coss was a businesslike administrator ... The only course in the Philosophy Department that he taught was one entitled 'Business Ethics.' He had almost no interest in either logic or truth

and very little in philosophy. He probably found the way I had expressed my emotions about these subjects a little embarrassing, perhaps ungentlemanly, and certainly typically Jewish.

Even if I had not been Jewish, the paper that I had read before the Philosophy Department would have put me in Professor Coss's black book, because it contained slurs on pragmatism and pragmatists.[24]

Sure enough, Coss wrote a dismissal letter searing with condescension, which concluded, 'While money remains in this world a real consideration you must think of that along with other things ... Think of something other than advanced study in philosophy. It might be worth your while to take psychology, pure or applied.'[25]

Adler did indeed finish a PhD in psychology. He tells us that he hammered out his seventy-seven-page research dissertation in a twenty-hour stint at the typewriter. This dubious account cannot be verified, but it certainly offers a window into young Adler's resentful soul. His studied effort at nonchalance about meeting graduate requirements seethes with rage. The whole process, he insists, bored him. He writes, 'I must confess that I had little or no interest in this Ph.D. project; in fact, little or no interest in getting a Ph.D. I had not yet read William James's telling attack on the Ph.D. octopus in American institutions of higher learning.'[26] Rejection by one discipline, and active dislike for another, tempered his attitude toward higher education for the rest of his life, making this very public intellectual thoroughly anti-academic and in many respects anti-intellectual. Subsequent events at Chicago would only reinforce his dislike. One can only speculate whether later on, minus his resentments, Adler would have received a better hearing on those matters that he thought most important: (1) carving out adequate space for general education free from the pressures of disciplinary specialization, a kind of general education today that usually goes under the banner of the humanities, and (2) insistence on a pedagogy based primarily on text-based discussion rather than lectures.

The Great Books experiment at the University of Chicago

Shortly after he arrived at the university in 1929 as its new president, Hutchins offered Adler a job that featured appointments in three different departments – philosophy, psychology, and the school of law.[27] The decision immediately set much of the faculty on edge, and it initiated years of recrimination between the Hutchins-Adler combine and numerous departments, including the natural sciences and history. These felt their turf invaded. Moreover, they perceived – accurately – that most of the time, Adler had Hutchins's ear.

Adler very quickly took bold steps that alienated him from the professorial ranks. According to historian Mary Ann Dzuback, one of his first acts at the University of Chicago on behalf of a reformed undergraduate curriculum was to 'argue for four lists of books corresponding to the divisional academic fields. Most of the books were written before the twentieth century, and excluded much of the work by University of Chicago faculty in the sciences, humanities, and social sciences.'[28] This proposal met predictable outrage. Here was Hutchins's New York upstart, usurping the role normally reserved for the expertise of entire departments, blithely squashing individual egos in the process.

But Hutchins was not interested in enhancing the power of departments, and the ruckus Adler had raised was one to his liking. The new president aimed to develop a larger conception of what undergraduate education could be, and it was the sort of vision that could only threaten departmental fiefdoms. He articulated this vision in his landmark book, *The Higher Learning in America*, published in 1936. There he said genuine education must counteract negative forces at work in the land: 'overspecialization, crass vocationalism, academic disciplinary isolation ... and anti-intellectual tendencies'.[29] In Hutchins's view, an alternative program of 'permanent studies' would help students develop an understanding of their own 'intellectual inheritance' to be found in the 'greatest books of the western world'.[30]

For his part, Adler – Hutchins's co-architect, and likely master planner of the new Bachelor of Arts program – was more than happy to sharpen the agenda's definition, and began to flesh out his idea of a four-year general education curriculum. How do we explain Adler's desire to displace academic departments with what was, in effect, an Über-department of his own creation? After all, the course of study at Columbia that had lit up Adler's youthful mind, John Erskine's General Honors course in great books, a book-a-week program spread over two years, was not the hegemonic recipe for four years of study that Adler wanted.[31] Adler's thirst for curricular empire was matched by his desire to stamp out competing disciplines and departments. By 1940, feeling roughed up by the curricular struggles that he had helped initiate, Adler was boiling with rage against academics everywhere. In a speech he gave in New York, he sounded a near-hysterical note when he said, 'Until the professors and their culture are liquidated, the resolution of modern problems will not begin' because 'democracy has more to fear from the mentality of its teachers than from the nihilism of Hitler'.[32]

The speech in its entirety, which included Adler's praise for Hutchins's failed efforts at curricular reform, was published in the student newspaper, *The Maroon*.

Yet if his ability to incur the wrath of academic colleagues is at times breathtaking, his ideas by the late 1940s made him a popular educational consultant in colleges around the country. He is disarmingly honest about his inclination toward impolitic behaviour and speechifying. But he doesn't seem to understand that the reforms he called for in higher education would make most academics in America his permanent enemies. In the first volume of his autobiography, *Philosopher at Large*, Adler reminisced:

> During the late forties and early fifties, I was frequently asked by one institution or another to meet with a curriculum committee which had been set up to reform the collegiate course of study. On such occasions, I laid out a set of negative conditions which I regarded as prerequisite to any reform aimed in the right direction ... The conditions were as follows: (1) there should be no vocational training of any sort; (2) there should be no electives, no majors or minors, no specialization in subject matter; (3) there should be no division of the faculty into professors competent in one department of learning rather than another; (4) no member of the faculty should be unprepared to teach the course of study as a whole; (5) no textbooks or manuals should be assigned as reading material for the students; (6) not more than one lecture a week should be given to the student body; (7) there should be no written examination.[33]

Across America, these reforms, with the exception of the first, met a deaf ear. Only at St John's College, where Adler's friend Scott Buchanan became president, was there instituted what Harry Ashmore calls a 'hundred-proof Great Books curriculum'.[34] The most radical proposals – eliminating all majors, minors, and academic departments, and requiring all faculty to be able to teach every part of the curriculum – are so astonishingly out of step with the way higher education generally works today that we must wonder at Adler's audacity in putting them forward. (Even the most rabid contrarians occasionally show some moderation. In spite of his love for Aristotle, moderation doesn't seem to have figured that often in Adler's repertoire.) And his imperative that all faculty function as interchangeable cogs in the generalist wheel suggests he did not quite grasp how knowledge gets created through dialogue within a disciplinary field, or between disciplines. Adler considered 'specialization' practically a curse word. In *Liberal Schooling in the Twentieth Century*, he wrote: 'college teachers ... should not be expected to carry on specialized research. They should win the honors and emoluments appropriate to their careers by their excellence as teachers, not by their contributions to the advancement of knowledge.'[35] Writing in his introductory volume to the Britannica Great Books of the Western World series, Adler would fume: 'By the end of the first quarter of this century great books and the liberal arts had been destroyed by their teachers. The books had become the private domain of scholars.'[36] The sweeping generalization is typical Adler, and one wonders if indeed there were no professors to be found who saw some kind of relationship between good teaching and good scholarship. Adler habitually dichotomized teaching and scholarship. Both his discouragement of student written exams and of faculty research would indicate his belief that while we should be filling ourselves up with Great Books, we may not want to try and write any books of our own – unless we are Adler.

To read the accounts of the battles Hutchins and Adler fought with many faculty and powerful department chairs, one feels surprise that Hutchins was able to achieve any of the reforms he sought in undergraduate education. Adler's role as provocateur created openings for Hutchins, but also roadblocks. Yet in spite of the resistance, a four-year liberal arts college was in place at the University of Chicago by 1937,[37] and if it did not carry the strictly Great Books pedigree that Adler coveted, by the mid-1940s its curriculum was primarily Great Books.

Many intellectuals of that generation were deeply influenced by that program – Saul Bellow, Susan Sontag, and Joseph Epstein, just to name a few. But the dismantling of the program would begin shortly after Hutchins left the university in 1951, as disciplines and departments reasserted their might.[38] Thereafter, St John's College, Shimer College, and a handful of other programs across the country embraced Great Books curricula, and Columbia University continued its commitment to great works at least in the first two years of its undergraduate program. But these were the exceptions, not the rule.

Mary Ann Dzuback suggests that Hutchins's mistake during his presidency was that he didn't listen to his faculty enough and listened to Adler too much.[39] One can understand her perspective, given Adler's impolitic style and frontal assaults on academe. In higher education circles, Adler's jagged personality and diatribes against professors harmed more than helped the Great Books cause. At the same time, I am dubious whether there would have ever been a Great Books cause without Adler, whose ideas thoroughly shaped the Hutchins plan.

In his last couple of decades, Adler started a new project, the Paideia movement for school reform. This diversified his repertoire of approved teaching methodologies to include student 'coaching' as well as lecture components to stand alongside the text-based, Socratic methodology that he had so tirelessly, and single-mindedly, advocated.[40] And the very fruitful close of his career contains several ironies worth mentioning. One of the people to whom he dedicated *The Paideia Proposal* was John Dewey, his old nemesis, which maybe shows that even old, stubborn warriors can sometimes manage to make peace and see things whole. But to add to this irony, Adler's start-up of the Paideia group led to his ousting from the Great Books Foundation's board of directors in 1987, on grounds of conflict of interest. To the end, ever the educational entrepreneur, Adler was better at burning bridges than he was at building them. Perhaps no educator of the twentieth century more completely embodies Joseph Schumpeter's spirit of 'creative destruction'.

Cindy Rutz, a young colleague of Adler who knew him in his later years when he was heading the Paideia project, once observed him conduct a seminar for teachers at the Goldblatt elementary school in Chicago. A teacher in the training seminar made an offhand comment, saying, 'This is what I think; Aristotle thinks something different. So what?' Adler went apoplectic. He pounded his fist on the table, looked directly at her, and said, 'If you're not looking for truth in these books, then don't bother.'[41]

Some of Adler's most vocal critics attest to the spirit if not the letter of his teaching. In what was one of the most scathing obituaries written about Adler, even Joseph Epstein had grudgingly positive things to say about the man, although he conveyed them indirectly:

> I was myself the recipient of a partial great-books education at the University of Chicago, which Hutchins was able to install after the smog of controversy had cleared. Mine was assuredly better than a bad-books education, such as is nowadays offered at almost every school in the land, but education, I have come to conclude, is mostly luck in finding good teachers. I myself never found any at Chicago ... What I did discover at Chicago was an atmosphere where erudition was taken seriously. Because all the books taught were first class – no textbooks were allowed, no concessions were made to the second-rate for political reasons, and one was graded not by one's teachers but by a college examiner – I gradually learned on my own the important writers and eternal issues, and where to go if one wished to stay with the unending work in progress called one's education.[42]

Twilight of the Great Books gods: Hutchins on the ramparts

After resigning his presidency at the University of Chicago, Hutchins sought career projects that developed organically out of his Great Books commitment, and in this respect he resembles Adler, whose efforts on behalf of school reform grew out of a concern for the troubled state of American education. But in Hutchins's case, the ideological and civic cast of his thought remained transparently and unabashedly that of a deeply liberal thinker – of the sort so well described by Kevin Mattson in his recent book, *When America Was Great: the Fighting Faith of Postwar Liberalism*.[43]

In 1951 Hutchins took up a new position, as one of three associate directors of the Ford Foundation, with assignments in the areas of education and peace. The initial mandate there was pleasantly daunting: give away more than $100 million to worthy causes. Hutchins promptly set up the Fund for the Advancement of Education and the Fund for Adult Education, and by 1954, when he left the Ford Foundation, he had supervised educational grants totalling $89 million. (Grants of $826,000 went to the Great Books Foundation; $640,000 was allocated to Adler's Institute for Philosophical Research in San Francisco.) Hutchins also awarded sizeable grants for curricular reform in college teacher-training programs, which were, in his estimation, unduly burdened with 'methods' courses and notoriously light on actual subject matter.[44]

Hutchins also advocated the funding of progressive organizations such as the American Friends Service Committee, and the hue of his political commitments, not entirely to Henry Ford II's liking, became altogether clear when he lobbied for a new fund to help battle abuses perpetrated by anti-communist and McCarthyite crusaders. In October 1951, Ford Foundation director Paul Hoffman (who in the next year went to work on Eisenhower's presidential campaign) proposed to the board of directors a new corporation to be called the Fund for the Republic. This entity would eventually be spun off in 1954 as an entirely separate corporation, with Hutchins at the helm and with an endowment of $15 million. In 1959 it would be renamed the Center for the Study of Democratic Institutions.[45] Hutchins's memorandum detailing the agenda for the fund is altogether revealing:

> The Fund should feel free to attack the problem of the freedom of the press; of migrant workers; of the immigration laws and the McCarran Act; of loyalty investigations; [of] the House Un-American Activities Committee; of conscientious objectors; of academic freedom and teachers' oaths; of racial and religious discrimination in all

its manifestations, from lynching to inequality of educational opportunity; of disenfranchisement; of dishonesty in government; of the liberties guaranteed by the First and Fourteenth Amendments ...[46]

Connoisseurs of the culture wars in recent decades may find this catalogue jarring, if for no other reason that its author, in the following year, would announce in New York that the Great Books of the Western World were 'an act of piety'. Hutchins explodes our era's simple-minded equation between Great Books commitment and reactionary politics. Indeed, it is necessary to see that at least in Hutchins's mind, the connection between Great Books and progressive politics was a natural one. Recalling again his assertion that the Syntopicon provided a toolkit of ideas that would potentially 'save the world from destruction', we are inclined to hear the words as a particularly poignant moment in the history of American kitsch; we can practically hear the rumble of footsteps as that phalanx of Great Books salesmen begin to fan out across America, selling the tomes to anxious readers who, like Hutchins, genuinely hope they won't be living under a mushroom cloud.

But another possibility – behind the advertising copy jingle – is that Hutchins meant what he said in 1948. For at that moment most of the country was thinking quite seriously about the mushroom cloud. How else to save the world from self-destruction unless by learning from the best ideas of the world's greatest thinkers? If I may speculate further, perhaps at that moment Hutchins was hoping the gift of Great Books might offset some of the other gifts inflicted on the world, including that radioactive entity called 'The Pile' that took shape under his university's empty football stadium only a few years before. Maybe he was thinking deep apocalyptic thoughts, a little bit like his Calvinist Presbyterian preacher father used to think back in Oberlin, Ohio.

In many accounts of twentieth-century American education, Hutchins is portrayed as out of touch with the progressive tradition epitomized by his and Adler's enemy, John Dewey. In this caricature, Hutchins wants students to fossilize amidst the dusty tomes, Dewey wants education that will make a difference and build democracy. Hutchins wants to find eternal truths and 'first principles', Dewey wants to help the republic evolve.

The picture is a grotesque distortion. The scope of Hutchins's activities suggest a restless and progressive spirit at work, a man hardly content to be a caretaker of the wisdom of the past, but rather eager to discern – and help shape – the future. His efforts at the Ford Foundation were not surprising to those who knew him; the signs of his deepest commitments were already well in place by the time he left the University of Chicago.

When virtually all university presidents were being cowed and silenced by the McCarthy witch hunts of the late 1940s, Hutchins spoke out boldly for freedom of expression before a committee of the Illinois House of Representatives. In 1949, Hutchins defended his students who had noisily protested a bill in Springfield that would have made loyalty oaths mandatory for teachers and public employees. It did not help the university's image downstate when this protest morphed into an impromptu integration of a drugstore lunch counter, with black and white students mingling dangerously together. Hutchins acknowledged to his critics that the students might have been 'impolite', but that 'rudeness and Redness are not the same'.[47]

If Hutchins's stance against McCarthyism contributes to his heroic profile, his effort to convene scholars on the subject of world government now looks a bit quixotic and out-of-touch. It is worth remembering, however, that following the use of atomic weapons in 1945, leading intellectuals including Albert Einstein saw nationalist interests as potentially fatal to the planet's future. The dropping of the atomic bombs had shaken everyone, perhaps the physicists most of all. But the reaction of the national media to Hutchins's establishment of the Committee to Frame a World Constitution was profoundly negative. Hutchins joked that it should have been called 'The Committee to Frame Hutchins'.[48] It did not help matters when Adler was quoted in a Cleveland speech as saying, 'We must do everything we can to abolish the United States.'[49] Some ideas are ahead of their time, and in this case Hutchins knew well enough to let it go.

Entering the final phase of his career in sunny California – the Center for the Study of Democratic Institutions would be located in Santa Barbara – Hutchins cut a jaunty figure. Milton Mayer describes him as typically bedecked in a Hawaiian shirt, comfortably behind the wheel of his Thunderbird convertible.[50] But the appearance shouldn't hide the reality that Hutchins was intent on thinking seriously about topics of grave concern. At his liberal think tank, he set an agenda for global ways of thinking. After Pope John declared the Peace on Earth (*Pacem in Terris*) encyclical of 1963, Hutchins called on the fellows of the institute to focus their efforts on conflict and conflict resolution. The Center sponsored four peace conferences as a result. The first of these took place in New York in 1965, three days after President Lyndon Johnson's carpet-bombing campaign, Operation Rolling Thunder, commenced in Vietnam.[51] The second conference, in Geneva in 1967, was actively undermined by the US State Department. Perhaps this had to do with Hutchins's call for a withdrawal from Vietnam early in 1966.

William F. Buckley would call the gathering the 'Hutchins International Conference to Hate America'.[52]

One of the last things that Hutchins wrote for the Center's newsletter, published shortly before his death in 1977, ended with these words: 'We have to stop throwing our weight around. We have to stop talking about being the most powerful nation on earth. We have to think of the nurture of human life everywhere, otherwise we return to Matthew Arnold's Dover Beach, written a hundred years ago.' Then Hutchins quoted from that original theorist of the Great Books, the late Victorian who recommended that we 'learn and propagate the best that is known and thought in the world':

> ... the world which seems
> To lie before us like a land of dreams,
> So various, so beautiful, so new,
> Hath neither joy, nor love, nor light,
> Nor certitude, nor peace, nor help for pain;
> And we are here, as on a darkling plain
> Swept with confused alarms of struggle and flight,
> Where ignorant armies clash by night.[53]

Almost a century has passed since a professor at Columbia named John Erskine pioneered a reading seminar for soldiers one step removed from the bloody trenches of the First World War. His course, titled War Studies, was later renamed General Honors.[54] When Adler and Hutchins got hold of the notion and called it Great Books, and started proselytizing for it on Chicago's Midway, their zealous advocacy resulted in some overselling. Their faith in the idea grew, at times, well – a little windy. Thinking back to Hutchins's sanguine feeling roughly sixty years ago, I suspect the Great Books are not quite 'the reading toolkit that will save the world from self-destruction', because the academy has inculcated in me certain sceptical habits of mind. The very notion of the Syntopicon seems preposterous. Yet I will confess that here, too, my heart is with Hutchins and Adler, for at the end of the day, when the respective ideas are put on the scales, who does not hope that love will outweigh both sin and eternity?

Notes

1. 'The 102 Great Ideas: Scholars Complete a Monumental Catalog', *Life*, 26 January 1948, 92–3.
2. Ibid., 92.

3. James Sloan Allen, *The Romance of Commerce and Culture: Capitalism, Modernism, and the Chicago–Aspen Crusade for Cultural Reform* (Chicago: University of Chicago Press, 1983), 97.
4. 'There Are Only 102 Great Ideas' (publication unknown, 1948?), Great Books Foundation archives, 61.
5. Gary Schoepfel, conversation with the author, 3 February 2004.
6. 'There Are Only 102 Great Ideas', 58.
7. Harry Ashmore, *Unseasonable Truths: the Life of Robert Maynard Hutchins* (Boston: Little, Brown, 1989), 336–7.
8. Tim Lacy, 'Making a Democratic Culture: the Great Books, Mortimer Adler, and Twentieth-Century America', unpublished dissertation, Loyola University, Chicago (2006), Chapter 3, 129.
9. William H. McNeill, *Hutchins' University: a Memoir of the University of Chicago 1929–1950* (Chicago: University of Chicago Press, 1991), 151.
10. Marshall McLuhan, *The Mechanical Bride: Folklore of Industrial Man* (1951; Corte Madera, CA: Gingko Press, 2002), 43.
11. Mike Elsey, conversation with the author, 28 January 2004.
12. Dwight Macdonald, 'The Book-of-the-Millennium Club', in *Against the American Grain: Essays on the Effects of Mass Culture* (New York: Vintage, 1962), 243–4.
13. Robert Maynard Hutchins, *The Higher Learning in America* (New Haven: Yale University Press, 1936), 107.
14. Donald Whitfield, conversation with the author, November 2003.
15. Mortimer J. Adler, *Philosopher at Large: an Intellectual Biography* (New York: Macmillan, 1977), 55–6.
16. Ibid., 56–7.
17. Milton Mayer, *Robert Maynard Hutchins: a Memoir* (Berkeley: University of California Press, 1993), 109.
18. Sidney Hyman, 'Mortimer J. Adler (1902–2001): a Century of Great Books', *The Common Review* 1, 2 (Winter 2002): 37.
19. Adler, *Philosopher at Large*, 139–40.
20. 'Worst Kind of Troublemaker', *Time* (21 November 1949), 59.
21. Ashmore, *Unseasonable Truths*, 130.
22. Ibid., 132.
23. Adler, *Philosopher at Large*, 27, 28, 49.
24. Ibid., 43–44.
25. Ibid., 44.
26. Ibid., 124.
27. Hyman, 'Mortimer J. Adler (1902–2001)', 36.
28. Mary Ann Dzuback, *Robert M. Hutchins: Portrait of an Educator* (Chicago: University of Chicago Press, 1991), 119.
29. Ibid., 125.
30. Ibid., 125.
31. Joan Shelley Rubin, *The Making of Middlebrow Culture* (Chapel Hill: University of North Carolina Press, 1992), 188.
32. McNeill, *Hutchins' University*, 79.
33. Adler, *Philosopher at Large*, 214. It is interesting to note that Adler changes this account somewhat in the second volume of his autobiography, *A Second Look in the Rearview Mirror: Further Autobiographical Reflections of a Philosopher*

at Large (New York: Macmillan, 1992). There he claims that he began to moderate these demands as time went on (64–5).
34. Ashmore, *Unseasonable Truths*, 189.
35. Adler, *Reforming Education: the Opening of the American Mind*, ed. Geraldine Van Doren (New York: Macmillan, 1988), 145.
36. Adler, *Great Books of the Western World, Vol. I, The Great Conversation* (Chicago: Encyclopedia Britannica, 1952), 27.
37. Dzuback, *Robert M. Hutchins*, 128.
38. Ashmore, *Unseasonable Truths*, 309–10.
39. Dzuback, *Robert M. Hutchins*, 206–7.
40. Adler, *The Paideia Proposal: an Educational Manifesto* (New York: Macmillan, 1982), 49–54.
41. Cindy Rutz, telephone interview with the author, 11 February 2004.
42. Joseph Epstein, 'The Great Bookie: Mortimer Adler, 1902–2001', *Weekly Standard* (23 July 2001). Epstein writes memorably: 'I have seen him lecture – browbeat is closer to it – a room of specialists on each of their own subjects for ten hours, do a two-hour call-in radio show interview afterwards, return home to work on a book (he liked to turn out one a year), and, I should not have been in the least shocked to learn, end the day by making vigorous love to his thirty-odd-years-younger wife, and at last fall asleep doubtless while attempting to draw a bead on some tangled epistemological problem.'
43. Kevin Mattson, *When America Was Great: The Fighting Faith of Postwar Liberalism* (New York: Routledge, 2004).
44. Ashmore, *Unseasonable Truths*, 311–14, 319, 321.
45. Ashmore, *Unseasonable Truths*, 319–32, 392. See also Frank K. Kelly, *Court of Reason: Robert Hutchins and the Fund for the Republic* (New York: Free Press, 1981), 3–8.
46. Ashmore, *Unseasonable Truths*, 330–1.
47. Dzuback, *Robert M. Hutchins*, 201.
48. Ashmore, *Unseasonable Truths*, 263.
49. McNeill, *Hutchins' University*, 179.
50. Mayer, *Robert Maynard Hutchins*, 468.
51. Kelly, *Court of Reason*, 244.
52. Ashmore, *Unseasonable Truths*, 457.
53. Matthew Arnold, 'Dover Beach' (c. 1851), quoted in Mayer, *Robert Maynard Hutchins*, 504.
54. Gerald Graff, *Professing Literature: an Institutional History* (Chicago: University of Chicago P, 1987), 135.

5
'I Used to Read Anything that Caught My Eye, But ...': Cultural Authority and Intermediaries in a Virtual Young Adult Book Club

DeNel Rehberg Sedo

Introduction

> *Are you There God? It's Me Margaret* by Judy Blume
> *The Handmaid's Tale* by Margaret Atwood
> *Story of O* by Pauline Réage

These were the most memorable books of my teenage years. They were books recommended to me by a friend or teacher, or pilfered from secret sources. Maybe I noticed one of them on the shelf in the one-room public library in my small hometown. At the time, I neither thought about how I got these books nor what they meant to me. I just knew I liked them, and I remember them. These are books that, on reflection as a reading researcher, certainly must have guided the questions I asked of the larger world and helped to form my identity as a young reading woman. Most likely, readers of this chapter can think of special books that did the same for them.

In small town USA, talking about books in the early 1980s was definitely not a 'cool' thing to do. Representations of readers were limited to the likes of Mary and Laura reading to Ma and Pa or vice versa in Laura Ingalls Wilder's *Little House on the Prairie* on television, and readers were virtually nonexistent in the movies. If you were a reader, you had to seek out other like-minded people. This meant that choosing books, and talking about them, was limited to carefully selected reader friends, or the school or public librarian. If you were lucky, you could find the enthusiastic ear of a trusted teacher.

How do young adults make reading choices at the turn of the twenty-first century? Who facilitates their process of choosing a book, interpreting its content and the experience of reading it? This chapter reports the findings of a case study investigating an Internet book discussion group. The membership is mainly public librarians, teachers or teacher librarians, book industry publication editors, reviewers, publishing representatives and parents. According to the definitions provided by French sociologist Pierre Bourdieu, the membership of The Young Adult Book Club (TYABC)[1] can be considered part of the 'new petite bourgeoisie' and are 'cultural intermediaries'.[2] They are cultural workers who mediate the space between the online Young Adult (YA) literature reading community and the off-line communities in which young adults live.

Through an analysis of this online book club, I illustrate how Elizabeth Long's argument that book club investigations can demonstrate the 'infrastructure of literacy and the social or institutional determinants of what's available to read, what is "worth reading," and how to read ...'[3] within the contemporary milieu of Young Adult Fiction.[4] The chapter begins with a brief introduction to the few relevant online book club studies that have been published. The discursive practices in this virtual interpretative community illustrate how agency, power, norms, rules, and authority within the group can function simultaneously to oppress and give voice to individual readers. The community is a site of subjection to group norms and authority figures and at the same time it is a site of active individual resistance to group norms and authority figures. The chapter ends with a discussion of how these interactions might work to influence which YA books are prioritized in contemporary print culture.

Online book club studies

Scholarly examinations of face-to-face (herein f2f) book clubs by Jenny Hartley, Elizabeth Long, Elizabeth McHenry, Heather Murray, and Marilyn Poole demonstrate that book clubs are important sites for cultural consumption and participation, and in some instances, the acquisition of cultural capital.[5] Elsewhere, Norma González, Linsey Howie and I each argue that the cultural competencies expressed in book clubs are influenced in unique ways by specific members' perceived cultural authority. That authority is informed by individual member's gender, ethnicity, social class, political, and religious beliefs.[6] While cultural authority legitimates certain kinds of literary values and modes of reading, f2f book club members often simultaneously validate and resist this authority in differing degrees.

Does this happen in the same way in a virtual environment? What roles do cultural authority and cultural competencies play in the textual interpretation that is evident in online book club dialogue? Scholarship in virtual book reception and collective reading practices is a small field that covers a narrow range of reading communities.[7] Barbara Fister's constructive illustration of the social dynamics and reading practices of the 600-member online mystery book club 4MA[8] is particularly relevant to this discussion of power and authority in online book clubs. Her case study illustrates the ways in which norms are negotiated by club members and patrolled by powerful members, including in one instance, a somewhat cheeky online moderator.[9] According to Fister,

> 4MA members only rarely need a gentle reminder that some issues have the potential to upset other members... 'Let's remember we're at a party and that politics and religion and causes are subjects that should always be avoided to ensure a peaceful, successful party,' one of the moderators posted when members wandered into an area that invited discord.[10]

Like many online book discussion lists, 4MA posts 'acceptable' and 'unacceptable' topics for discussion, identifying the normalizing influences and power relations within the online communities. In the group that Fister investigated, readers tried to maintain congenial relationships by avoiding hot topics.

> Though controversial issues often surface in the discussion of a book, since social conflict and troubling ethical issues are so commonly the subject matter of crime fiction, members generally are careful to focus their comments on interpreting the texts to minimize any potential to cause offense.[11]

These club norms demonstrate how politeness masks 'rules', while illustrating the role of moderators as discussion custodians and members as compliant followers, in reinforcing the online book club as an apolitical space. Who then is silenced by these club norms?

Long's brief introduction to online reading communities in her seminal work, *Book Clubs: Women and the Uses of Reading in Everyday Life* outlines some power dynamics in the online book discussion lists she observed.[12] While she hints at the power that list 'owners' and moderators have, such as 'making the rules for suggesting and choosing books ... surveying members ...and vetting the incoming messages...' it is Trysh Travis's work that specifically considers the lack of agency in some online book clubs.[13] According to Travis, both Long and Janice Radway view women's reading communities through a liberal feminist lens.[14] She argues that 'the cultural studies lens empowered the subjects

Radway ... viewed through it, and ennobled women historically overlooked by the feminist vanguard. Thus a mindless, bamboozled female public unwittingly contributing to its own oppression was transferred into active agents.'[15] While Radway argues that readers can have dominant, negotiated or oppositional readings of the text that are influenced by the social context in which reading occurs, Travis argues that both Long and Radway's analysis offers 'partial and indeed ambivalent character of the "resistance" to cultural authority'.[16] Travis's examination goes even further, to highlight the importance of not only cultural capital, but also material capital, in online communities. She draws connections between authority in the discussions and its explicit connection to the larger goal of increasing sales by projecting a particular image among readers of Rebecca Wells's *Divine Secrets of the Ya-Ya Sisterhood: a Novel*. Using Travis's nudge to evaluate online reading communities through a more critical lens, this chapter interrogates the extent to which readers demonstrate agency under the influence of 'real' or 'perceived' cultural authorities and suggests that material culture (that is, publishers' profits and individual professional advancement) also has much to gain from asserting cultural authority in the area of YA fiction.

TYABC

This chapter is the outcome of my involvement as a participant observer in an online group dedicated to reading Young Adult fiction. I intentionally sought out an online book club that did not share my own genre preferences, and chose to join TYABC, which is hosted by a for-profit website. Now more than 13 years old, the current membership is more than 960, which is double the number when I was part of the group. Moderated by the founder, a teacher who wanted to discuss YA fiction, the core group of book discussants number only 30 to 40 posters in any given month. Like f2f book clubs in North America, and reflective of the gender imbalance in the professions the members occupy, there seem to be more female than male readers. Most members appear to live in the USA, but readers in Canada, the UK and Australia also participate. At least one member lives in the Netherlands, and another in Thailand. Of those who posted or responded to my questionnaire, few appear to be teens or young adults themselves. Most members range in age from their twenties to forties. From the signatures used in the postings, and evident in the discussions themselves, we know that the members work predominantly as librarians or teachers, and there is at least one member who is an editor of a children's literary magazine. At least four of the active members review titles for publishers. During my tenure with the group, two members sat on national (US) YA literary fiction award panels. Five YA authors participate in the club. Few members work in other fields; most are the parents or relatives of teens. The members seem well educated, and all have a personal or professional interest in and passion for YA literature.

I was a group member for a one-year period during 2002–03, after gaining access through the moderator and group members. While I consider my overall experience with the group in making my conclusions, I am using only the discussions from my first four months with the group for reporting purposes because of ethical research arrangements I made with the group. As a participant observer, I took part in the discussions when I had access to the books and when I felt comfortable doing so; at other times, I lurked. My position as a book club researcher surely influenced some member's postings, but I believe that I did not have the same cultural authority as other educators in the group. 'Expert' status is reserved for those with proven experience within the arena of YA fiction.

While I was with the group, members posted 5464 messages. I analysed the online discussions and the off-line discussions I had with some members. I kept records of my own thoughts and interpretations of my online experiences and the texts. In addition, I posted a 25-question open-ended survey at the end of my time with the group. Fifteen surveys were completed and returned. The findings from this small sample have been incorporated into this chapter.

Finding an online book club to join is not difficult. One can participate in synchronous chat in a 'discussion room', mimicking the collective space of a f2f book club, or in an asynchronous discussion, such as those found in a listserv. There are also book-related blogs that allow readers to communicate directly with authors, reviewers, and other readers. A simple search of 'book clubs' on Google.com yields more than fifteen million hits.[17] Chat groups on large for-profit sites such as iVillage.com or on Yahoo.com produce another deluge of choices. Media such as newspapers, magazines, radio, and television also host online book clubs linked to their home pages, and/or mediated through broadcasts. In some instances, commercial associations and affiliations may not be immediately apparent.

With such a wide choice of options, how would a reader choose which group to join? Or, perhaps more importantly, *why* would someone choose an online book club?

I argue elsewhere that some readers feel more comfortable in virtual book clubs than in a f2f situation.[18] Virtual clubs may also be the only option if a reader cannot find a f2f group or cannot attend meetings for various reasons ranging from work schedules to physical limitations. Long demonstrates the unique ability of virtual book clubs to bring together readers from different social locations. This, she argues, is a result of online clubs emerging more from like interests than from daily interactions, such as friendships, work places, neighbourhoods and life stages as is usually the case in f2f book clubs.[19] Online book clubs tend to attract younger readers and readers with lower levels of formal education, and to represent more divergent socio-economic backgrounds.[20] Internet clubs also provide access to group members in different geographical areas. In TYABC, for example, members live on at least three different continents. A virtual club might also enhance one's membership in a f2f club by providing fodder for book discussion, or more likely, as Fuller, Squires, and I argue in Chapter 9 below, as a source for title recommendations. Online book clubs can provide space for specialized interpretative communities, or reading genres that are usually not readily available or may be deemed less valuable in f2f clubs, such as romance, mystery, or science fiction reading clubs. All this is not to say that virtual book clubs are utopian spaces. They are not. They illustrate the complexities of contemporary reading communities where vernacular reading practices are negotiated and normalized by the membership. I am interested in how these practices influence the cultural production and interpretation process because I see the members of this book club as educational theorist Henry Giroux sees teachers: 'cultural workers who provide the theory, language, and skills to dissect the dominant culture and construct a new, more democratic culture and more empowered and ethical identities'.[21]

Like many online book clubs, TYABC formed through the work of one woman who was interested in creating an online forum to talk about a genre of books that held particular interest for her. Demonstrating the viral influence of the Internet, membership is promoted mostly through word-of-mouth connections. Attempts to create personal links are common in this geographically diverse – albeit mostly within the USA – group. In an effort to create interpersonal associations that mimic f2f relations, members try to forge links to other members through individual salutations or observations about similar weather patterns, or more importantly for this study, through references to shared f2f or virtual meetings to which not all other members of the group are privy. These latter subgroups take the form of individuals meeting f2f after participating in the group, or more likely, when several members sit together on national association and/or literary award committees. Moving back and forth between virtual and 'real' spaces, the social networks embody the process of distribution and consumption of YA literature.

Cultural authority in text selection

Each month, TYABC selects book choices by membership vote. The moderator suggests titles sent to her by individuals several months in advance in response to this request: 'Nominations should be books appealing to an adolescent audience (between ages 10–18 or some segment of that group), in print, and not previously discussed as a TYABC monthly selection …' Suggestions put forward by members typically come from three sources: advanced reading copies received from publishers by the reviewers on the list, award shortlist announcements, and reviews from respected sources in the members' networks. Title recommendations originate only occasionally from teens themselves but are instantly popular once announced online, suggesting that the young adult reader confers a type of cultural authority within the group.

Relatively few members vote for the monthly book choices. This may be an apathetic response. Or, this might be because this is not the primary reason for participation and less active discussion members use the club instead to seek out title recommendations to share with their students and/or their own children. Generally, they 'trust' the active voices in the group. 'I usually have to force myself to read a book that has gotten a lot of buzz and publicity from sources other than the ones I trust (like TYABC) …' wrote Wanda. 'I'm not much of a poster but I enjoy what people say and it always makes me think twice about what I've read.' The 'use' of the club for reading recommendations is not problematic in itself because it can illustrate a form of individual agency, the choice to actively post, or to 'lurk'. My concern lies with *who* in the club is providing the recommendations because title recommendations largely come from a small group of members who are deemed 'YA Experts'. That is, those who appear to have the cultural capital necessary for book recommendation are those whom Bourdieu identifies as consecrators of literary value: teachers or librarians who use book discussion activities with their students, or employees of publishing companies.[22] In this case, it also includes those who sit on YA book award panels, editors and reviewers of YA books and industry magazines, and published YA authors, who stand to gain in reputation and in some instances professionally, from their perception as YA experts. There are financial outcomes to the promotion of some individuals as cultural authorities, and because there are gains to be made, there is a need to 'police' behaviours.

I am also concerned with the extent to which individuals defer to those with symbolic and cultural authority. Consider, for example, Shanna's post after she volunteered to lead the discussion of *Fire and Hemlock* by Diana Wynne Jones:

> I just thought I'd introduce myself since I'm going to be leading (or at least attempting to lead) the discussion for *Fire and Hemlock*. I've been following this list for about a year and a half now but mostly just lurk due to the fact that I'm a little shy with posting my own words to huge groups of people I don't really know. Though, on second thought, I do feel like I know some of you pretty well after all this time, which is great since, like many of you, I can't really find too many 'real' people who share my love of YA books. It's funny because reading about the many teachers and librarians on this list sometimes tempts me to go into those fields, even when I'm still just beginning in the one I've chosen ... Right now I'm trying to finish up a PhD in Neuroscience at SUNY ...

Obviously no intellectual dud herself, Shanna's self-deprecating comments make evident the symbolic capital of other members and reinforce Bourdieu's thesis that the cultural consumption process is informed and limited by the resources of cultural capital – whether embodied, inherited or institutionalized – that individual members possess. Within this group, a neuroscientist will not have the cultural authority that a middle school teacher might have *until* she is able to prove herself as a cultural authority and that authority is accepted and reinforced by other group members. Bourdieu's ideas are also helpful as we consider the tensions between readers and their text selection process. When I asked in the questionnaire how readers choose books, a 14-year-old Canadian boy wrote: 'I used to read anything that caught my eye, but lately I have adhered mostly to what other people recommended to me (mainly recommendations I received from members of TYABC) or books that have won awards ... I trust the opinions of the experts, and they are rarely wrong.' The influence of the group members and their discussions can change an individual's text selection processes. He '*used to* read anything', but the 'experts' have focused his choices. He implies that he has read the texts, and he is satisfied with the reading experiences. What we don't know from his response, however, is if the cultural competence he garners as a participant in this group translates into cultural capital in his classrooms. What is evident is that he has unfortunately relinquished his own legitimate judgement to those with cultural authority. Ironically, I suspect members of TYABC would prefer *he* recommend to them selections so that they can increase their own personal capital with the young people in their lives.

The cultural authority of the community as a whole appears to influence not only what readers as young as this one read, but also to extend to other members of the group. To gain authority, members must provide evidence of (a) knowledge of the YA genre, (b) experience with and access to young adults, and (c) industry experience. That is to say it is neither sufficient to write that 'I liked this book' nor to post a lot. Those who fulfil the three aforementioned criteria are rewarded with personal accolades and correspondence; they are given access to the inner circle of a coterie. Consider Robert, who posted thoughtful, analytical analysis almost daily. Indeed, the transcripts demonstrate that Robert – a teacher and a reviewer – received and gave the most referrals, responses, and comments of all the TYABC members who post. Discussions even ventured off into what kind of dog he should get, a discussion that would most likely not be tolerated from any other member, but because Robert has 'earned' his status within the group, he is able to use the community for more than book talk. The survey respondents referred to Robert as a member whose opinions and interpretations held considerable value. This was evident, too, in the postings when members would write to him specifically. When Robert had questions about a book he, too, would ask specific members for their thoughts. Those of us outside the conversation were then privy to perceived authorities' opinions not only for title recommendation, but also to what might be perceived as informed analysis or, more frequently, as informed title choices.

When asked what appealed to her about the recommendations made by this book club, Candace, a foster mother and teacher, said that the books 'are quick reads with usually well portrayed characters. I have 6 children and I work in a school with high school students. I have used the books I've learned about here at TYABC with my classroom students.' Her response is not only interesting in that it articulates the aesthetic and practical appeal of YA literature for a busy woman, but also because it illustrates the power the list can have in determining which books are purchased for school and home libraries, kept in circulation, read and valued by multiple readers. Consider also Katherine's response to a fellow member's review of *The Life and Death of Adolf Hitler* by James Cross Giblin. 'I'd like to further endorse (both Jamie's pick and) this Sibert winner and recommend that [you] give this incredibly informative and well-written title a read. Seriously, if your library doesn't have it, insist they get it!' Jamie passes on information on how list members can influence the process: 'Our library system has always been open to suggestions from patrons about new books that should be acquired. Supporting reviews or printed-out posts will give such requests added weight and after doing this a few times could give your opinions extra credence with the powers that be. I've always been proactive in getting them to acquire the occasional books they missed that I'd been recommending.'

In his review of Henry Giroux's critical pedagogy, educational philosopher Douglas Kellner posits Giroux's identification of 'children' and 'youth' as a 'complex site of hope and possibility, as well as domination and exploitation'. Quoting Giroux, Kellner argues that it is important to critically question 'the specific cultural formations and contexts in which childhood is organized, learned, and lived' because 'culture is the sphere in which adults exercise control over children and a site where children and youth can resist the adult world and create their own cultures and identities'.[23] While this examination focuses specifically on discussions in the group and does not explicitly detail how the practices of TYABC influence the activities in the members' classrooms, libraries and homes other than what was reported online, I question the unequal powers that some members wield in the 'creation' of book culture with their students.

After Robert posted a list his students had compiled for their own book competition based on his recommendations, he was asked by Katherine, 'Tell me how many, if any, of your students read anything non-fiction? <g> I mean, did any student read anything NF? Not like it? Just felt ho-hum about it? What's the poop? And what NF titles were you "pushing" – er, book-talking-to your class this year?' We are not privy to Robert's private response to Katherine, but it may be assumed, based on Robert's posts and recommendations to the book club, that there were few non-fiction titles. With what are I believe to be the best intentions, teachers and librarians recommend to their students the titles they learn about from TYABC members. We are left to hope that these young readers also seek other books for themselves.

The books chosen for discussion and for the annual internal TYABC award are often those that have also appeared on book prize lists, or will do so in the following year. Table 5.1 illustrates the parallels between some of the prominent US YA prize lists – the Newbery Medal (awarded by the Association for Library Service to Children); the Michael L. Printz Prize for Excellence in Young Adult Literature (sponsored by the Young Adult Library Services Association); and the National Book Award for Young People's Literature – and those chosen for discussion or prizes in TYABC.

Table 5.1 TYABC titles that are also YA Book Award winners (USA), 2002–05

	TYABC monthly picks	Newbery	Printz	National Book
November 2002–January 2003	*The House of the Scorpion* Nancy Farmer	2003 Honor	2003 Honor	2002
	Postcards from No Man's Land Aidan Chambers (Winner of the 2002 TYABC Award)		2003 Winner	
March 2003	*Pictures of Hollis Woods* Patricia Reilly Giff	2003 Honor		
August 2003	*A Northern Light* Jennifer Donnelly		2004 Honor	
November 2003– January 2004	*Fat Kid Rules the World* K.L. Going		2004 Honor	
	The First Part Last Angela Johnson		2004 Winner	
	The River Between Us Richard Peck (Winner of the 2003 TYABC Award)			
March 2004	*The Tale of Despereaux* Kate DiCamillo	2004 Medal Winner		
October 2004	*Doing It* Melvin Burgess	2005 Honor		
	Lizzie Bright and the Buckminster Boy Gary D. Schmidt		2005 Honor	

(continued)

Table 5.1 Continued

	TYABC monthly picks	Newbery	Printz	National Book
November 2004–January 2005	*Airborn Kenneth Oppel *How I Live Now Meg Rosoff *Sammy and Juliana in Hollywood Benjamin Alire Sáenz (Winner of the 2004 TYABC Award)		2005 Honor 2005 Winner	

Note: *TYABC nominees.

Considering that an institutional prize-winning book is in circulation the year before the award is presented, TYABC members frequently choose to read and discuss books that will also appeal to award committees. There are, as already mentioned, book prize committee members who are also members on TYABC, suggesting that the book club may act as a test 'market', and illustrating close connections between club members and institutional structures of YA distribution. I discuss this interconnection in the next section, and the response to YA texts pointing to a larger interpretative community. What literary judgement is being made about these books? While this study does not analyse the discussions that take place behind the scenes of literary awards, we should consider the discussion of this online book club to gain insight into the values embraced by these cultural workers.

Politics, power, and discourse in TYABC

Janice Radway's identification of romance readers as members of an 'interpretive community' is helpful to this research in that her Smithton romance readers shared a bond of cultural competence in reading romances even though they may have never met one another in person.[24] Does this same bond exist in TYABC? Is there a common cultural competence exhibited in reading the YA text, and if so, what is it and what does it mean? I begin to investigate this question by using Thomas Lindlof's extension of Stanley Fish's original conceptualization of 'interpretive communities'.[25] Fish argued that while each reader might have individual interpretations of the text, consistent responses emerge as a result of the interactions within the interpretative community to which one belongs.[26] The reader is not an independent agent, but rather a reader whose learned strategies are part of a community.[27] According to Lindlof, interpretative communities also define rules of social action, a concept that explains how the members of TYABC make use of the texts and discussion about those texts. The strategies and norms of the interpretative community guide the text's social uses.[28]

Cultural competency in TYABC has to be earned and proven. The welcome note upon joining the club attempts an accessible tone, 'We welcome any messages about young adult books and related issues, including but not limited to reading, teaching, and learning. TYABC members tend to branch off from original topics and discuss all sorts of things. These discussions can be passionate, funny, informative, and thought-provoking. This kind of meandering is encouraged – it is exactly what good books should make people do.' The moralizing expectation of what 'good books should' do is one that can be heard in many book programmes across Canada, the USA, and the UK.[29] However, the space in which the discussion occurs in this book club is fraught with complications that affect how much liberty members have in their posts. While analytical techniques and articulation of YA literary analysis are revered, but not an absolute necessity, readers must first prove that they understand the genre.

A member can demonstrate her or his cultural competence by volunteering to lead a book discussion and by asking thought-provoking questions, to which other members will respond with personal accolades, questions, and comments. For example, prior to Colleen leading a discussion, she received little feedback from her comments; afterwards, readers responded to her on a more regular basis. Similarly, members of the list most often responded to the members who wrote analytic responses to texts, and those members who were on the production side of YA literature seemed to garner more respect and response than some others.

Let us return to Kellner for a moment. He has written that 'Because youth today are the subjects of education, critical teachers must understand youth, their problems and prospects, hopes and fears, competencies and limitations.'[30] The active members of TYABC appear to share this idealism and are attempting to learn about the young people in their lives through the literature they read and, though perhaps to a lesser extent, through their discussions with one another. Whether discussing the monthly pick or another text, members will ask how students of other members have reacted to texts and will post reports from their own homes, libraries, and classrooms. Only rarely, however, does this specific discussion go past 'they loved this book' or 'they thought that book was boring'.

Members' own interpretations of the texts delve into deeper analysis even though typical posts are short, often consisting of no more than two paragraphs. Common discussion topics include characterization, setting, form, style, and theme of the monthly pick. When analysing this discourse, we find evidence of the conservative norms and values of group members. Consider Lily's post in response to Ellen Wittlinger's *Hard Love,* a story about two teens, one a lesbian and one a straight young man who become friends through the world of zines: 'I, like the rest of you, work with teens, and these characters were real to me. Palpable. I kept on laughing a [sic] certain passages and near the end of the book I began to jot down the phrases that got me. "suicidal goldfish" "lesbian tent" "naïve straight kid" just to name a few. Wittlinger was able to capture these teens on paper, and I think her language selection was central here.' The only response Lily received was from Carol that same day: 'Thanks for the wonderful comments! I especially found amusing the whole thing Marisol did in her zine with quoting Shakespeare instead of swearing.' There were no discussions about gay and lesbian issues in the classroom; however, the broader issue of teen alienation was taken up. In a flurry of messages in response to the two main characters (one straight, one a lesbian) going to a prom together, active members argued about the normalizing of teen spaces through institutionalized events such as a high school prom. Julie, a Canadian, expressed dismay in what she viewed as a 'discriminatory policy'. The apology that she adds at the end of her argument demonstrates nicely how the discourse in this club is patrolled – often by the members themselves – and how those same responses can begin to take up broader social issues: 'Sorry for the strong opinions. It's just that book after book is about teenage alienation and policies that further this are a big part of the problem.' One of the dominant behaviours of this group is to approach topics of a political nature rather gingerly as is evident in Julie's response. These carefully-constructed political discourse boundaries were evident in discussions of abortion, book censorship, mental illness, and race conflict. The silence around their discussion is notable because the themes are often found in contemporary YA fiction. Also evident, however, was a sense of trust and genuine curiosity among several of the active posters when the theme was one that had less potential to cause conflict among the members, such as questions around children with disabilities and teens who self-mutilate.

Active club members generally work together to negotiate peaceful dialogue. However, the virtual space of this online club neither reflects the democratic ideals that early champions of virtual communities reported nor does it enable Nicholas C. Burbules's 'third space' potential of dialogue, which is a 'zone in which semantic frames meet, conflict, and get attached with meanings neither original party intended or could have intended'. The possibilities that Burbules so rightly connects with online discourse – which is frequently criticized – lies in third-space distinctiveness, which is 'not about bridge building, fusing, blending, or reconciling; it is about a conflict, a disruption of ordinary meanings that leads to a new possibility'.[31] While there is little flaming or direct attacks on individual members of TYABC, the dialogue can silence those who are not perceived as part of the dominant core of members. Instead of posting whatever interpretation or thought one might have to create the new meanings Burbules calls for, less active members of the club often remained in 'lurkdom'. This became especially obvious in the survey responses. Barbara told me that she felt 'The same people who post constantly state their opinions as though they're the authority on the topic, and that's that. I often feel as though my opinions are completely ignored. My posts are often completely ignored.' And, when I asked her if she thinks the group embraces controversy, Janice responded, 'I think controversy for controversy's sake is discouraged; putting forth ones [sic] opinions, even if it creates a controversy, is encouraged. Though, when some people talk about "silly" posts I begin to wonder if there are some members who would prefer that opinions be not as diverse as they are.' So controversy is only encouraged if the ideas advanced fit the norms of the group. On the other hand, there are several members who feel comfortable enough posting their interpretations even though they may be 'flamed', or considered 'silly'.

As with the f2f groups I study, discursive norms within TYABC are learned over time and through experience and are reinforced by members.[32] What was unusual about this group was that it offered the opportunity to evaluate how these processes shift when several authors are part of the interpretative community. One author who frequently participates in the discussions told me that she learned early in her days as a member what was acceptable and unacceptable behaviour. She wrote:

> Since I am an author – I am restricted from saying negative things about a book. I didn't know that early on. I was naïve. I did so and got slammed. A lurker on the list sent my comments to the author of the book I commented about. Author contacted my editor. What a mess. I was chastised by some on the list. Now some of the posters on list were saying the same things, but as an author, it seems that's a no-no. So I learned a big lesson. Wish I had known the rules. So while the discussions go on, the negatives are pointed out with great abandon and I can only state the positives. That's not a bad thing, but sometimes I see a weakness that goes unnoticed and I grit my teeth. But that's only happening to me and a few other authors on the list.

This reader/author articulates the complex cultural authority within the group, one that is not without social, emotional, and perhaps financial, repercussions. Even though members openly welcome authors to the list and ask questions about inspiration, the writing process, and character/plot/setting development, the club members' responses towards this author suggest that there are different expectations of specific types of cultural authority figures. The challenging of the authority (cultural or otherwise) traditionally lent to authors reshapes the power relations within the community: the readers enact their own authority, which ends up messy when a person who holds the traditional authority role plays the dual role of cultural participant and worker. Another author on the list suggested that positions of authority are in flux in this online community. She wrote: '... there are occasionally some pretty catty remarks about books. As an author, I tend to cringe, hoping the writer isn't on the list. When I have a book available for discussion (I joined right after the last book would have been discussed) I plan to leave the group, at least for a while.' This response is telling in its assumption that 'resistant' comments might be interpreted more harshly if the person is an author herself. The comment also illustrates the fluidity of this online community, where a member can enact resistance by leaving the community and then return when they deem it appropriate.

Collective textual interpretation in TYABC mimics f2f book club readers' vacillation between critical detachment from the text and reader-character-place affiliation.[33] These reading practices are reminiscent of earlier reading-response studies of women and men's involvement in texts, which found that women readers tend to become more involved with the story, setting, and characters than do men.[34] Courtney explained to the group why she found Aiden Chambers's *Postcards* a better book than *The Lightkeeper's Daughter* by Iain Lawrence. As she explained her familiarity with the European setting, the familial context and the similarity in juvenile experiences, Courtney herself timidly suspects 'out loud' that her gendered reading practices may have an influence on her responses to the book. She writes:

> In fact, (I know I'm a distinct minority on this), I found none of the characters particularly engaging. Interesting, yes. But I couldn't relate to any of them in the way I could relate to those in *Postcards* or in *Gingerbread* (which I finally read and loved!) I'm wondering if it has something (and this may be strongly and hotly disputed which is fine!) with my gender. I found the males unattractive and could simply not relate to the mother or daughter. Could not imagine being in their situations. For some reason I was able to relate personally much more to the characters of *Postcards* ...

No one on the list responded to Courtney's gender observation and self-reflection. This silence suggests that articulation of gendered reading practices might be, in some way, a challenge to the cultural authority in TYABC. It allows an individual to establish their credibility based on a position that is difficult for others to challenge. At the same time, it also comes close to – hence her hesitation – broaching topics that may be construed as political (in this case, feminism) and as attempting to establish resistance to the very limited forms of critique that are tolerated.

Conclusion

The online space of TYABC serves as an apolitical – that is, non-threatening – space for discussion of YA fiction. It is a space that works to establish and reinforce cultural authority for some individuals in the area of YA fiction, from which they may derive personal benefits, such as with one's students and/or children, and/or positive cultural and professional returns. Through TYABC, a member can garner reading recommendations that boost their status as a cultural authority, particularly among young people. In the club, members' reader-responses serve as a 'pre-test' to YA prizes. The club also functions as a space for aspiring YA authors to seek advice about writing and publishing. Interestingly, one of the things that this space does not do is to provide a space for young adults to discuss books and what they are reading. It does not provide a site of interaction between readers and potential readers and YA authors.

TYABC members are limited in their articulation of different interpretations of the book, and of different social issues presented therein, because of group norms and rules established over time through the online discussion. Active members who have cultural authority inside and outside the community create norms and practices in the interpretative community of cultural workers, which influence cultural production processes.

Jody's comments illustrate what some individual readers take from membership in the community. While she would not be considered by members to be an authority figure in the group, she articulates the different ways readers use this book club. In her response to my question about what set of skills someone might need to participate in this community, she said, 'I guess just the desire to talk about the books. Or rather, they don't even have to talk, just read the conversation. Some of the members are reviewers or take this very seriously. Some (like me) just read and don't feel the need to analyze. I have a gut feeling and often can't explain it, but I'm still a full participant.' Choosing not to participate in the discussions, whether through felt intimidation, lack of time or interest in a particular book, demonstrates resistance not only towards a text, but also resistance to a particular set of practices.

This particular research cannot draw a complete picture of the effects of the group on the distribution, production, and reception of YA literature, but it provides important glimpses of what individuals might *do* with their membership. Jody, for example, used the book club as a study group to advance her professional career. 'My knowledge of YA literature has improved so much since I joined TYABC. I went from being a generalist paraprofessional library tech who kind of enjoyed that type of book to being the YA librarian.' Julie, too, used the group to satisfy both emotional needs and practical ones: 'I joined this list when my son was 10 because I wanted to find some great books for him. He's 14 now and I've done more than that, I've reawakened my passion for books and turned it into a career in publishing.' Others might see the group as a place for pleasurable professional development. 'Coming at it from a teacher's perspective, I know very few teachers who purposely set out to bore students or destroy their natural curiosity and love of reading. Understanding why that's happening gives us more insight into how to change things for the better', wrote Michaela in a discussion of required classroom reading.

The complex concern over the 'infrastructure of literacy and the social or institutional determinants of what's available to read, what is "worth reading," and how to read'[35] identified by Long become especially interesting when analysing YA fiction choices, reading practices, and the subsequent discussion. *Are you There God? It's Me Margaret*, *The Handmaid's Tale* and *The Story of O* are three titles that I particularly remember from my youth. All three illustrate the importance of considering contemporary young adult cultures of reading where meaning is made, produced, and reproduced. Judy Blume's *Are You There God? It's Me Margaret* spoke to me as a sixth grader about to begin menstruating and as a young woman wondering about the power of God. Margaret was 'just like me', and Blume offered me an insight into books that I hadn't experienced before. Books became my life guide. While the small public library did not ban Blume's award-winning book, I do remember trying to check out books from the adult section and being told that 'those aren't for girls your age'. Having read everything in the small YA section, and not wanting to be told what I could and could not do, I turned to my mother's garage-sale book purchases. From that pile came *The Handmaid's Tale* and *The Story of O*, both texts that are 'outside' the genre of young adult fiction and were intended for adult readers.

In fact, all three books might appeal to young readers because they are novels broadly concerned with sexual discovery in some respect: *Are You There God? It's Me Margaret* and *The Story of O* are (generally speaking) stories of sexual awakening; *The Handmaid's Tale* is about a repressive regime intended to usurp and counter women's sexual awakening and freedoms. Both adult novels, however, were best-sellers and no doubt heavily promoted through the popular press (our small North Dakota town is not known as a hotbed for literary reading so knowing about non-best-sellers was unlikely).

Kellner argues that 'Culture is the sphere in which adults exercise control over children and a site where children and youth can resist the adult world and create their own cultures and identities.'[36] Young adult book culture offers opportunities for resistance and identity formation, but we must ask ourselves, to what extent? Further study is necessary if we are to better understand how cultural mediation influences young adult's reader reception. We need to understand more fully the influence that the 961 members of this particular community of readers – and others similar to it – wield when off-line. As teachers, librarians, reviewers, and parents, they are all in positions of cultural authority and have an influence on the next generation of readers.

Notes

Sincere thanks to Danielle Fuller, Anouk Lang and Katherine Side for their helpful comments on earlier drafts of this chapter. They confirm that scholarship is an interactive process that can be enjoyable.

1. The name of the reading group and its members have been changed to protect their identities.
2. Pierre Bourdieu, *Distinction: a Social Critique of the Judgment of Taste*, trans. Richard Nice (1979; Cambridge, MA: Harvard University Press, 1984), 359–60.
3. Elizabeth Long, 'Textual Interpretation as Collective Action', in *The Ethnography of Reading*, ed. Jonathan Boyarin (Berkeley: University of California Press, 1992), 193. See also Pierre Bourdieu, *The Field of Cultural Production* (New York: Polity Press, 1993).
4. 'Young Adult Fiction' is a subjectively defined genre. For purposes of this study, I rely on members of TYABC who themselves spent several days discussing the categorization. While there was no consensus among the active members, YA texts are generally written for readers aged 12–24.
5. Jenny Hartley, *Reading Groups* (Oxford: Oxford University Press, 2001); Elizabeth Long, *Book Clubs: Women and the Uses of Reading in Everyday Life* (Chicago: University of Chicago Press, 2003); 'Textual Interpretation as Collective Action', *Discourse* 14, 3 (1992): 104–30; Elizabeth McHenry, '"Dreaded Eloquence": the Origins and Rise of African American Literary Societies and Libraries', *Harvard Library Review* 6, 2 (1995): 32–56; Heather

Murray, *Come, Bright Improvement! The Literary Societies of Nineteenth-Century Ontario* (Toronto: University of Toronto Press, 2002); Marilyn Poole, 'The Women's Chapter: Women's Reading Groups in Victoria', *Feminist Media Studies* 3, 3 (2003): 263–81.
6. Norma Linda González, 'Nancy Drew: Girls' Literature, Women's Reading Groups, and the Transmission of Literacy', *Journal of Literacy Research* 29, 2 (1997): 221–51; Linsey Howie, 'Speaking Subjects: a Reading of Women's Book Groups', PhD dissertation, La Trobe University (1998) and Chapter 7 below; DeNel Rehberg Sedo, 'Badges of Wisdom, Spaces for Being: a Study of Contemporary Women's Book Clubs', PhD dissertation, Simon Fraser University, Burnaby, BC (2004).
7. Several studies investigate the Internet portion of Oprah's Book Club (http://www.oprah.com/entity/oprahsbookclub). See, for instance, Yung-Hsing Wu, 'The Romance of Reading Like Oprah', in *The Oprah Effect: Critical Essays on Oprah's Book Club*, ed. Cecilia Konchar Farr and Jaime Harker (Albany: State University of New York Press, 2008), 73–87, which uncovers reader agency in Oprah's Book Club online discussion boards.
8. Barbara Fister, 'Reading as a Contact Sport: Online Book Groups and the Social Dimensions of Reading', *Reference & User Services Quarterly* 44, 4 (2005): 303–9.
9. Ibid.
10. Ibid., 306.
11. Ibid.
12. Long, *Book Clubs*, 206–17.
13. Ibid, 208; Trysh Travis, 'Divine Secrets of the Cultural Studies Sisterhood: Women Reading Rebecca Wells', *American Literary History* 15, 1 (2003): 134–61.
14. Janice Radway, *Reading the Romance: Women, Patriarchy, and Popular Literature* (Chapel Hill and London: University of North Carolina Press, 1991).
15. Travis, 'Divine Secrets', 137.
16. Ibid., 138.
17. The same process in 2004 yielded only a little more than one million pages.
18. DeNel Rehberg Sedo, 'Readers in Reading Groups: an On-Line Survey of Face-to-Face and Virtual Book Clubs', *Covergence: the Journal of Research into New Media Technologies* 9, 1 (2003): 66–90.
19. See also Jenny Hartley, *Reading Groups*, 14–15.
20. Rehberg Sedo, 'Readers in Reading Groups'.
21. Henry Giroux, as cited in Douglas Kellner, 'Critical Pedagogy, Cultural Studies, and Radical Democracy at the Turn of the Millennium: Reflections on the Work of Henry Giroux', *Critical Studies/Critical Methodologies* 1, 2 (2001), 236.
22. Bourdieu, *The Field of Cultural Production*.
23. Kellner, 'Critical Pedagogy', 224.
24. Radway, *Reading the Romance*, 5. Radway discusses reading habits within a community to which she gives the pseudonym Smithton.
25. Thomas R. Lindlof, 'Media and Audiences as Interpretive Communities', in *Communication Yearbook*, ed. James Anderson (Newbury Park, CA: Sage, 1988), 81–107.
26. Stanley Fish, *Is There a Text in This Class? The Authority of Interpretive Communities* (Cambridge, MA: Harvard University Press, 1980).

27. Stanley Fish, *Doing What Comes Naturally: Change, Rhetoric, and the Practice of Theory in Literary and Legal Studies* (Oxford: Clarendon Press, 1989). While useful for its foregrounding of the collective, there are problems with attributing too much determinism to the regulatory norms in Fish's model. First, Fish's readers might be characterized as imprisoned in communal norms of interpretation, coerced by their authority as noted in Elizabeth Freund, *The Return of the Reader: Reader-Response Criticism* (London: Methuen, 1987). Second, authority, according to Fish's outline, is usually androcentric – see Patrocinio P. Schweickart, 'Reading Ourselves: Toward a Feminist Theory of Reading', in *Gender and Reading: Essays on Readers, Texts, and Contexts*, ed. Patrocinio P. Schweickart and Elizabeth A. Flynn (Baltimore and London: Johns Hopkins University Press, 1986). Schweickart's critique is an important one because she argues that by focusing on the processual as Fish's model does, we lose sight of the underlying social structural forces that may allow a preferred or dominant interpretative community/or reading to emerge, and a minority one to recede. Agency is always constrained by social structure, and the power of class in acculturation.
28. Lindlof, 'Media and Audiences as Interpretive Communities'.
29. Danielle Fuller and DeNel Rehberg Sedo, 'A Reading Spectacle for the Nation: the CBC and "Canada Reads"', *Journal of Canadian Studies* 40, 1 (2006): 5–36.
30. Kellner, 'Critical Pedagogy', 227.
31. Nicholas C. Burbules, 'Rethinking Dialogue in Networked Spaces', *Cultural Studies – Critical Methodologies* 6, 1 (2006), 114.
32. Rehberg Sedo, 'Badges of Wisdom'.
33. Ibid.
34. Elizabeth Flynn and Patrocinio P. Schweickert, eds, *Gender and Reading: Essays on Readers, Texts and Context* (Baltimore: Johns Hopkins University Press, 1986).
35. Long, 'Textual Interpretation', 193.
36. Kellner, 'Critical Pedagogy', 224.

6
The Growth of Reading Groups as a Feminine Leisure Pursuit: Cultural Democracy or Dumbing Down?

Anna Kiernan

According to Nicholas Clee, former editor of the *Bookseller* (the UK's leading publishing trade magazine), 'the rise of book clubs has coarsened literary debate'.[1] Reflecting on how opinion makers in publishing are now largely dominated by television personalities, Clee's article considers how book groups work and suggests that the empathy often evoked in readers of book club books is not always compatible with the experience of reading 'great literature'. Despite his attempted deflection of anticipated criticism in the opening line of his *New Statesman* article – 'to criticise book clubs and reading groups is an act of a snob' – Clee's subsequent musings evidence such a tendency. The piece functions as a reiteration of the type of 'difficult' critical reception that book groups/clubs, and in particular television book clubs, have garnered from the literary establishment (see references to literary critics McCrum and Cusk later in this chapter), with an inherent devaluation of such forms of gendered cultural consumption.

In *A History of Reading* Alberto Manguel recounts a similar bookish tension emerging in fifteenth-century France. Here, the narrator of the *Évangils des quenouilles* (Gospels of the Distaffs) visits a household of women spinners set on countering the tendency of men to 'incessantly write defamatory lampoons and infectious books against the honour of the female sex'.[2] Over six days, within the context of this prototype book group, the narrator witnesses the women as they 'read, interrupt, comment, object and explain, and seem to enjoy themselves immensely, so much so that the narrator finds their laxity tiresome … [and] judges their comments "lacking rhyme or reason". The narrator is, no doubt [concludes Manguel] accustomed to more formal scholastic disquisitions by men.'[3] Manguel's account suggests that reading groups have historically been marginalized as a 'feminine' leisure pursuit. Over five centuries later this viewpoint, to some extent, still prevails. This begs the question: why are the reading habits and patterns of literary consumption among women – the dominant market force – still treated with a degree of derision?

In this chapter, I consider the possibility that television has, paradoxically, contributed to the development of a new demographic of readers, so that in this context, it may be that the mass media does not necessarily signify cultural 'dumbing down'. In the light of this shift, I assess the impact of new (book club) readers on notions of dominant cultural divisions between 'high-' and 'low-brow'. Drawing on my experience as a fiction editor at Simon & Schuster and my work as a reviewer, I consider how publishing and reviewers view book club books and the influence of TV book clubs. I also draw on posts from a discussion forum I set up on the Richard and Judy website and on interviews.

My starting point in this discussion is the premise that the cultural value ascribed to a given media text is often seen to be inversely proportionate to its popularity, so that the more popular the text, the less cultural value it is perceived to have.[4] This appears to be the case with book clubs – despite many of the texts selected belonging to the category of literary fiction. I will suggest that certain 'feminine' reading habits and preferences are given short shrift by some critics because of their association with mass media and 'low-brow' culture. I will go on to consider how television book clubs have become one of the most important contributors to potential growth in the book publishing market, since, as my online discussions of the Richard and Judy forum indicate, television book clubs have the power to influence reading habits.

The format of television book clubs emulates the usual setting of a book group by attempting to recreate the intimate and informal exchanges that would occur, but with the addition of authors and the show's host. By creating a seemingly cosy intimacy between the host and the audience in this way, the shows rehearse a situation that many viewers are comfortable with. Thus, the usual binary split between masculine forms of high culture in the public sphere and feminine forms of low culture in the private sphere is reconstituted, so that the experience of reading and discussing texts within a private setting is publicly valorized. Context is in many ways as significant as content here: women often read at home, entertain members of their book group at home, and watch daytime television at home (though daytime television is of course not solely the domain of women, since other demographics, such as students and the unemployed, are also consumers). In other words, mass market and other female 'audiences' are bound to be frequently situated in the home, since that is so often their place of (domestic and maternal) work.[5] Despite this contextual obligation – or perhaps because of it, as I will explain – the localized, and often domestic setting of such activity presumes the rationale of the reading group, in particular, as being predicated on an appreciation of writing/literature, rather than its analysis. The counterpoint of the usual reading group context is of course the university – a place in which a very different sort of cultural and literary engagement is assumed to take place. Reading groups are therefore often ascribed a low cultural value as opposed to the high cultural value of discussing a Great Work of Literature in an academic context.

In 'Reading in Groups: Women's Clubs and College Literature Classes', Jane Missner Barstow explores this delineation in reading practices through observing both reading groups and groups of college students in class. She concludes that, 'Women look to reading as a source of affinity and connectedness, whereas for men reading is part of an ongoing process of individuation and separation.'[6] Citing Patrocinio P. Schweickart's call for a 'dialogical model of reading which combines personal meditation with literary analysis' as a possible outcome may offer a solution for renegotiating abiding views of the value of various cultural outputs.[7] The notion of sharing both subjective and objective perspectives within a classroom, or indeed a reading group context, offers a pragmatic counterpoint to accepted literary discourse.

Schweickart's equalizing impulse is, however, more difficult to apply to daytime television, the setting for television book clubs, configured as it is in terms of its low, gendered cultural value.[8] Television book groups appeal to viewers through their 'affinity and connectedness' but are not interested in emulating the cultural authority of an academic context. Furthermore, critics conclude that watching television leads to a decline in literacy and it has therefore historically been viewed as having little to add to the forum of literary production or reception.[9] The recent union of television and books, however, has resulted in something of an anomaly. Wendy Bloomer, librarian at Kingsbridge library in Devon, one of the libraries participating in both 'Richard and Judy's Summer Read 2004' and the BBC's 'Big Read' in 2005, suggests that the newfound relationship between television and reading has catalyzed an unexpected cultural exchange. She explained to me that, 'some people have watched the programme and thought that the books look interesting. And some see [the] library displays [of Richard and Judy titles] and think, "gosh, they look interesting, I must go and watch the programme."'[10] Bloomer's experience of the cultural exchange promoted by Richard and Judy's

Book Club signifies a shift in consuming practices – and in particular, the view that TV and reading audiences are mutually exclusive.[11] It may be that the combination of 'personal meditation' and 'literary analysis' are not so far removed in the context of television book clubs and that the sense of self-development afforded by an engagement with television book club books is partly dependent on some level of critical engagement with the text.

The same possibility of resistance that Ien Ang and Janice Radway identify in readers reading genre fiction can be applied to viewers reading TV book club books. Ang and Radway explore those tensions between 'reaffirmation of patriarchy' in texts belonging to genre fiction, such as the romance, and the 'declaration of independence' made by women in the actual practice of reading, either in isolation or together with a reading group made up of women.[12]

My own approach, as a former fiction editor and book reviewer, might be categorized as that of a 'redemptive reader' of popular culture: someone who 'seeks to identify the "progressive" potential of the popular text'.[13] In order to make the case for the significance of popular culture, and particularly popular fictions, it will be useful to consider the cultural hierarchy within which mass market fictions are located.

'Official' discourses and 'the popular aesthetic'

The *idea of culture* largely conforms to an assimilatory hierarchy dependent upon the western patriarchal aesthetic tradition. French sociologist Pierre Bourdieu's *Distinction* is a useful thesis on how 'taste' aligns with class and, in my view, gender.[14] As Thornham has noted, '[Bourdieu] argues that "nothing more rigorously distinguishes" the dominant class from the working class than the former's "disposition" towards the legitimate consumption of legitimate works, the aptitude for taking a specifically aesthetic point of view on objects already constituted aesthetically.'[15] Bourdieu identifies 'cultural practices' with education, so that artistic or literary merit might be understood as deriving from a shared understanding between critic and artist based on an equivalence in terms of educational attainment. Applied to my argument, the implication is self-evident: those who are highly educated have (apparently) a greater reverence for (and understanding of) 'high culture', which is directly correlative to their social status or class. This naturally tends to be inversely proportionate to a dismissive view of popular culture. Within Bourdieu's framework, Clee (a commentator with more cultural capital than most) having a dig at Richard and Judy's Book Club is, in many ways, typical.

In 'Literary Editors, Social Networks and Cultural Tradition' James Curran maps out some of the ways in which such a hierarchy bears upon the book world, through his examination of the quality press's review sections.[16] Curran's key finding is that literary editors' view of what they do is quite different from what they *actually* do. It also offers a useful context for considering the 'problem' of Richard and Judy's Book Club. Bourdieu argues that a 'financial' and 'cultural' economy coexist, but by dint of its ratings, Richard and Judy's Book Club has challenged the cultural dominance of the literary establishment, through its affinity with both cultural and financial capital.

In his paper 'Watching the Big Read with Pierre Bourdieu: Forms of Heteronomy in the Contemporary Literary Field', David Wright takes issue with the abiding perception of a binary division of 'high' and 'low' culture within the book trade. He argues that mass media has become an 'active partner' of literature and that, 'Mass mediated publicity for books, via such broadcasting initiatives as Oprah's Bookclub in the US and Richard and Judy's Bookclub in the UK, is celebrated within the book industry for precisely "spreading the word about books."'[17]

What emerges from Wright's analysis of the Big Read is that the mass media appears to draw more coherently on the preferences of the general reader and to reflect – and reflect upon – their preferences more easily than the traditional arbiters of taste, literary critics.[18] While the Big Read called for viewers and listeners of the BBC to nominate favourite novels, resulting in 140,000 votes in the first instance, when Curran interviewed 11 literary editors of national newspapers and weekly periodicals he discovered that a 'stock response' was that 'literary editors merely respond ... to the external world'.[19] They deciphered a 'pre-set agenda shaped by what readers are interested in, and what is being talked about' alongside a need to cover new works by 'important authors, with established reputations and track records'.[20] More confusingly – and this is the nub of Curran's findings – literary editors appeared to be unclear about what it was, exactly, that they did, despite believing their roles to be well defined: 'One account invoked a theory of predestination in which books were not chosen but chose themselves. The other summoned up an image of improvisation and randomness, of actions governed by instinct and insight, without a clear pattern.'[21]

Such a view is of course consistent with romantic notions of artistic genius, innate aesthetic judgement, and the continuation of an entrenched and unquestioning form of social hierarchy. Arguably and in keeping with Bourdieu's conception of cultural capital, only the privileged can afford to be wilfully eccentric in this way.

Curran notes four key areas that comprise the bulk of the book review sections, namely biography, literary fiction, history and general humanities. Of these categories, Curran's content analysis reveals that in 1997 the *Observer* reviewed 14 works of literary fiction for every four popular novels, the *Sunday Times* 19 works of literary fiction for every four popular novels, and the weekly *New Statesman* reviewed 16 works of literary fiction and no popular fiction. The ratio of the coverage of literary to popular fiction in quality newspapers evidenced little change, while the *Daily Mail* saw an inversion of ratios from 14 literary fiction to 11 popular fiction in 1984 to 11 literary fiction and 14 popular fiction in 1997.

Curran concurs that 'twas ever thus, particularly in the allocation of reviews to specific tropes and genres: 'Over half the review space of the *Sunday Times* was given in 1870, as in 1997, to literary fiction, history and biography.'[22] One explanation for this disparity is the cultural elitism that editors tend to naturalize: 'Literary editors in 1999 were predominantly middle-aged, and educated at elite universities – as were their predecessors in 1986.'[23] This begs the question, what possible interest could they have in Richard and Judy's Book Club or Oprah's Book Club?

Very little, it would seem. Despite recognizing the significance of the democratization of literature that the hybrid of TV book clubs has produced, the legacy of over 100 years of engagement with a very particular sort of literary culture and criticism is, unsurprisingly, resistant to the influence that non-specialist celebrity readers/reviewers (that is, Richard, Judy and Oprah) are able to extend to book-buying trends. Resistance to the pressure of mass media trends within the book pages (which is by no means absolute) goes some way to addressing James English's concern (as noted by Wright) that, 'Society ... is fast replacing a rich and varied cultural world with a shallow and homogenous McCulture based on a model of network TV.'[24] Such resistance may also be seen as a reiteration of Bourdieu's identification of literary production of high cultural value being uninterested in generating financial capital, since it exists, as it were, for its own sake.

The Oprah effect

Oprah Winfrey's apparent lack of interest in the views of the literati combined with her love affair with leading publishers was bound to irritate some less powerful opinion makers and also to trouble some advocates of 'high art'. Since its inception in 1996, Jenny Hartley notes that Oprah's Book Club has generated 10,000 letters per month and 28 consecutive best-sellers. Over 500,000 viewers have read at least some of the titles chosen. Even at its lowest ebb (in April 2002) books endorsed by the programme sold 600,000 copies (down from one million), at which point the first iteration of the book club stopped.[25] Winfrey's explanation for this was that, 'It has been harder and harder to find books on a monthly basis that I feel absolutely compelled to share.'[26]

Following Winfrey's lead, Richard and Judy's Book Club was launched in January 2004 and has made Richard and Judy very powerful players in UK publishing, guaranteeing best-sellers, producing readers who buy every selected title, and leading to Amazon selling out of copies.[27] The books selected for Richard and Judy's Book Club, or for that matter Oprah's Book Club, rely on a very particular set of criteria that reflects those listed by Malcolm Gladwell in his discussion of *The Divine Secrets of the Ya-Ya Sisterhood* in *The Tipping Point*. Gladwell defines a book group book as being 'emotionally sophisticated, character-driven, multi-layered [which] invites reflection and discussion'.[28] The producers dedicated to the Richard and Judy project seemed to reiterate these criteria, looking for stories that speak to the human spirit and that might move and inspire readers. Maria Rejt, publishing director for Pan Macmillan and judge of the Richard and Judy novel prize, described the short-listed authors as taking readers on a journey with great skill and *empathy*.[29] While not exclusively so, books that invite reader empathy, identification and emotion are the mainstay of the book club choices. However, these 'feminine' conventions are the cause of much of the bad press that book club books have garnered – on both sides of the Atlantic. This, I would argue, is because empathizing is an emotional rather than an intellectual response and, as such, is presumed to be a *feminine* response.

In an article on book groups in 2005, Robert McCrum, literary editor at the *Observer*, foregrounded the diversity, integrity and influence of book clubs/groups but based his thesis on a number of inaccuracies. He wrote: 'Last year, amid some surprise, the Penguin/Orange Reading Group Prize went not to that popular book-club stereotype – a group of middle class chardonnay-swilling, middle-aged women – but to the Racketeers, a Manchester-based circle of blokes, passionate bibliophiles who meet each month at a local pub to discuss their reading of the Booker Prize shortlist.'[30] According to Hartley in *The Reading Groups Book*, in 2002–03 all-female reading groups (in the UK) constituted 66 per cent of all groups, while all-male groups accounted for 6 per cent. Yet to admit this commonly accepted fact (the source, presumably, of the 'book-club stereotype') is regarded as conceding something that is in some way unsatisfactory. The more typical book group member tends to be one of two types: the now well-known middle-class woman, who is most likely to be 30–39 but is often older or the daytime TV viewer turned reader typified in this response: '… A 46-year-old woman confessed that until her conversion to reading through Oprah she had not read more than five books in her entire life.'[31]

McCrum could be interpreted as regarding both the highbrow literary critic – Oxbridge educated, middle-class and male, as identified by Curran – and the self-taught Mancunian 'bloke' as being of more value to the development of literary culture than the typical 'chardonnay-swilling', female book groupie. As Fuller, Squires and Rehberg Sedo observe in Chapter 9 below, 'typical' book group texts have now been identified by all major publishers (HarperCollins, Random House, Penguin, Bloomsbury), and are targeted through the addition of book group notes on publishing websites as a matter of course. However, McCrum goes on to say that the diversity of the short-listed groups for the Penguin/Orange Reading Group Prize proves 'that most publishers know only too well that you simply cannot – thank God – predict the reading preferences, or profiles, of the fiction-buying public'.

As David Wright's work on the Big Read shows, the initiative began with a call for nominations of favourite novels by BBC viewers and listeners, resulting in 140,000 votes. The nation's reading preferences are thus fairly transparent in the 100 favourite reads that resulted from the vote. McCrum's mystification of literature seems to advocate exclusivity or cultural capital over the reality of the book trade and its acceptance of the industry driver, economic capital: that is, sales.

Of course McCrum is not alone in feeling discomfort regarding the co-opting of high culture by the mass media. Jonathan Franzen, author of *The Corrections*, was one of the few 'highbrows' to acknowledge, quite openly – at least in the first instance – that he was not thrilled to have been picked by Oprah, since he viewed Oprah's choices as being 'schmaltzy' and 'one dimensional'.[32] He saw his own work as being 'solidly within the high-art literary tradition' and therefore, it was to be understood, not appropriate reading for the masses of (largely female, partially educated) viewers and readers of Oprah's books and shows.[33] The cultural split implied here – between high-brow and low-brow – resists a simple application of class structure and snobbery: McCrum's ideal is the 'noble' working-class hero. But the prognosis on gender has a certain congruence: either from the chattering or lower classes, women's book groups do not represent the eminent intellectual's 'ideal reader'.[34] Whose cause such assumptions serve, and whose they ignore will be explored in the next section.

The Richard and Judy demographic

In 'Extra-Curricular Activities: Women Writers and the Readerly Text' and '"Out of Category": the Middlebrow Novel' Hilary Radner suggests that textual consumption, or reading the text 'for pleasure', is characteristic of the type of novel that Roland Barthes has called the readerly text. She argues that readers of genre fiction, and notably romances, have an expectation of narrative structure and character that is satisfied each time they consume a text from their chosen genre. Thus the reading process is unchallenging and pleasure is derived from narrative expectations being met. The 'writerly text', according to Barthes, has a very different expectation of the reader, in that it 'offers the reader the impression of writing his [sic] own narrative'. The writerly text demands a reader initiated into those cultural codes which will enable him [sic] to re-inscribe the text for himself [sic] 'as a sign of his position of master'.[35] The readerly style, Radner suggests, is typical of the romance reader, while the writerly text is characteristic of, for instance, textual studies in academia. Because the outcome can be anticipated in formula fiction, the former is process driven, whereas the latter is product driven. That is, the pleasure comes, as it were, with the finale. The process here is best understood as the reader succumbing to fantasy.

In *A Feeling for Books: the Book-of-the Month Club, Literary Taste and Middle-Class Desire*, Janice Radway explains this in terms of a formative personal experience:

> These [popular books] prompted physical sensations, a forgetting of the self and complete absorption in another world. The books that came to me as high culture never seemed to prompt the particular shudder, the frisson I associated with the books of my childhood, because they carried with them not mere promise alone but also a threat, the threat that somehow I might fail to understand, might fail to recognize their reputed meaning and inherent worth.[36]

Radway's ethnographic thesis, *Reading the Romance*, an earlier exercise in audience studies based on researching an all-female reading group in 'Smithton', observed an important difference between the continuation of a patriarchal hegemony in the genre romances themselves and a moment of resistance in the act of reading. The 'resistance' here was in the act of the romance reader distancing herself, through the act of reading, from her obligations as wife, mother, carer – that is, from being secondary to someone else's needs.[37]

Ang tests Radway's view that romantic fiction is 'compensatory literature' in 'Feminist Desire and Female Pleasure: On Janice Radway's *Reading the Romance*'. Radway's assertion of the possibility of readerly empowerment being realized through the redemptive potential of romances to allow (women) readers briefly to escape the perceived limitations of their marriages and lives is radically redressed to take in the possibility of a more active engagement with genre romances. Ang suggests that engaging with fantasy is not merely a strategy for escaping from an inadequate reality but rather that fantasy is an alternative reality, and that women who read in this way may be utilizing a 'psychical strategy' in which they 'empower themselves in everyday life, leaving apart [the] ideological consequences in social reality'.[38] Ang's argument is not concerned with promoting the literary value of romances but rather with identifying the potential of genre fiction to instil the consumption of mass media texts with imaginative potential.

In the tradition of the French post-structuralist feminists and notably with Julia Kristeva, Ang seems to be most interested in the pleasure – or *jouissance* – that can be derived from the practice of reading. It is the absence of pleasure, or rather the lack of acknowledgment of reading as a transcendent activity, that Ang notes as a major omission in Radway's early 'recruitist' approach.[39] Ang's readers are motivated by pleasure, not resistance, and Ang is less interested in limiting readerly pleasure to a feminist framework.

Drawing on Radway's work in this way, Ang introduces a secondary characteristic to the process of reading romances that invites further reflection on forms of readerly engagement. In the quote that follows, Manguel's categorization and characterization of processes of reading owes a debt to Barthes (see above) but his interpretation is, unusually, dually feminine:

> At least two different sorts of reading seem to take place within a segregated group. In the first, the readers, like imaginative archaeologists burrow their way through the official literature in order to rescue from between the lines the presence of their fellow outcasts ... in the second, the readers become writers, inventing for themselves new ways of telling stories in order to redeem on the page the everyday chronicles of their excluded lives in the laboratory of the kitchen, in the studio of the sewing-room, in the jungles of the nursery.[40]

By re-inscribing domestic space as one of industry, in these admittedly rather laboured metaphors, Manguel redresses the implicit gendered oppositions mapped out by Barthes and picked up on by Radner, both of whom can be seen as largely unconcerned by the reductionism implied by simplifying the processes of reading different types of text.

The difficulty with such a division is that writing – even genre writing – is not always so predictable in the responses it generates. By the same token, all TV viewing, read from this perspective, would surely be perceived as 'readerly', or passive.

The 'ideal (or "writerly") reader' versus the reading group

Novelist Rachel Cusk's 2005 feature-length article in the *Review* section of the *Guardian* reveals a barely-concealed contempt for the all-female monthly book group session that she attended on moving to a new locale. She writes:

> The problem, I immediately saw, was that, though different, they had all read the same book. One dress would not have suited them all: by the same token one author could not hope to appease them. They read as though reading were a mystery they hoped one day to resolve … it was as though not merely the texts but the experience of reading itself was encrypted. They couldn't break through it, to a place of silent comprehension. As if for the first time I understood that reading is a private matter.
>
> I believed [Chekhov] would transform them. I believed in his power of verisimilitude, of true emotion, of human understanding. I believed in his art. I imagined the serious book group convening in a new and luminous spirit, reborn, having felt the incomparable benediction of recognition, of the vanquishing of time by truth. I imagined them becoming serious.[41]

To view an engagement with literature in this way is a reiteration of modernist negotiations with form in which the negation of an ultimate meaning infers a denial of narrative authority. It is of course a far more realistic view. There is no happy ending. But even in that most incomprehensible of modernist writers, Joyce, we can find moments of meaning. And is that not the same impulse? Decontextualizing meaning-making is a moment in which authentic meaning is made.

According to Cusk, the goal is to become 'serious' and 'silent'. The notion of intellectual enquiry finding expression in conversation is mocked here: 'they read as though reading were a mystery'. Yet this description of a group of readers might sit just as easily with a class of undergraduates embarking on an analysis of Derridian theory. More than likely, they won't understand it all; they will attempt to make sense of it by applying a linear narrative, and they will feel baffled and possibly alienated by the jarring language and oblique reasoning. Would it be better that they retreated to a place of 'silent comprehension', or is such an expectation untenable? Furthermore, is it fundamentally elitist?

Cusk's description returns in some sense to Elizabeth Long's notion of the idealized reader: the solitary female figure, silently absorbed and observed, in Long's account, by the male gaze. In *Soap Opera and Women's Talk*, Mary Ellen Brown suggests that much of the pleasure derived from soap operas is gleaned from discussing them, from gossiping about 'what happened' last night on the soap of the moment.[42] Applied to readers and reading groups, this view is a counterpoint to the historical notion of the 'ideal' reader, configured as a silent and passive female figure. This notion of the 'ideal' writer has no place in the book group, a place in which politicized, vocal 'gossip' about literature can take place – often in an intellectual way. The sense in which the idealized reader constitutes a threat to the status quo is most obviously outside the cultural context of my discussion up to this point.

Reading Lolita in Tehran by Azar Nafisi is an autobiographical account of life in Tehran after the revolution. Nafisi writes that because of the constraints imposed by the Islamic authorities and university management that served to limit the intellectual and imaginative content of her lectures and the books she was allowed to discuss, she is forced to give up her job as an English lecturer. So she sets up a book group at her home, in secret, to which she invites a number of her best students to discuss Great Works of English Literature, which are more often than not 'banned' novels such as *Lolita*.[43]

The limitations that the fundamentalist authorities put on intellectual endeavour, particularly that of women, are questioned through the very practices of reading and discussion that form the basis of Nafisi's memoir. Each novel under discussion is subject to an in-depth critical analysis but relates to the readers' lives, through what might be regarded as a 'universalizing impulse'. Nafisi writes:

> Modern fiction brings out the evil in domestic lives, ordinary relations, people like you and me – Reader! *Bruder!* as Humbert said. Evil in Austen, as in most great fiction, lies in the inability to 'see' others, hence to empathize with them. What is frightening is that this blindness can exist in the best of us (Eliza Bennet) as well as the worst (Humbert). We are all capable of becoming the blind censor, of imposing our visions and desires on others.[44]

Her suggestion – that 'we are all capable of becoming a blind censor' – could be read as a riposte to Cusk's diatribe against book groups. Afisi's group convenes in contravention to Islamic law because voicing experience, desires and ideas, and debating intellectual concerns, as a group of women, in private, is a necessary act of political resistance. It is also the source of solace: 'At some point, the truth of Iran's past became as immaterial to those who appropriated it as the truth of Lolita's truth, this is how I read Lolita. Again and again as we discussed Lolita in that class, our discussions were colored by my students' hidden personal sorrow and joys. Like tearstains on a letter ...'[45]

According to Clee, 'Great literature does not necessarily encourage reader empathy; or it may encourage it, as for example *Lolita* does, for subversive purposes. A novel's worth is not determined by the relevance of its themes or the moral values it espouses.'[46] Nafisi and her group's application of themes, narratives and textual dilemmas is less to do with the material implications of subscribing to moral values than uncovering a flash of insight. In Nafisi's Iran, a red-painted nail spied beneath a burqa is a punishable offence; and such subtle dissent is what Great Literature might hope to inspire, rather than 'reader empathy' per se. But such a view brings us back to Radway's thesis on the romance, the least reviewed, lowest form of genre fiction. That women read romance not merely to escape, but rather to resist the apparent limitations of their lives, however briefly, is central to the sense in which such reading habits are not dismissible as complicit with patriarchal culture.

Nafisi's group finds a particular empathy with the romance in Jane Austen's *Pride and Prejudice*:

> The sense of touch that is missing from Austen's novels is replaced by a tension, an erotic texture of sounds and silences. She manages to create a feeling of longing by setting characters who want each other at odds. Elizabeth and Darcy are placed near each other in several scenes, but in public places where they cannot communicate privately. Austen creates a great deal of frustrated tension by putting them in the same room yet out of reach.[47]

Unspoken tension and repressed desire are trademarks of romance, the genre of which Austen was an early, and exceptional, proponent. The tension here though is perpetrated on a historically determined assumption of idealized feminine passivity; Elizabeth must wait for Darcy to come to her. Like the 'ideal' reader she must suffer – indeed she must experience every nuance of emotion – in silence, in an unobtrusive imaginary context. Not so the reading group, that place in which opinions are exchanged, emotions are heightened, gossip is shared. The ideal reader knows her place but book groupies care less for such traditional constraints. As librarian Wendy Bloomer tentatively exclaimed when I suggested that the cultural establishment look down their noses at book groups, 'Sod the critics!'

Conclusion

By investigating the phenomenon of book groups in general and television book clubs in particular through several literary and critical perspectives, I have sought to identify and defuse simplistic divisions between high and low culture and reading practices. In so doing, I have argued that television book clubs have been shown to create new readers and that new readers' approach to analysing literary texts may be more complex than some reader-response studies and a number of critics suggest.

As cultural critics, it is vital that we review the ways in which we attribute worth to cultural practices. Of course, there are degrees of intellectual engagement and 'high-brow' culture continues to challenge where some 'low-brow' culture does not. Elitism here, though, has gendered implications. Women's fiction is not, it seems, as highly valued as fiction by men. Lisa Jardine and Annie Watkins's study of reading habits among academics, writers and critics shows that four out of five of the male respondents said that the last book they had read was by a man.[48] This suggests that there is still a disparity in how women's writing is viewed by men, which may go some way to explaining the subtle suspicions harboured by the cultural establishment towards book groups and television book clubs, which are largely female and often discuss fiction by women. This is a pity, because, rather than dumbing down as I have shown, television book clubs, through massive sales and the creation of an expanded market for books, have contributed to both the literacy and literary potential of a demographic of readers who will determine the direction of the book trade in an era of massive change.

Notes

1. Nicholas Clee, 'The Book Business', *New Statesman*, 21 March 2005, http://www.newstatesman.com/200503210047 (accessed 5 December 2009).
2. Alberto Manguel, *A History of Reading* (New York: Penguin, 1996), 117. See also Jenny Hartley, *Reading Groups* (Oxford: Oxford University Press, 2001).
3. Manguel, *A History of Reading*.

4. Pierre Bourdieu, *Distinction: a Social Critique of the Judgment of Taste*, trans. Richard Nice (1979; Cambridge, MA: Harvard University Press, 1984).
5. Traditionally (and enduringly), women are more likely to work part-time and act as the primary care-giver for their children. Indeed, as Sue Thornham explains, it is the 'family structure which assigns the nurturing role to women ... male subjectivity is constructed through separation and difference, whilst female subjectivity is constructed always as a "self-in-relation"'. Thornham, *Feminist Theory and Cultural Studies: Stories of Unsettled Relations* (London: Arnold, 2000), 107.
6. Jane Missner Barstow, 'Reading in Groups: Women's Clubs and College Literature Classes', *Publishing Research Quarterly* 18 (2003): 15.
7. Ibid. See also Temma Berg, '"What do you Know?"; or, the Question of Reading in Groups and Academic Authority', *LIT: Literature Interpretation Theory* 19, 2 (2008): 123–54.
8. Thornham, *Feminist Theory and Cultural Studies*, 109–10. See also Christine Geraghty, *Women and Soap Opera: a Study of Prime Time Soaps* (Cambridge: Polity Press, 1991); Verina Glaessner, 'Gendered Fictions', in *Understanding Television*, ed. A Goodwin and G. Whannel (London and New York: Routledge, 1990). Ien Ang's 'Feminist Desire and Female Pleasure: on Janice Radway's *Reading the Romance'*, in *Living Room Wars: Rethinking Media Audiences for a Postmodern World* (London: Routledge, 1996) offers a useful further discussion.
9. Donald Lazere, cited in Kathleen Rooney, *Reading with Oprah: the Book Club that Changed America* (Arkansas: University of Arkansas Press, 2005), 11; and Donald Lazere, 'Literacy and Mass Media: the Political Implications', *New Literary History* 18, 2 (1987): 289.
10. Wendy Bloomer, conversation with author, 31 October 2005.
11. When I posted the question 'Has the Richard and Judy Book Club changed your reading habits?' on the Richard and Judy discussion forum, I was taken to task regarding the meaning of a 'feminine leisure pursuit'. In this sense, I am referring to Jenny Hartley's argument that reading groups are historically, culturally, and typically made up of women; and notably women over thirty. The semantic discussion that ensued following my initiating a forum resulted in 24 postings, 425 views and some interesting online debate. For me, it offered evidence that there might be a chiasmic split between what this demographic is and how they are perceived. Such a split is worth noting because it highlights an ongoing compulsion within the intelligentsia, literati and critics to ascribe cultural values in very particular ways. (The archive has been removed.)
12. The essence of this argument can be found in Ang's 'Feminist Desire and Female Pleasure', 98–108.
13. Thornham, *Feminist Theory and Cultural Studies*, 112–13.
14. Bourdieu. *Distinction*. For further critical feminist interpretations of Bourdieu, see Lois McNay, *Gender and Agency: Reconfiguring the Subject in Feminist and Social Theory* (Cambridge and Malden: Polity Press, 2000); Lisa Adkins and Beverley Skeggs in *Feminism after Bourdieu* (Oxford and Malden: Blackwell, 2004); and Elizabeth B. Silva in 'Gender, Home and Family in Cultural Capital Theory', *British Journal of Sociology*, 56, 1 (2005): 83–103.
15. Bourdieu, *Distinction*, cited in Thornham, *Feminist Theory and Cultural Studies*, 109.

16. James Curran, 'Literary Editors, Social Networks and Cultural Tradition', in *Media Organizations in Society*, ed. James Curran (London: Arnold, 2000).
17. David Wright in 'Watching the Big Read with Pierre Bourdieu: Forms of Heteronomy in the Contemporary Literary Field', CRESC working paper series, 45 (2007), 4.
18. Ibid., 6.
19. Curran, 'Literary Editors, Social Networks and Cultural Tradition', 216.
20. Ibid.
21. Ibid., 216.
22. Ibid., 231.
23. Ibid., 222.
24. Wright, 'Watching the Big Read with Pierre Bourdieu', 10; citing James F. English, *The Economy of Prestige: Prizes, Awards and the Circulation of Literary Value* (Cambridge MA and London: Harvard University Press, 2002), 3.
25. Hartley, *Reading Groups*, 5.
26. Chris Lehmann, 'Oprah's Book Fatigue: How Fiction's Best Friend Ran out of Stuff to Read', 2002, http://www.slate.com/id/2064224/ (accessed 10 April 2002).
27. Katie Allen, 'Ross Confident of Book Club Future', *thebookseller.com*, 2009 at http://www.thebookseller.com/news/ross-confident-book-club-future.html (accessed 4 April 2011).
28. Malcolm Gladwell, *The Tipping Point: How Little Things Can Make a Big Difference* (Boston: Little Brown, 2000), 173.
29. Richard and Judy Website (4 October 2005). No longer available.
30. Robert McCrum, *Don't Judge a Book-Reading Group by its Cover*, 24 July 2005, available from http://books.guardian.co.uk/news/articles/0,6109,1534954,00.html (accessed 5 August 2006).
31. Hartley, *The Reading Groups Book*, 173; 5.
32. Chris Lehmann, 'Literati: the Oprah Wars', *American Prospect Online*, 12 March 2001, available from http://prospect.org/cs/articles?article=literati_the_oprah_wars (accessed 4 April 2011).
33. Franzen subsequently retracted his criticisms of Oprah but was unable to repair relations with the TV star, having questioned her 'economic clout, calling the Book Club seal a corporate logo'. See Celia Konchar Farr, *Reading Oprah: how Oprah's Book Club Changed the Way America Reads* (New York: University of New York Press, 2005), 77. In December 2010, Winfrey invited Franzen to appear on her programme with his novel *Freedom*.
34. That literacy has a natural affinity with democracy, in the sense that to exercise choice, one must understand the choices being offered, could be viewed as a given. What then of Elizabeth Long's discussion in *Book Clubs: Women and the Uses of Reading in Everyday Life* in which she situates women readers, historically, as being – ideally – in isolation. She notes in particular, the recurrence in high art of the solitary female reader as signifying an ideal, for instance in Johannes Vermeer's 'Women in Blue Reading a Letter' and Vittore Carpaccio's 'The Virgin Reading'.
35. Hilary Radner cited in Clare Hanson, *Hysterical Fictions* (Basingstoke: Palgrave Macmillan, 2000); Hilary Radner, 'Extra-Curricular Activities: Women Writers and the Readerly Text', in *Women's Writing in Exile*, ed. Mary

Lynn Broe and Angela Ingram (Chapel Hill: University of North Carolina Press, 1989), 254.
36. Janice Radway, *A Feeling for Books: the Book-of-the-Month Club, Literary Taste and Middle-Class Desire* (Chapel Hill: University of North Carolina Press, 1997), 3–4.
37. Janice Radway, *Reading the Romance: Women, Patriarchy and Popular Culture* (1984; Chapel Hill and London: University of North Carolina Press, 1991).
38. Ang, 'Feminist Desire and Female Pleasure', 107.
39. Ang, 'Feminist Desire and Female Pleasure', 114, refers to this as 'the feminist cause'.
40. Manguel, *History of Reading*, 233.
41. Rachel Cusk, *The Outsider*, Guardian, 20 August 2005, available from http://books.guardian.co.uk/review/story/0,12084,1551867,00.html (accessed 6 October 2006).
42. Mary Ellen Brown, *Soap Opera and Women's Talk* (London: Sage, 1994).
43. Azar Nafisi, *Reading Lolita in Tehran* (London: Fourth Estate, 2004), 315. For a critical account of the marketing of, and the guide to, Nafisi's memoir, see Catherine Burwell, 'Reading Lolita in Times of War: Women's Book Clubs and the Politics of Reception', *Intercultural Education* 18, 4 (October, 2007): 286–7; 290–4.
44. Nafisi, *Reading Lolita in Tehran*, 315.
45. Ibid., 37.
46. Clee, 'The Book Business'.
47. Nafisi, *Reading Lolita in Tehran*, 306.
48. See David Smith, 'Women Are Still a Closed Book to Men: Research Shows Men Mainly Read Works by Other Men', *Observer*, 29 May 2005, available from http://books.guardian.co.uk/news/articles/0,6109,1495060,00.html (accessed 29 May 2005). Smith noted that 'The research [on gender and reading] was carried out by academics Lisa Jardine and Annie Watkins of Queen Mary College, London, to mark the tenth year of the Orange Prize for Fiction, a literary honour whose women-only rule provoked righteous indignation when the competition was founded. They asked 100 academics, critics and writers and found virtually all now supported the prize. But a gender gap remains in what people choose to read, at least among the cultural elite. Four out of five men said the last novel they read was by a man, whereas women were almost as likely to have read a book by a male author as a female.'

7
Speaking Subjects: Developing Identities in Women's Reading Communities

Linsey Howie

Introduction

Group reading has its own rhythm, a movement between reading a book, usually in the comfort of home, followed by a meeting to discuss the book with book group friends. This cycle is characterized by solitary activity followed by monthly gatherings where rituals associated with 'book talk' or social 'chat' are interspersed with routine practices designed to make group members feel welcome. Each group has its own way of marking arrivals to meetings: rooms are prepared, seating is arranged to support the expression of views about the book or the author or more intimate exchanges between group members. Most provide light refreshments; some showcase the cooking prowess of members. As the meeting closes, members anticipate the book selected for the month ahead, and ascertain who chose the book or who is hosting the next meeting. There is security in the knowledge that the cycle of group reading will be repeated.

Women's book groups, it appears, are distinguishable from other community-based groups in that reading a book is a vehicle for expressing one's ideas or opinions about a text or author, and in so doing developing a growing self-awareness, a sense of identity that is developed in the company of others at monthly meetings. Reading groups also sustain an experience of an evolving sense of self. Over time, regular meetings which lead to meaningful (not superficial) conversations measure or reflect a growing sense of who one is in the world and how change in attitudes or beliefs might be effected. Women's particular capacity for building and sustaining relationships supports this process.

Teresa De Lauretis argues that 'the practice of self-consciousness – of reading, speaking, and listening to one another – is ... the best way we know to analyse our differences and contradictions'.[1] John Sturrock's translation of Marcel Proust's *On Reading*, notes 'the Proustian reader is made more, not less alert to the activity of his own mind by reading, [and] is provoked into attending as he might otherwise not be to the mysterious resonances of his "*moi profound*" or "deep self"'.[2] In a similar vein, Sven Birkets observed that 'reading a novel is not simply a matter of making a connection to another person's expression. Over and above the linguistic connection, the process makes a change in the whole complex of the self.'[3] Talking at book group as practice that attends to the self, and how reading might support this practice are the central concerns of this chapter.

The study

In the mid-1990s I undertook a large-scale study of women's book groups in Australia. Initiating this study I enlisted the support of the Council of Adult Education (CAE) which manages book groups across the eastern seaboard of Australia. With approval from La Trobe University Faculty of Health Sciences Human Ethics Committee and permission to access the CAE's data bank of over 780 book clubs in 1994, I designed a multi-strategy research project. This project included a qualitative component of informal interviews and reading to support the design of a questionnaire, followed by a survey of a 10 per cent random sample of the CAE book groups (8800 members). Individual surveys were sent to group secretaries and members of 91 book groups. Eighty-seven secretaries and 727 members responded, 98 per cent of whom were women. Following analysis of the survey, and in light of the predominance of women in the groups, I interviewed 21 women who indicated their interest in continuing involvement in the study. In this stage of the study I utilized a grounded theory methodology to guide data collection, theoretical sampling and data analysis[4] and the computer program NUD.IST (1995) to support categorizing and retrieval of large volumes of narrative data. This chapter relates to one aspect of this larger study, namely 'developing identities' at book group.

Two salient themes were derived from analysis of the interview data with respect to developing identities at book group. The first, *relational ways of being*, considers the centrality of relationships between book group members in promoting grounds for self-awareness; and the second, *subjects-in-process*, examines book group dynamics and personal experience as self-reflexive practice that supports the development of shifting self-knowledges. These themes frame the remainder of this chapter. In conjunction with each theme, I will discuss the literature illuminating the data, drawn from self-in-relation theories and concepts of subjects-in-process, in philosophy, sociology, psychoanalysis and feminism. These theories support the development of my central argument about book groups and chart the structure of this chapter.

Relational ways of being

The characteristics of relations at book group provide an interesting consideration in exploring the interview data. The participants' tales of 'book talk' (discussion of the text) versus 'social talk' and the value accorded to each during the group meeting, particularly in light of women's predominance in book groups, reveals how these women welcomed the free exchange of ideas whether or not these ideas were strictly related to the text in question. One participant commented that were men involved, they might expect the conversation at book group to 'stick to the book' more than female group members did, or that men would want it 'more structured' or 'more organized' than it generally was in her group. Fay said:

> Well I think we probably say a lot more things than we would in mixed company and I think we're probably more open with each other than men would be. And recently, it tends to keep coming up with ageing parents and how we feel responsible for them, and how they've regressed to children, and we have to look after them, and how we feel about that ... and we share that information. It's more personal about family lives and feelings.

What can be made of Fay's remark that in the absence of men, women are more open, more personal with each other? She went on to say that men might think the things they talked about were not important, 'they wouldn't be so willing to recognize that yes, you [women] do feel angry about your ageing parents when they make demands on you ... [whereas men might] sort of say well that's nonsense and whatever'. Her response reveals the indignation of someone accustomed to having her conversation or ideas dismissed. Importantly, however, it suggests the potency of being in the presence of people who are prepared, or inclined to listen to what you say. Jessica Benjamin's argument is pertinent here, she states, '(r)ecognition is the essential response, the constant companion of assertion. The subject declares, "I am, I do," and then waits for the response, "You are, you have done." Recognition is, thus, reflexive; it includes not only the other's confirming response, but also how we find ourselves in that response.'[5] Women in these groups tolerate a departure from strict adherence to discussion of the book as they appreciate the benefits of freer conversations that allow exploration of things that matter to them.

Caring and support are recurring themes in the participants' different ways of relating at book group. For example, Marion said, 'everyone really cares about each other ... I've never been in a group of this sort before. There's a great feeling of personal support.' 'Nurturing', 'supportive', 'accommodating', 'sharing', 'safe', 'accepting', 'comfortable', 'tolerant', 'respectful' and 'non-threatening' are all words that the women use repeatedly when they talk about their book group. While participants experience relations at book group as sometimes competitive, argumentative, irritable or envious, their emphasis on 'considering others' needs' suggests the importance that the women place on relations that support the 'open' expression of opinions and reflection on others' views. Bea said that for her group it was important that they were 'harmonious within the ability to go hammer and tongs at each other without any after effects'.

The pursuit of harmony and concern for procedures that manage relationships are important to almost all of the women I interviewed. The participants construct particular ways of relating at book group to support self-expression, acknowledge differences and reflect upon their personal responses to the book and to others. Naomi's comment foreshadows aspects of this discussion. She said: 'This is the only group that I belong to that we go into things more deeply. Yeah it would be. It would be the only group that I'm associated with, that you would have their opinions bouncing back to me. And then you might think to yourself, well maybe, you know she's got a point.' In another interview, Marg said:

> And we don't feel less respected because someone holds a different viewpoint to our own ... It's fairly, it's a great atmosphere ... I'm not out in the paid workforce ... I'm not pushing a barrow ... or cause, or anything like that. So I'm not mixing with people to whom I can vent my viewpoint or listen to theirs in return ... And I think they help you, the views that are expressed by the other people in the group, help one formulate your own viewpoints about things.

These are two tantalizing descriptions of the discursive interplay of introspection with social processes in group reading. The participants' involvement in book group is characterized by particular relations that support the expression of opinions and differences that in turn contribute to self-reflection. And it is these practices, routinely revisited, that lead to engagement with alternative subject positions and to changing self-knowledge.

While a desire for, and enjoyment of, companionship exists as an aspect of the participants' experience of book group, it is sustaining connections and the interplay of ideas and 'chit-chat' at meetings that generates a range of emotions from pleasure to comfort, support to excitement. If relations at times are irritating or exasperating, participants in the study find ways to manage their aggravations so that book group is infused with more congenial relations.

A concern for connectedness is further exhibited in participants' accounts of feelings for the text, authors or characters that are drawn into their relational sphere. In Fiona's case, and in that of other women in this study, for reading to be meaningful, or to inform her about living, she requires a relationship with the characters. Fiona said:

> Reading doesn't imitate life, in a way it *is* life. And so it demonstrates how life can be lived. How you can do things, how you can actually have strength, or courage, or motivation to actually achieve things. So it really does talk about life, whether it's fact or fiction, it is life ... So it's not really a story, I get really so involved in books that I do believe that the characters exist and the situation is real and true.

Figure 7.1 Book club members meet author Loranne Brown

Speaking of her group's response to a book about an unhappy marriage, Ann reveals a multiplicity of connections between book group members and authors inspired by the text. She said:

> One of the books that we read that everybody loved was a Doris Lessing book ... set in Africa ... she was a very clever writer. And that seemed to connect with us in our lives and you can imagine this woman being really lonely in an unhappy marriage and being isolated and needing human contact ... and for some reason that connected with us all, because we were all in relationships, whether daughters or sisters, got husbands or boyfriends or whatever.

Lisa provides another example of how readers experience relationships with authors. In commenting on authors Tim Winton and Anne Tyler she said, 'It just seems to be, you click ... you feel drawn to (them) and feel at home ... it's a strange feeling ... mmmm, like I ... actually know this person.'

Lisa's comment highlights how the author becomes a vital presence, someone to know and to relate to, if only through their choice of words or their use of language. There is a comfort in returning to favourites, as Lisa's remark suggests, when she refers to feeling 'at home' with particular authors. The participants' accounts of reading or discussing a book creates a strong impression that their world of relationships (real and imagined) expands and is hence enriched by friendships fostered through group reading. In another conversation Judith observes:

> Perhaps you don't even realize that you're intimate until over a period of time you actually build up knowledge of other people, an instinctive feel for them. Which, if you stop and think about what you've gained through what they've shared over the years about books ... you know from their reactions to things a lot about how they think and feel.

Participants' relational thinking is also made manifest in their references to reading or book group as 'someone' in their life with whom they have a relationship. Commenting on her book group, Rachel observes, 'You know its survived serious illnesses and marriage break-ups and all sorts of stuff and keeps going.' Kate agrees: 'it's like an old friend that you don't have to see that often to feel okay when you meet up'. Ann, too, spoke of her group in a similar vein saying, 'It's like a relationship. It's something you work at all the time.'

Self-in-relation theory provides an explanation for the participants' emphasis on relationships at book group. The significance of relationships to individual psychological growth is apparent in most psychological theories and clinical accounts of human psychological development.[6] Where the majority of psychological theories differ from the self-in-relation theory is in their greater concern with relationships during the first years of life, particularly the mother-child relationship. In asserting the desirable outcome of adult psychological development in terms of separation from primary relationships and the achievement of differentiation and self-sufficiency, these theories have regarded reliance on intimate, interpersonal connections in adulthood as a regressive account of human maturation,[7] a move 'into more primitive functioning'.[8]

In contrast, the basic tenets of the self-in-relation theory are that interpersonal relationships are crucial in achieving maturity and that a 'feminine sense of self' is developed through connections.[9] Psychoanalytic feminist writing on women's personality development has elaborated this further,[10] as has Carol Gilligan's research on moral development.[11] The influence of these theorists, together with the contribution of clinicians at the Stone Center at Wellesley College,[12] has produced a body of work that specifically theorizes the relational dimensions of women's psychology as well as inspiring novel interventions in clinical practice.[13]

In her research on gender differences in moral decision-making, Gilligan draws on Nancy Chodorow's influential psychoanalytic assessment of women's development to explain the differences she observed between men and women's moral viewpoint.[14] Gilligan concluded that women's moral actions are embedded in an ethic of care, characterized by taking responsibility for preventing harm, attending to others' needs and preserving interpersonal relationships.[15] Women's moral behaviour and sense of self, she maintained, are infused with notions of attachment, relationship and interdependence.[16] Her emphasis on principles of caring as integral to women's sense of self is a central theme of Jean Baker Miller's work as well, though Miller uses the word 'caretaking' to frame her discussion of the process and benefits of 'attending to and responding to the other'.[17]

Miller, a psychoanalyst, brings a political and social sensibility to her account of women's psychological development, noting that for many women their inclination towards affiliation can be experienced as a source of strength and empowerment. Recognizing that relationships are central to women, she stated, is an important step towards supporting their growth and development.[18] Miller stresses the importance of caretaking as fundamental to all continuing psychological growth. 'All growth', she insists, 'occurs within emotional connections, not separate from them.'[19] All children's sense of self is developed within relationships, however, caring for others is not seen as a *human* requirement, rather it has been assigned to women and their mothering role.

This aspect of Miller's thesis is important for my argument. In describing women's involvement in caretaking as a central feature of their psychological development and sense of self, she explains the fundamental appeal of relationships to women. Attending to others is not necessarily experienced as limiting, but rather it promotes feelings of well-being and satisfaction. Beyond that, she asserts, engagement in relationships encourages experiences of feeling knowledgeable, increasing one's self-esteem and sense of being competent and effective. Further, she states, 'picking up the feelings of the other and attending to the "interaction between" becomes an accepted, "natural seeming" way of acting and being'.[20] Miller appears to be arguing that in the reciprocal give and take of relationships, women experience a sense of their capabilities that relies on the presence of others to support self-knowing.

A further dimension of the self-in-relation theory that is pertinent to this discussion relates to the concept of empathy. Janet L. Surrey observes that to be in a relationship requires a capacity for empathy that is central to women's psychological development.[21] There are several aspects to her and Judith Jordan's account of empathy that resonate with dynamics at book group.[22] Surrey focuses on the mother-daughter relationship as the key site for an examination of the development of empathy.[23] In this relationship, she argues, theorists have observed that the ability of the mother to 'listen and respond, empathize or "mirror" the child's feelings', is 'the beginning of the development of the experience of the self'.[24] Both Surrey and Jordan observe that in this relationship, the daughter's increasing capacity for mutual empathy is sustained, and her feelings of being understood or recognized are facilitated. The implications are that in this arrangement of shared emotional and cognitive connections, mother and daughter are mutually empowered to respond to feelings, and to enjoy the gains that come from responding assuredly to the needs of others. In this sense, empathy that is reciprocated works to underpin women's self-esteem.

Further, Jordan and Surrey also note that empathy plays a significant part in people's experience of difference. As Jordan argues, 'in order to empathize, one must have a well-differentiated sense of self in addition to an appreciation of and sensitivity to the differentness as well as the sameness of the other'.[25] In this respect, an ability to experience one's separateness in connection with others is an important aspect of empathy. An additional feature of the empathic process, according to Surrey, is that in observing the other and making one's own process known, self-knowledge expands, while the growth of both participants is nurtured. Accordingly, she argues, mutual empathy is fundamental to learning, and is a forceful element in mobilizing self-empowering practice.[26] Surrey further argues that 'the relational line of development ... suggests that relationships and identity develop in synchrony'.[27] This point warrants emphasis as it encapsulates the hypothesis I am proposing: that women's capacity for relationships is central to developing identities at book group.

Surrey concludes that reciprocity in relations is an essential component of empathy and a source of mutual self-esteem, and that it comprises a core feature of the self-in-relation theory.[28] Jordan also observed the role of empathy in validating experiences of self and other. With reference to the work of Jean Piaget, she notes, 'growth occurs because as I stretch to match or understand your experience, something new is acknowledged or grows in me'.[29] Her comments reflect the dynamics present in book group discussion. An openness to listening to each other allows members to enter into one another's worlds in support of their own growth.

To summarize, in making sense of the participants' accounts of relationships, including social and 'book talk' at book group meetings, feminist and psychoanalytic theories on women's psychological development and self-in-relation theory illuminate the data and help to clarify the project of book groups. From this perspective, we can conceive of book group as a space in which women develop a sense of self through their relationship to the author, characters and text, and importantly, create connections between members of the group and the group itself. Book group creates particular relationships and environments – a climate in which women feel enabled to 'discover' the self.

Subjects-in-process

While relationships at book group were a dominant topic in the interviews, equally interesting were the ways the readers made reference to more personal notions of an evolving sense of self in the context of self-expression at meetings. The assessment of speech as an indicator of agency and enabling practice described by bell hooks parallels the participants' tales of finding their voice at book group. She argues that the act of speaking cannot be viewed as 'a mere gesture of empty words', rather, it can be viewed as a political act for those who use speech to make sense of their circumstances, express their dissatisfaction or hope for a different way of being in the world.[30] Her argument resonates with participants' self-assessment and stories of belonging to their reading group.

Several participants in the study spoke of feeling inadequate or intimidated when they first joined book group, as they viewed others in the group as 'intellectuals' or 'brainy lasses'. A few spoke of lives in which they had few opportunities to think about issues, formulate opinions, or to 'present something in the way they were thinking', especially in front of a group of people. Fiona noted that 'book club has been nice in a way because it's allowed me the opportunity to reflect and discuss, and that's something that I've never had before'. Bea admitted that '[speaking in public] doesn't upset me as much as it would. I couldn't have done it once, that's all about it. That might have just come with age anyway. But I do think book group's helped in that regard.' Hilda also spoke of feeling nervous at even commenting on a book when she first joined, but of changing her attitude to 'truly [being] able to comment' now that she saw the others as equals. Samantha spoke of the reward of book group, in 'broadening' her thoughts, and feeling 'more flexible in expression'. Val said, 'when I look back on it, I was unable to express myself'. Two members in her group who had 'a searching manner', and 'saw the metaphysics in everything they read', had taught her a lot.

The participants' early experiences of belonging to book group identify pervasive feelings of limited agency, powerlessness or inadequacy, a loss of voice, and limited opportunities to speak. Their shift over the years to greater comfort, confidence or self-esteem is noteworthy, taking place usually slowly, sometimes painfully, and accompanied by considerable work and self-reflection. Rosalie said:

> You know if you get that funny feeling inside and you think, oh you know I don't know about this, but I know I've got to say it ... Then you know one just has to be brave and say it. Sometimes those sorts of situations are quite confronting just to oneself, nobody else probably even notices that you're under a bit of a strain. But that's been very helpful, too, to have to come out with something that you were a bit frightened about saying in public, because you know it's about you, about yourself.

Rosalie's touching description of her experience of disclosing aspects of herself to the group is an account of summoning courage to publicly reveal something that is essentially personal. It illustrates the benefits of this challenging experience, and illuminates the struggle to place herself as subject in the discussion. Naomi also reveals the personal challenges that can be posed during book group and the way discussion mobilizes self-reflection. 'We try to be open-minded and not to be too straight-laced. Somebody made a remark to me last Monday and I don't think it's true really. But you know we were sort of joking in a way ... she said ... "it's amazing how you always seem to think there might be incest." I don't think I do at all!'

Interactions lingered in her thoughts, because, as she said later, 'one always thinks beyond the book'. Naomi was left wondering about her interpretation of the text, the group response to her reading of it, and her own growing self-awareness. Naomi's description of this event is a window on to the nature of discussions at book group and the trail of thoughtfulness that accompanies group reading. This idea supports a comment made by Simone who said, 'Sometimes I have a lot to contribute, other times I just sit back and I think, "oh I didn't get any of that, that's amazing." And of course then it triggers off a whole lot of thoughts ... that make much more sense or whatever.' These comments invite a reading of book group as a forum for challenging long held views or prejudices, a site in which it is possible to scrutinize ideas about the self and others. Self-discovery in this context is a gradual process embedded in robust discussion and self-reflection.

Vicky's view of her development at book group is expressed slightly differently in a context of wider societal changes and her fear of 'stagnating'. In emphasizing the need to 'keep growing' and 'try different things' she acknowledges the role of her book group in 'forcing' her 'to try something a bit different', to expand herself and try to understand 'various viewpoints and just keep abreast of things'. Reading and book groups are capable of disturbing conventional views of women in society, and as these participants testify they bring forward for scrutiny a range of topics that might otherwise have been left in abeyance.

In many respects, book groups are consciousness-raising groups by another name. Consciousness-raising groups of the 1960s and 1970s provided a forum for women to discuss a variety of personal, social and political issues. However, although allowing members to raise pertinent issues in the safety of a small group, the book group differs from consciousness-raising groups in the prominent position of the text. The text, however, as we will continue to see, is the springboard for a range of relevant and stimulating discussions in which the participants respond to their changing interests and circumstances. In the free talk generated by the safety of all-women groups, where personal stories are interwoven with interpretations of the text, participants move towards greater self-knowledge.

As in consciousness-raising groups before them, group reading is a social outing, a 'sounding board', a place 'to bounce ideas off one another', a source of comfort and support in knowing that 'you are not alone'. Theresa describes her book group as showing her how to put her foot down, to fight for what she wants. Lisa, too, notes that their discussions are marked by being 'very frank, very open, very much air the dirty laundry a lot ... very much a release, as well'. Kate's comments reveal that aspects of her group operate very much like a consciousness-raising group. Her group provides much required self-validation, where she could see herself 'reflected in others' before she was able to accept her 'own opinion or feel comfortable talking about' her own ideas. This is a clear evocation of the development of subjectivity in social contexts. In experimenting with novel ideas, the participants use other group members as a mirror to their emerging self-knowledges.

Susan sees her group in more therapeutic terms. People can come to book group and talk about the 'terrible time' they are having, and others say, 'oh yeah I've been through that, I know what it's like'. It was, she says, 'good to have the book to hide behind ... rather than just being dumped in a social group'. Several participants spoke of sharing problems, or finding solutions to issues around raising children, being a single mother, caring for ageing parents, or managing difficult teenagers. Judith offers an insight into the breadth and depth of discussions at her group and their relevance to the members' immediate concerns. She said, 'It's usually [at] quite a deep level ... we'll often discuss issues like death ... A lot of soul-searching, a lot of ... you know, especially for ... a few of us, who are sort of re-entering the work force after a period out ... [it is] more about us, than about people in our lives.' Her reference to 'a lot of soul-searching' highlights how book discussion is an opportunity to go beyond superficial exchange, such as 'weddings and clothes', for instance. This sentiment of seeking answers to deeply held questions is apparent in Lisa's comment. She said, 'One of our members must have been going through a very searching stage about her role as a woman, and when we originally put the list together of the books that we select, hers were all along the same line on women's roles and responsibilities.'

The word 'search', to look carefully in seeking to find something derives from the Latin *circus,* or circle. It is tempting to juxtapose Judith and Lisa's comments about searching at book group with the idea of the reading circle as a forum for the discussion of a broad range of psychological and social issues. For many participants this was a richly rewarding aspect of book club.

Texts also raise discussion of political, historical or social events. Talking about *Wild Swans* Simone said, 'we just got so much into China and politics and change and reliving our own experiences of when it was happening. I probably liked that part almost the best.' Marg said:

> I'm just trying to think of the book that provoked the discussion about homosexuality and its acceptance in the community. It could have been any book mind you, that we got onto that topic. But you know we were talking about that and you know we're not allowed to discriminate against people on that basis. Well that's quite difficult when you've been cast in a different sort of mould and the mould says well that kind of behaviour isn't right. So you've got to redevelop and change your ideas and learn acceptance ... So that was a very provocative evening ... it was one where we felt, or I felt, that I had to think about this issue more and ... because you can't go around like this all the time.

This is a striking description of the facility of book group to engage members in contemporary life issues, and the way book discussion can unsettle dominant values to produce novel understandings and different subject positions. Through group discussion, Marg's deeply held beliefs are dislodged, 'you can't go around like this', and she realizes that her views on homosexuality do not need to be fixed.

As book group members give voice to their experience and new understandings, they enter new or different speaking positions, in which their subjectivity is challenged or re-assessed. Marg's account, like that of other participants elucidates this process. As Chris Weedon observes, 'as we move out of familiar circles, through education or politics, for example, we may be exposed to alternative ways of constituting the meaning of our experience'.[31] Book group, as these participants described it, may best be interpreted as a move away from enduring self/other representations, to an acceptance of more fluid or changeable alternatives as suggested by poststructuralist and psychoanalytic thinking.

The participants' references to shifting subject positions in response to others' viewpoints can be aligned with Julia Kristeva's concept of subjects-in-process.[32] Their comments are best understood in terms of psychoanalytic and poststructuralist notions of subjectivity as discursively constructed, producing shifting and changeable self-understandings. The participants' active engagement with the uncertainty generated by this process is noteworthy. Their references to lively debates in which they explore their differences and wonder about alternative attitudes or behaviours are indicative of subjects who are prepared to reflect on limiting self–other definitions, and are prepared, as Rachel remarks, 'to be different, to question, wonder, and bother about oneself and one's experience of the world'.

Analysis of the interview data confirms that group reading for women is an important forum for self-expression where supportive relations and emotional connections are regularly guaranteed, and where differences between women are both encouraged and respected. In this sense group reading facilitates opportunities for women to surmount constraining representations of women in society, and to speak, imagine or live alternative subjective positions that are relevant to their own changing needs and interests.

The argument put forward in the earlier discussion of self-in-relation theory emphasizes theories of the subject that confirm its foundations in a relational context. However, here my focus is on how subjectivity is discursively constructed in the social practices of ordinary life. This claim requires a return to psychoanalysis and its understanding of subjectivities as incomplete, contradictory and progressing,[33] and an assertion of the decentred subject of feminist poststructuralist theory, as produced in particular historical, cultural and social contexts and constituted in many and varied discursive fields.[34] In these debates, subjectivity is formulated in different discourses that generate conflicting ways of making sense of life circumstances and experiences. Feminist poststructuralist theory revisits knowledges of language, subjectivity, social and institutional relations in order to understand contemporary power relations and their implications for change.[35] It does this through a focus on discourse which is seen as a principal organizing factor in society; language being the dominant mode in which subjectivity is constituted. In an attempt to understand how different discourses reflect different political interests and power relations, and to explain people's diverse lived experiences, both poststructuralist and feminist theory focus on studying the subject as it is influenced by the intersection of gender, class, race and culture.[36]

It is now difficult to argue for the un-gendered, unified and fixed subject of the Enlightenment. Psychoanalytic concepts of the unconscious, which question the possibility of a clear distinction between mind and body, and feminist studies on gender, which assert the varied ways of expressing or experiencing being a woman or a man, make it difficult to hold on to any unitary concept of subjectivity.[37] Postmodern theories on the discursive constitution of the subject also unsettle this concept.[38] In the following discussion, I utilize the psychoanalytic theory of the subject-in-process as the concept that best explains the participants' experiences of growing self-development and self-awareness through involvement in book group.

Psychoanalysis explains the ambiguity of subjectivity in terms of unconscious processes, which challenges the idea of the unitary subject and reveals the subject to be both temporary and unstable, and as such, providing grounds for 'the articulation of the subject-in-process'.[39] Kristeva argues that all language is structured by both the expression of rationality and by unconscious material. While rational language maintains the symbolic order, where meaning is fixed in the unitary subject, semiotic aspects of discourse threaten this stability by situating meaning in diverse subjective experiences.[40] Thus Kristeva's concept of subjectivity as a site of disruption is formulated, taking its place alongside notions of subjects-in-process, and dissident speech.[41]

Kristeva takes the process of making conscious the contrary elements of subjectivity to be an essential and enlivening step in becoming aware of, and asserting one's choices in societies which enforce restrictive social norms.[42] Her notion of the 'unsettling' or 'questionable' subject-in-process[43] views subjects as participating in the shifting ground between the illusion of a coherent, unified subject, and as Meyer argues, the 'outcroppings of nonconscious material that bedevil conscious life'.[44] Accessing the unconscious and giving voice to its desires, is, in Kristeva's words, a dissident act, and she argues for people to engage in 'aesthetic practices' through which they can figuratively express this 'nonconscious material'.[45] Aesthetic practices, expressed in ways that generate 'pleasurable contemplation' she argues, ameliorate the threat and anxiety posed by the unconscious when it is projected onto others or expressed as prejudice. Kristeva nominates several manifestations of aesthetic practice as dissident: rebels against political power, psychoanalysts, writers and women.[46] I argue that women's book groups based on the discussion of a text lend themselves to Kristeva's concept of dissident practice. This concept can be compared with Radway's account of the Smithton women, romance readers who perceive reading as 'mild protest' and 'combative … in the sense that it enables them to refuse the other directed social role prescribed for them by their position within the institution of marriage'.[47] Participants in the book group study reveal how finding their voice and articulating ideas, changing values and opinions, and experiencing lingering reflections on discussions that broaden or subvert prevailing beliefs and attitudes are testament to the relevance of speaking at book group to changing subjectivities.

Meyer argues that in 'freeing the imagination and mobilizing its powers of representation, the established order is "demystified" and alternative social norms can be envisaged'.[48] Responding to Kristeva's idea of loving connections between women, Meyer notes, along with other feminist writers,[49] that women need to experience love for themselves as women, in order to overcome limiting and alienating representations of women so prevalent in society. While Meyer prefers the term solidarity to love, she develops an argument for members of socially excluded groups to collectively articulate 'shared figurations', in order to construct and value an 'evolving collective identity for themselves'.[50] This, she maintains, would constitute dissident speakers as 'collective' subjects-in-process.

Adopting Meyer and Kristeva's line of argument,[51] and the writing of Weedon and Lugones, I am drawn to conceptualizing the phenomena of book groups in terms of collective subjects-in-process. Book groups appear to sustain the development of 'alternative ways of constituting meaning of our experience',[52] and as Meyer indicates, in relation to socially excluded groups,[53] they allow for members to gather, not to seek definitive truths, but to share ideas or interests of their own making. Such groups are highly significant in allowing the development of a 'self-generated identity' counter to views held by the dominant culture.

Conclusion

This chapter has examined women's experiences of book group and two theories of the subject that contribute to understanding group reading as concerned with the construction of self-identity: self-in-relation theories, and the theory of subjects-in-process. Feminist clinicians and theorists have built upon psychoanalytic concepts to highlight how subjectivity, for women in particular, is constructed in relationships that nurture mutual empathy and recognition. In exploring feminist and psychoanalytic contributions to these theories, which advance concepts of the decentred subject and the significance of relational and social practices to these concepts, my aim has been to direct attention to complex notions of multiple and evolving subjectivities, and the idea that in collectives, individual subjectivities evolve through the expression of opinions and the recognition of difference.

The capacity of book discussion and social talk to contribute to developing self-understanding is a meaningful dimension of group reading that to date has attracted limited attention.[54] The opportunity provided by book group to reflect on oneself or one's relationships, to explore ideas and feelings with others, or to publicly present aspects of oneself which are not generally given expression, have been presented along with an account of how participants make connections with the book, the author or characters, or with group members to articulate different ideas or knowledges of the self, a self which they affirm is not static. Further, I have described how conscious or unconscious responses to reading a book, or engaging in group discussion facilitated the expression of differences between group members. In this move, I argued, the aesthetic practice of group reading, the capacity to play with, or assert different ideas, or adopt different subject positions in the presence of others, lends weight to the contention that book group is important in disturbing confining self-representations, and in offering novel ways of perceiving oneself as a subject-in-process. Accordingly, book groups may be interpreted as collectives, where group members appropriate relationships, books and language to effect socially-constructed and fluid subjectivities.

Notes

1. Teresa De Lauretis, ed., *Feminist Studies, Critical Studies: Theories of Contemporary Culture* (London: Macmillan, 1986), 8.
2. John Sturrock in Marcel Proust, *On Reading*, preface and translation by John Sturrock (London: Penguin, 1994), vii.
3. Sven Birkets, *The Gutenberg Elegies: the Fate of Reading in an Electronic Age* (Boston: Faber and Faber, 1994), 81.
4. Kathy Charmaz, 'The Grounded Theory Method: an Explication and Interpretation', in *More Grounded Theory Methodology: A Reader*, ed. B.G. Glaser (Mill Valley, CA: Sociology Press, 1994) and *Constructing Grounded Theory: a Practical Guide through Qualitative Analysis* (London: Sage, 2010); B.G. Glaser, 'The Constant Comparative Method', in *More Grounded Theory: A Reader*, ed. B.G. Glaser (Mill Valley, CA: Sociology Press, 1994).
5. Jessica Benjamin, *The Bonds of Love: Psychoanalysis, Feminism and the Problem of Domination* (London: Virago, 1990), 21.
6. Jerome David Levin, *Theories of the Self* (Washington: Hemisphere Publishing Company, 1992); Jean Baker Miller, 'The Development of Women's Sense of Self', in *Women's Growth in Connection: Writings from the Stone Center*, ed. Judith V. Jordan et al. (New York: Columbia University Press, 1991); Donna M. Orange, *Emotional Understanding: Studies in Psychoanalytic Epistemology* (New York: Guilford Press, 1995).
7. Judith V. Jordan, 'The Meaning of Mutality', in *Women's Growth in Connection: Writings from the Stone Center*, ed. Judith V. Jordan et al. (New York: Guilford Press, 1991); Miller, 'The Development of Women's Sense of Self'.
8. Judith V. Jordan, 'Empathy and Self Boundaries', in *Women's Growth in Connection: Writings from the Stone Center*, ed. Judith V. Jordan et al. (New York: Guilford Press, 1991), 68.

9. Nancy Chodorow, *The Reproduction of Mothering: Psychoanalysis and the Sociology of Gender* (Berkeley: University of California Press, 1978).
10. Benjamin, *The Bonds of Love*; Nancy Chodorow, *Feminism and Psychoanalytic Theory* (New Haven: Yale University Press, 1989); Miller, 'The Development of Women's Sense of Self', and *Toward a New Psychology of Women* (Boston: Beacon Press, 1976).
11. Carol Gilligan, *In a Different Voice: Psychological Theory and Women's Development* (Cambridge, MA: Harvard University Press, 1982).
12. Judith V. Jordan et al., eds, *Women's Growth in Connection: Writings from the Stone Center* (New York: Guilford Press, 1991).
13. Janet L. Surrey, 'The Self-in-Relation: a Theory of Women's Development', in Jordan et al., *Women's Growth in Connection*, 51–66.
14. Gilligan, *In a Different Voice*, 7–8.
15. Ibid., 62.
16. Ibid., 170.
17. Miller, 'The Development of Women's Sense of Self', 14–16.
18. Ibid., 16.
19. Ibid.
20. Ibid.
21. Surrey, 'The Self-in-Relation', 53.
22. Jordan, 'Empathy and Self Boundaries', 69.
23. Surrey, 'The Self-in-Relation', 54.
24. Ibid., 56.
25. Jordan, 'Empathy and Self Boundaries', 69.
26. Surrey, 'The Self-in-Relation', 59.
27. Ibid., 63.
28. Ibid., 57.
29. Jordan, 'The Meaning of Mutuality', 89.
30. bell hooks, *Talking Back: Thinking Feminist, Thinking Black* (Boston: Sheba Feminist Publishers, 1989), 9.
31. Chris Weedon, *Feminist Practice and Poststructuralist Theory* (Cambridge: Blackwell, 1987), 33.
32. Toril Moi, ed., *The Kristeva Reader* (New York: Columbia University Press, 1986).
33. Jane Flax, *Disputed Subjects: Essays on Psyschoanalysis, Politics and Philosophy* (New York: Routledge, 1993), 92–103.
34. H.L. Moore, *A Passion for Difference: Essays in Anthropology and Gender* (Bloomington: Indiana University Press, 1994), 54; Weedon, *Feminist Practice*, 74.
35. Weedon, *Feminist Practice*, 21.
36. Ibid., 32–5.
37. Flax, *Disputed Subjects*, 16.
38. Ibid., 100.
39. Weedon, *Feminist Practice*, 89.
40. Kristeva, cited in ibid., 89.
41. Diana Tietiens Meyer, *Subjection and Subjectivity: Psychoanalytic Feminism and Moral Philosophy* (New York: Routledge, 1994).
42. Moi, *The Kristeva Reader*, 293–5.
43. Julia Kristeva, *Revolution in Poetic Language*, trans. Margaret Waller (New York: Columbia University Press, 1984).

44. Meyer, *Subjection and Subjectivity*, 58.
45. Ibid., 59.
46. Moi, *The Kristeva Reader*, 292.
47. Janice A. Radway, *Reading the Romance: Women, Patriarchy and Popular Literature* (Chapel Hill: University of North Carolina Press, 1984), 211.
48. Meyer, *Subjection and Subjectivity*, 59.
49. Maria Lugones, 'Playfulness, "World"-Travelling, and Loving Perception', *Hypatia* 2, 2 (1987): 3–19.
50. Meyer, *Subjection and Subjectivity*, 105.
51. Kristeva, *Revolution in Poetic Language*.
52. Weedon, *Feminist Practice*, 32.
53. Meyer, *Subjection and Subjectivity*, 59.
54. Elizabeth Long, *Book Clubs: Women and the Uses of Reading in Everyday Life* (Chicago: University of Chicago Press, 2003).

8
Leading Questions: Interpretative Guidelines in Contemporary Popular Reading Culture

Anna S. Ivy

> *Lidie Newton* provides a novel perspective on antebellum America. What other historical events need telling from a woman's point of view?
> Reading Group Question for Jane's Smiley's *The All-True Travels and Adventures of Lidie Newton*[1]

> JANICE: I think it's a luxury to have a mental breakdown. I really do.
> WINFREY: Oh, that's a great comment, Janice.
> MITCHARD: True. It is an interesting comment.
> *Oprah*, 18 October 1996

Book groups, as Margaret Atwood comments in her Foreword to the third edition of *The Book Group Book* 'are to early twenty-first century America what salons were to eighteenth-century Paris and what improvement societies were to the Victorians'.[2] That is, they provide a rubric under which people can come together for a variety of social and intellectual purposes. More to the point, they are the fashion. Certainly book groups are everywhere, and they take many different forms, so that to speak generally about them is risky.[3] However, one thing that *can* be said is that they take their cues from more than one tradition of communal discourse, among them literary criticism, 1970s feminism and the consciousness-raising movement, popular psychology and self-help, and the kind of talk show pedagogy emblematized by Oprah Winfrey. Atwood, for her part, claims that the book group is 'the graduate seminar, the encounter group, and the good old-fashioned village pump gossip session, all rolled up into one'.[4] But what happens when the graduate seminar meets the encounter group, given that they are so often perceived as *opposites*, poles of critical distance versus emotional intimacy? There are, after all, time-honoured distinctions between the professional and the lay reader, between institutional practice and personal exploration, between literary criticism and literary appreciation. However, this series of binaries (which often extends to include others such as form/content and male/female) is complicated by the fact that central to the development of a contemporary popular culture of reading has been the increased production and circulation of interpretative guidelines for reading fiction, among them the reading guides that go hand in hand with book groups and are sometimes called 'reading group guides' or 'discussion guides'. My concern here is with how such guidelines reflect and/or define a set of reading practices, and with the situation of those practices within other discursive and intellectual traditions, most notably at that confluence of the critical and the personal which characterizes reading group culture and is also a site for much feminist criticism.[5] Though 'feminist theory has always built out from the personal: the witnessing "I" of subjective experience',[6] it is also the case that the therapeutic ethos of the reading group model is often perceived as implicitly *un*critical because too subjective, too personal. What, then, might the function of 'interpretative guidelines' be in contemporary popular reading culture? What are they guiding readers toward?

Like reading groups, reading guides take many forms. Visit Oprah's Book Club online and you will be offered 'expert reading guides, fun facts, and interactive features' when you 'join the biggest book club in the world!' Sign up for free and you have access to chapter summaries, reading questions, and special messages from Oprah. In addition, of course, you can browse the archives of books featured, shop at the Oprah's Book Club Boutique, read and post to message boards, and so on.[7] Publishers' websites now regularly include reading guides, along with publication information and praise for the author, to support hot new titles and/or revive old standbys. Reading guides also exist in printed form. Some are pamphlet-style, available separately from publishers or displayed in bookstores along with the books they accompany (often in a freestanding display). Others are more substantial, like those in the Continuum Contemporaries series, small books produced by 'a team of contemporary fiction scholars from both sides of the Atlantic'.[8] More informative than most reading guides, each one contains chapters on the novelist, the novel, its reception, its performance on the market, and suggested further reading, along with questions for discussion; in offering ideas and inspiration for 'members of book clubs and reading groups, as well as for students of contemporary literature at school, college, and university', the guides in this series make no attempt to distinguish the academic from the non-academic, the specialist from the generalist. Indeed, they serve to break down these distinctions by providing a model for reading that is grounded in (and authorized by) academia but available for common use.

Most intriguing, perhaps, are those guides that are actually bound in with the books, as much a physical part of them as a title page or an introduction. They are, to use Gerard Genette's term, part of the 'paratext', that 'zone between text and off-text' that includes introductions, publication information, jacket copy, and everything else that serves to frame, present, and bolster the text.[9] These guides, incorporated as they are into the book-as-object, demonstrate most clearly the extent to which the modern publishing industry has been influenced by the book group phenomenon, and how intrinsic to the book itself the experiences and attitudes brought to it are perceived to be. To package a novel with a reading guide attached is, in a sense, to build in an idealized response, or at least the framework within which such a response might be articulated. Many publishers put out series of these guides, each published along with a novel and signalled by a logo on the front cover and a direction such as 'Discussion Guide Inside' or 'Ballantine Reader's Circle'. Like Oprah's Book Club logo, a reading guide logo is designed to catch the attention of bookstore browsers and/or reading group organizers, and to signal to potential readers that help is available. The books included in reading guide series, like Oprah books, tend to have a particular character: many are easily identifiable as reading group material even without the logos. Generally their design, cover copy, and blurbs mark them as 'reading group books'. Most are contemporary; I have seen relatively few 'classics' treated in this way.[10] As for what is between the covers, the majority of 'reading group books' feature conventional narrative structures with dramatic, even melodramatic, story lines. Most also feature one or two clear protagonists with whom the reader can be expected to identify, and the by-now familiar emphasis on family trauma, tragedy, and noble suffering is very much in evidence.[11] But what of the guides themselves? Despite their differing sizes, formats, and styles, they generally have one thing in common: they consist primarily of questions, sometimes accompanied by 'conversations' with the author, presented in a Q&A format.

The fact that reading group guides usually take the form of 'reading questions' or 'questions for discussion' suggests, to begin with, that the selfsame tools are being put to work in the service of academic instruction (what teacher has not struggled to come up with questions that will prompt students to read and/or write more effectively?) and the marketing of popular fiction. Indeed, it may be the fundamental *similarity* between the class discussion plan and the reading group guide that creates a need to distinguish them. In drawing on a variety of competing ideas about the nature and function of reading (and in particular of women's reading), the contemporary culture of 'book talk' raises important questions about where and how academic interpretative discourse meets popular reading practice, and about how the practitioners of academic reading, those who identify as scholars and critics, engage with the kinds of interpretation common to this area of popular culture. For the female and/or feminist critic, this may be a particularly vexed question, since popular reading culture enacts ideas about the value and the experience of women's reading that can be politically useful and, at the same time, slightly embarrassing. While Oprah's readers may appear perfectly comfortable discussing their emotional responses to books, focusing on 'real life' applications, and entering into fantasy conversations with characters, many professionals feel the need to distance themselves from such naive engagements.[12] For a scholar, the accusation of an unsophisticated or politically disengaged critical practice can be damaging, and studies of popular culture must defend themselves particularly stringently, lest they be said to replicate the kind of 'bad' reading – the absorbed, uncritical reading – so often attributed to consumers of popular culture. So academics tread warily when it comes to expressing serious, considered opinions about phenomena like reading groups and reading guides, although this is changing. There is, for example, an ever-growing body of scholarship devoted to Oprah Winfrey.[13] There have even been a number of courses taught at university level that deal exclusively with Oprah's Book Club, courses designed not to mimic but to define and understand her cultural function.[14]

Nonetheless, academic embarrassment surrounding popular reading guides, and the culture they represent, can in fact be acute. For the reasons I have suggested, academics often feel the need to distance themselves from questions such as these, for example, taken from the reading guide to Ruth Ozeki's 1998 novel *My Year of Meats*: 'Of all the women in the novel, with whom did you most identify? Do you feel that the novel is optimistic about intimacy? Are you?'[15] Academic responses to questions like this tend to range from derisive laughter to outright horror and, not surprisingly, parody. Dennis Baron's 'I Teach English – and I Hate Reader's Guides' contains a series of mock discussion questions which are, he suggests, practically indistinguishable from the real thing.[16] A professor of English at the University of Illinois, Baron accuses questions like 'What do you think of Daniel and Jo's marriage?' and 'Would Jo's betrayal of Daniel have been more profound if she'd actually had an affair with Eli?' of reading 'like a lit final mixed with soap-opera summaries'. He offers up a series of mock questions such as the following for Helen Fielding's *Bridget Jones's Diary*: 'Do you think Bridget could gain more control of her life if she used a Palm Pilot? Explain.' What is interesting about Baron's resistance to reading guides (and he points out that he has no objections to reading *groups*, merely to the use of reading *guides* to prompt discussion within them) is that it is based, not on some snooty distinction between the scholarly and the middle-brow, but rather on the fact that the questions in these guides remind him of the worst kinds of questions in a high-school lesson plan. As he puts it,

> The last time I saw questions like those, I was, in fact, a beginning high-school English teacher trying to lure a group of sullen, unprepared students into a discussion of the day's reading. Those kinds of questions fail because they reduce the text to safe formulas: Find the theme, discuss the moral, identify with a character, feel the imagery, locate the climax, describe the book's redeeming social value.

The problem, then, is not only that reading guides do the work that the readers themselves should be doing ('if some friends go to the trouble of choosing a book to read together and discuss, why do they require the prodding of an official reader's guide to get them talking?'), but that the questions they pose are *bad* questions, the same kinds of bad questions that show up in classrooms all the time. Baron is identifying a connection between bad teaching on the one hand, and bad reading group pedagogy on the other; what he is *not* doing is simply turning up his nose at 'those educated adults who have joined the craze of reading groups' and their pseudo-intellectual practices. This is, then, a very different kind of critique than it might at first seem to be, and in its own way it poses a challenge not only to reading guides but to the importation into popular reading culture of all the worst traits of institutionalized literary criticism.[17]

In an article on book club guides, William McGinley et al. explore the role of the publishing industry as a source of cultural authority for the reading public, and suggest that 'book guides endorse a pedagogy reminiscent of the early days of English studies wherein authorized histories, criticisms, biographies, and specialized questions were taken to be more important than the literary text itself – as prerequisites for reading, enjoying, and ultimately understanding particular works'.[18] So reading guides not only pose bad questions, they pose questions and model interpretative practices that are dated, even quaint, but that are nonetheless an acknowledged part of the discipline. Perhaps the embarrassment of the trained critic is based in part, then, on a kind of horrified recognition. The hierarchy of cultural values that emerges from discussions of reading groups and reading guides, essentially a hierarchy of 'good' and 'bad' questions, reflects a similar hierarchy *within* the academy.

Take another example: the series put out by the New American Library called 'Fiction for the Way We Live'. Jessica Barksdale Inclán's 2001 novel *Her Daughter's Eyes*, a novel about a young woman attempting to give birth secretly at home, is part of that series and contains, on the inside of the front cover, a mission statement:

> Written by today's freshest new talents and selected by New American Library, NAL Accent novels touch on subjects close to a woman's heart, from friendship to family to finding our place in the world. The Conversation Guides included in each book are intended to enrich the individual reading experience, as well as encourage us to explore these topics together – because books, like life, are meant for sharing.

This description is a classic of its type: it invokes those subjects 'close to a woman's heart' in a pleasantly alliterative fashion; it speaks of the enrichment of the individual; it concludes with an emphasis on the fundamentally communal nature of the ideal reading experience (and the ideal life experience). In the conversation guide at the end, after an author Q&A, we find 'questions for discussion' that include the following:

> New York Times bestselling author Sally Mandel said, 'Jessica Barksdale Inclán brings a profound understanding of human nature to her characters – each is flawed, each is heroic, and their lives are comic and tragic, often simultaneously.' Why do you think she feels this way?

> Redemption is a recurrent theme in this novel. Describe how each of the characters compensates for a previous failure.

> How do you imagine the lives of these characters progressing? Discuss where you think they might be – emotionally and psychologically – five years after the novel ends.

Such questions are absolutely characteristic of the genre in that they move easily back and forth between interpretation of the text and imaginative self-exploration. The first presents the 'expert' opinion of a 'bestselling author', perhaps as a model for what interpretation should be, but then it invites readers, not to agree or disagree necessarily, but to speculate about why Mandel might 'feel this way'. The second is thematic, and perhaps comes closest to a conventional academic question, the kind that might be given to literature students as an essay topic. Typically, it focuses on the actions and experiences of individual characters and invites a storytelling approach, with the emphasis on description rather than interpretation.[19] The third does something else that is common in reading guides: it invites readers to forecast a future after the close of the novel, to answer the question 'what happens next?' Baron finds this kind of question particularly egregious and makes a mockery of it with suggestions of *Brideshead Re-revisited: the Night He Came Back* and *More Remembrances of Things Past*.

Each of these is, in its own way, a 'bad' academic question but a 'good' reading group question, at least from a marketing perspective. What might this tell us about reading groups? For example, what happens when readers are invited to speculate about the possible survival of characters into a future beyond the novel's end? To some degree, the integrity of the text, its aesthetic self-sufficiency, is thereby challenged, since the existing story needs to be augmented, elaborated upon. Of course, this desire to generate more narrative out of what is already in existence is something we also see in fan fiction (much of it internet-based) that builds on existing stories to produce 'what if?' scenarios in which events can develop and relationships can be pursued beyond the limits of the original literary, cinematic or (very often) televisual form. This kind of fan fiction is fundamentally resistant to the idea of completion, of finitude; the multiple 'spin-offs' of Jane Austen novels (fictions that pursue the lives of characters after the original novels' endings) reveal a deep-seated refusal to accept that the Austen canon is closed, completed, never to be reopened. But these novels, in so far as they are published and sold (as opposed to simply circulating in fan circles on the internet) are also *commercial* enterprises, more akin perhaps to those film sequels that nobody really believes are artistically necessary (or even viable) but which seem to be the inevitable result of a smash hit. In other words, there is still money to be made out of Jane Austen, and publishing companies are, after all, in the business of making money. The reading group guide phenomenon reflects current ideas about reading, but it also reflects a commercial awareness and encouragement of that desire for more narrative, that hunger for the continuation and proliferation of stories that makes serial and open-ended fiction so much a part of our common cultural life.

Whatever combination of philosophical and commercial motivations it suggests, the 'what happens next?' question exposes the extent to which the text itself is a *prompt*, a starting point, rather than a clearly delimited aesthetic object. Close textual analysis gives way to speculation about the possible implications of this story for a future that the reader is invited to imagine and to help create. Thus the reader's imaginative powers are called into play, and the reader becomes a participant, a collaborator, in the project of making the story mean something. This is typical of reading guides, many of which contain questions that invite readers to consider how they themselves might have acted in situations like those described in the book. For example, the 'reading group questions and topics for discussion' for Amy Ephron's 1997 *A Cup of Tea*, one of the books in the extensive Ballantine Reader's Circle series, include 'Could you imagine helping a homeless person on the street in the same way that Rosemary did?' and 'What might Rosemary have done to help Philip deal with his wartime experiences?' These questions assume a reader who has entered into the story, is closely identified with its protagonists, and is looking for the opportunity to learn from the reading experience through accurate diagnosis and imaginative prescription. It is not difficult to see in this type of reading question the 'encounter group' mentality to which Atwood was referring.

It is no secret that the language of therapy and self-help pervades contemporary culture. What *is* perhaps surprising is the extent to which this discourse shapes popular reading practice. In 'Heathcliff and Cathy, the Dysfunctional Couple', Trysh Travis records her discovery that the students in her college English courses were applying to the novels they read in class (and, she came to suspect, to everything they read) the interpretative tools of pop psychology and of the ubiquitous 12-step programme. She had already begun to notice that when students were asked to name a book they had recently enjoyed, 'a surprising number of plots (particularly, but not exclusively, in the novels chosen by female students) centered on family trauma and tragedy and the protagonist's struggle to overcome it'.[20] Having put this down to 'the persistent appeal of 19th-century sentimentalism, which was just then experiencing a glossy renaissance at the hands of Oprah's Book Club', Travis was jolted into awareness of the real state of affairs when her students produced a collaborative reading of *Wuthering Heights* that cast Heathcliff and Cathy as a dysfunctional couple with boundary issues, thrust into a relationship of co-dependency as a result of early abuse and a 'toxic' family environment. The answer to their problems? Couples therapy or Prozac, apparently. Travis goes on to detail the history of 12-step programmes in the United States and to suggest that these recovery programmes offer 'compelling narrative and interpretive rubrics' that have conspired with the 'precarious economics of late-twentieth-century publishing' to produce a popular book culture with its own interpretative practice.[21] As Travis points out, the limitations of this practice (from an academic standpoint), its 'downright hokiness' and belief in the power of books to 'heal', are also the measure of its belief that we need to be healed, that something is wrong. Hidden within the language of reconciliation and healing is a subtle critique of existing conditions.

I support Travis's conclusion that literary scholarship must 'reckon with the language of acceptance, forgiveness, and unconditional love' and must 'take seriously the cultural forces that have brought those terms, rather than a scholarly language of aesthetics and politics, into the foreground of readers' critical vocabularies, and thus into the fabric of their lives'.[22] She is not alone in reaching this conclusion. In 1992, Elizabeth Long noted that,

> for many, joining a reading group represents in itself a form of critical reflection on society, or one's place within it – because it demands taking a stance towards a lacuna felt in everyday life and moving towards addressing that gap. This action, in turn, reveals both to participants and to the analyst some of the ways in which contemporary society fails to meet the needs of its members, needs that correspond in patterned ways to their social situations.[23]

Travis and Long offer an alternative to the embarrassment, to the derision, and to the general effort among academics to dissociate themselves from 'bad' questions. The literary critic would do well to reckon with the fact that in the lexicon of reading group guides the goal or function of reading is more than textual insight. It is a whole experience, a deeply personal experience that has become the basis for a contemporary 'pronovel' discourse, a belief in the novel as a central component of the development of personal and social awareness. This is not to say that in a reading group textual insight is beside the point, but rather that it is a vehicle for a particular kind of reading *experience*, one in which pleasure is associated with identification, recognition, and 'healing'.

Janice Peck, in her 1995 study of TV talk shows, refers to a 'therapeutic ethos' in contemporary American culture, in which the vocabulary and sensibility of therapy (particularly the talking cure) has permeated all aspects of culture and, as a result, talk itself is presented as the only solution, the only possibility for resolution of social problems.[24] The internal contradiction of talk shows, for Peck, is that 'they address social conflicts that can never be fully resolved on television while holding out the possibility that talk will lead to, or is itself a form of, resolution'.[25] She goes on to emphasize that 'if talk shows cannot guarantee final solutions to the problems they present (indeed must not, if they're to stay on the air) their appeal is based on the *possibility* of resolution, and in particular on the premise that talking itself is a solution'.[26] Jane Shattuc makes a similar point in her 1997 *The Talking Cure*, a study of women and talk shows. She argues that on these shows 'labeling tends toward generic or psychosocial characterization rather than identity politics' and 'it is not understanding a social identity but creating identification with participants that is paramount'.[27] While it is true that talk shows like *Oprah* emphasize 'healing' over political change, Shattuc is reluctant to dismiss them, for as she points out 'daytime talk shows depend on a unity-in-diversity model as women share their individual, different experiences of the struggle of a shared female existence. The audience formulates a critique of the traditional methods of arriving at knowledge or truth through a demand for the test of lived experience.'[28] So, on the one hand these shows are driven by a liberal individualism that is inclined to be politically conservative in its failure to overtly challenge the system, and on the other hand these shows uphold female experience as 'evidence' and allow women to identify with each other, to formulate collective identity out of individual experience, a strategy that may itself show radical potential. For the most part, however, this is a form of multiculturalism that is really about familiarizing difference.

We can see this dynamic playing out in an episode of *Oprah*: the discussion on 8 March 2001 of *We Were the Mulvaneys* by Joyce Carol Oates. It is not uncommon for guests to be chosen as discussion participants because they have some sort of connection to the issues raised by the book; they embody its themes, so to speak. In this discussion of Oates's novel, for example, which deals with the prom-night rape of a teenage girl and the subsequent disintegration of her family around that event, two of the guests were presented as having personal connections to the story: one had a daughter who had been raped as a teenager and another had been banished from her home by her father when she herself was a teenager.

> WINFREY: When a tragedy happens, it happens not to one person. The family has to understand that it really does happen to everybody.

JAYNE: It slapped me in the face. We were all trying to help [my daughter]. It dawned on me, reading this book that we have all been raped.
Later
LAURIE: You don't have to have experienced what Marianne did. None of us are exempt from that. My family could unravel just like the Mulvaneys did ... You forgive your family for doing terrible things to you. I don't understand it a lot of the time, too. But people do. It's that bond that you have with family that you can forgive them for insane things.
WINFREY: My question then, is what is a family if you can't withstand the difficult times? If joy is only during the joyous times? If you can't have a faith that allows you to reach out during the most difficult times?
JOYCE: Families do evolve. I think sometimes it happens that there's irrevocable loss. And one person just shifts and has a personality change. A family is always evolving.
Later
CELESTE: This was such a beautiful family. I just couldn't believe that they let this gift that they had go. I couldn't forgive until talking to you now.
WINFREY: I've learned to surrender and forgive all characters, all things.
B.J.: Then you would be there at the hospital bed of the one who abandoned you. You just said what it would take for you to get there.[29]

The operation of authority in a discussion like this is fairly complex. The author, of course, occupies a privileged position, and indeed contemporary book culture relies heavily on interviews with authors and on speculation about authorial intention and biography. The author is invited to help us interpret the book, and to clear up points that make interpretation difficult. On the other hand, Oprah herself is in a position of undeniable authority, in part because this is her space, and her choice. She selects the books, and on some level it is her reading experience that is being modelled here, her pleasure in the text that functions as a lesson in how to read and how to love reading. By definition, any book showcased in this way has already been experienced, with pleasure, by her. As an experienced talk show host, she is also skilled in summing up and presenting in a digestible form the 'lessons' offered by emotional situations and, in this case, texts. She is confessor, teacher, and therapist rolled into one, but she is also reader and student, one who learns from the author and from the reading experience. She is, in some sense, a floating member of this exchange, inclined to ventriloquize, to translate when necessary. As Laurie Haag puts it: 'Viewers recognize the serious Oprah, the playful Oprah, the empathetic Oprah, the angry Oprah, the "just folks" Oprah ... More so than with the other talk show hosts, the audience knows when she is talking *for* them, and it knows when she is talking *to* them, even when she is not employing direct address.'[30] Oprah Winfrey teaches by presenting what she has learned, as for example when she says 'I have learned to forgive all characters, all things.' Then again, the guests who are connected to the themes of the book have a kind of authority attributed to them based on their experiences. Their reactions are valuable because the experience offered by the text can be measured against the real-life experience of dealing with the issues. In some sense, then, these readers are the authorities, the ultimate gatekeepers, since they can confirm or deny the truth of the fiction, its applicability to real life. B.J. responds to Oprah's claim by reapplying it to a possible real-life situation, and by proposing that what Oprah has learned from reading fiction she would necessarily translate into practice if the need ever arose. Since the average reader is presumably most closely allied with the guests, the average reader can also lay claim to this kind of authority. The point of these discussions is to suggest to ordinary readers that they too can read in authoritative ways, can engage with the text, the author, and the 'expert reader' on the strength of their own personal experiences.

Reconciliation is an ostensible project of the talk show, and it is woven into the reading group sensibility, but sometimes even Oprah has to work visibly to reconcile disparate goals and this speaks of the confusion between her own and other institutionalized forms of reading. On 6 March 1998, *Oprah* featured scenes from a discussion with Toni Morrison about her novel *Paradise*, that month's book club selection. It is a fascinating discussion, mainly because of the ways in which it is atypical and difficult to reconcile with the format of previous discussions. In a forum in which resolution and affirmation are highly valued, this show begins with an acknowledgment of difficulty and a lack of resolution: 'WINFREY: 'I warned you going into it ... You were going to get lost in the story. Our last book was challenging. By page, like, seven, eight, you're going, "What is going on?"' The show opens not with a greeting but with a disclaimer: I warned you. Winfrey acknowledges up front that this is a book that may not have given satisfaction, and that the reader may have gotten 'lost' in the story, may have failed to emerge triumphant. If ever a book needed a reading guide, this is apparently it. The danger here is that readers will be unable to respond to the novel because the possibilities for identification are blocked. Winfrey's opening is notable for the way she expresses (and ventriloquizes for her audience) anxiety about plot: 'what is going on?' She quickly reverts, however, to the pleasure of being 'taught' by Toni Morrison, pulling us back into fandom and into a model of reading that depends on faith in the guide, in this case the author, expert by virtue of a host of institutional and cultural credentials. Winfrey's answer to the difficulties posed by this novel, which diverges in a number of ways from the predominantly realist, linear narratives she generally chooses for her club, was to hold a mock class on Morrison's home turf, an encounter that, for once, made explicit the influence of the seminar on the reading group: as Winfrey puts it, 'twenty two of us went to Princeton to learn the secrets of *Paradise*'.

She begins by explaining the change of venue:

> WINFREY: I heard from many people this month. Some admitted that they could not make it to paradise, they just couldn't make it to paradise. And even readers who did finish still felt a little confused. So the first time our book club became a class, we needed help ... Our thirteenth book brought us to prestigious Princeton University in Princeton, New Jersey, where twenty viewers and I became *Paradise* pupils for a day. It's a natural setting, not only because it's a place of higher education – whoo, girl, do we need that – but because it's also where author Toni Morrison teaches. Could we find paradise inside Princeton?

Winfrey's metaphors are predictable (she likes to make connections, rhetorically, between the titles and topics of her books and the reading process) but interesting nonetheless. The question 'can we find paradise inside Princeton?' is a real one, because Winfrey's model of interpretation generally holds out the possibility of deep emotional satisfaction, a kind of paradise, and in this case that satisfaction is proving elusive. It is not, apparently, available to the average reader in her home, nor is it available on the usual sets; it must be sought in a place of higher education. It becomes obvious that there is here no clear distinction between reading for pleasure and reading for intellectual engagement. Rather, they are linked, the classroom functioning as a place wherein pleasure, as well as insight, can be taught.

What, then, takes place in this classroom? This is, of course, not a real seminar; it is a staged fantasy of classroom experience, and it is permeated by anxiety. In a voice-over, Winfrey modestly says 'we all tried to come prepared, but who could compete with these scholars?' And her 'we' establishes a distinction between lay readers and professional readers, 'these scholars'. As the participants ask questions of Morrison, many of them take a mock-humble attitude toward the author, calling her to task for having produced such a difficult read even as they seem to blame their own lack of expertise. At one point a reader (who is also one of Winfrey's close friends) says: 'Ms. Morrison, are we supposed to get it on the first read? Because I've read it – I'm not even trying to be funny – because I've read it and I called Oprah and I said "Please, 'splain it to me."' There is a real challenge contained within this comment, the challenge that readers who think of themselves as 'ordinary' or average pose to authors who for whatever reason seem to withhold or mystify the reading experience. If Winfrey can't explain it, then Morrison is going to have to, although as Winfrey points out in another voice-over, 'wise author that she is, she knows the rewards are twice as great when we readers get to unlock the secrets on our own. And that is paradise.' Morrison is thus therapist as well as author and teacher; she knows the answers (who better?) but her job is to guide the reader in 'unlocking the secrets' on her own.

The specific difficulty of this novel lies not in what it represents but in how it represents; it offers not just unfamiliar characters or situations (readers can often find ways to identify across cultural and historical boundaries) but an unfamiliar reading experience, one that for some of these readers is almost unrecognizable as reading. Even Winfrey makes a show (and how much of it *is* a show cannot be verified) of not knowing how to read this novel, of losing confidence in herself as a reader. Morrison refuses to accept this, telling Winfrey 'you got it and you didn't believe you got it'. Thus Morrison challenges Winfrey's pose, her lack of faith in herself and her ability to read in an 'expert' way; Morrison is more interested than many of the guests in breaking down the distinction between expert and lay readers, and between insider and outsider status in literary criticism. Much of the 'class' is geared toward emphasizing the power, the authority, of the reader, as when Morrison says she 'wanted the weight of interpretation to be on the reader' and that she 'wouldn't want to end up having written a book in which there was a formula and a perfect conclusion and that was the meaning and the only meaning'. In a sense, Winfrey and Morrison collude in harnessing this difficult text to the paradigm that is already in place for popular reading, a paradigm according to which personal experience, life experience, is the key to understanding.

The main lesson Winfrey culls from this scene of 'higher education' is that 'you have to open yourself up. You don't read this book with just your head. You have to open your whole self up. It's a whole new way of experiencing reading and life.' In fact, though, there is little about this that is new; the trip to Princeton has confirmed, not altered, her reading practice. After all, opening up and reading with more than just the head (with the heart, presumably) is the way of reading that women are most often encouraged to perform. It is perfectly in keeping with the reading group ethos, and the therapeutic ethos, in which meaning is seen as arising out of the shared experience of opening up, in this case to the novel. Winfrey takes her show to the academic stage, then, precisely in order to gain a kind of institutional permission to forgo the process of figuring out exactly what the novel means, of struggling to understand it. The key, she seems to suggest (in concert with Morrison) is to let go a little, to relax, to trust yourself. This intervention is, like all interventions, really an attempt to reboot the system, to harness that which is temporarily out of control. That the 'students' in Morrison's seminar should be reminded of their own natural authority as readers, their own ability to 'get it' just by being receptive to 'it' suggests that what is really at stake here is not cultural analysis, not the analysis of Morrison's depictions of racism or her handling of narrative technique, but rather the feelings of community and connectedness, of satisfaction, sought by her readers.

It is true that one reason why this novel was so difficult for Oprah readers to engage with is that it deliberately complicates the process of identification; Morrison says that she 'wanted to force the reader to become acquainted with communities' and thus chose not to present an obvious protagonist, a single character with whom readers could easily identify. The novel's deliberate obscurity about which characters are white and which are black (the opening line, 'they shoot the white girl first', prompts a question that many readers feel is impossible to answer, namely 'which of the girls is white?'), in a novel that deals centrally with racial history and politics, is one example.[31] Readers may not be sure whom to identify with, whom to approve of, whom to like. As Timothy Aubrey points out in his discussion of this episode:

> [Morrison's] hope is not to disable identification altogether, but to facilitate another form of identification: a structure of empathy difficult to imagine, less individual-centered, less competitive, and more inclusive. Interestingly enough, Morrison's strategy conflicts slightly with *Oprah*'s tendency to incite compassion through the presentation of individual narratives.[32]

This is an important distinction – Morrison is challenging individual identification as the basis for an effective critique of racism, pushing rather for a sense of the structures of community through multiple, conflicting, even irreconcilable identifications, which is indeed quite different from Winfrey's characteristic 'personalizing' of social issues through narratives of individual experience – but at the same time there is a sense in which Morrison's 'structure of empathy' is an organized, deliberate evocation of something that Winfrey is, perhaps, *unwittingly* generating. That is, one could argue that the Oprah Winfrey model of individual identification and personal connection is always being staged communally and that in some sense it is the communal, non-competitive practice of empathy – enacted through the sharing and pooling of individual responses, which are themselves multiple, variable, often irreconcilable, but all on some level valued *as* responses – that characterizes her reading culture. It is still of course quite true that the overall effect of Winfrey's model is to individualize social and political dilemmas and thus in some sense to discourage systemic critique; however, the cooperation of Morrison and Winfrey, 'this strangely matched pair',[33] shows how difficult it really is to distinguish the academic urge to multiply the possible readings of a given text from the popular/commercial urge to validate individual responses as such.

That neither Morrison nor Winfrey is interested, here, in distinguishing the two is part of the point. As John Young points out:

> By circulating her authorial image and her texts via Winfrey's book club, and by reading her abridged novels on tape, Morrison aims for the most popular audience for serious works of fiction. Through these kinds of promotional activities, Morrison does not so much reify the high-low cultural gap while seeking to bridge both sides of it as she denies the terms on which the dichotomy is grounded, finding no principled incongruence among *Oprah* viewers, audio-book consumers, and readers of 'demanding and sophisticated' fiction.[34]

If Young is right (and he bases his claims at least in part on statements Morrison herself has made) then this would suggest that the author is not *simply* being co-opted by Winfrey; the reinstatement of Winfrey's own habitual reading practice as a result of this mock-seminar is not *simply* an example of the multicultural middlebrow impulse to feel good about difference winning out. Instead, Morrison can be seen as strategically sacrificing something of the academic exclusiveness that is her right in order to replace 'separate black and white readerships with a single, popular audience'[35] and, by extension, to validate, not *all* of the individual responses proffered necessarily, but the idea of a popular response mediated both by individualism and communal discourse.

While Morrison's desire to create a popular audience for serious works of fiction, and to free herself from an 'exclusivity' that, after all, has historically excluded writers like herself, may be seen as presenting a radical challenge to the institution of canonicity, we cannot assume that it will lead to a radical reading practice. Indeed, it may be more likely, as we can see from the example of *Paradise*, that her works will be translated into popular terms, will be read according to the therapeutic models of the day. The lesson learned in Morrison's 'class' is remarkably similar to one described by Trysh Travis in her analysis of the 'cultural sisterhood' surrounding the popular novel by Rebecca Wells, *The Divine Secrets of the Ya-Ya Sisterhood*. As Travis remarks, the novel's early emphasis on the 'social pressures brought to bear on middle- and upper-class white women in the postwar years' gives way to 'a discursive space from which social history has been evacuated so that the rationale of recovery can have free reign'.[36] At the end of the novel, the daughter who has struggled to understand the history of her own abuse at the hands of a mother both ravaged and beautified by that history must abandon the desire to know, to understand: 'For Siddalee Walker, the need to understand had passed, at least for the moment. All that was left was love and wonder.'[37] As Travis remarks, '12-step logic dictates that Sidda's endeavor to understand her mother's behavior through intellect – to "solve" and "account for" it – is doomed from the beginning. Indeed, Sidda's intellect is both cause and emblem of her unhappiness, her ignorance of "how to love."'[38] Like Oprah's readers contending with *Paradise*, readers of Wells's novel may be getting a mixed message about the value of the pursuit of understanding: the novel itself poses an interpretative problem, something that the reader might feel herself obliged to (and indeed might want to) try to solve, yet the overarching message presented (by the novel itself in the case of Wells, and by Oprah's 'seminar' in the case of Morrison) is that certain things, the truest and most important things, cannot necessarily be understood intellectually, but must instead be *felt*. Crucially, Travis identifies the *Ya-Ya* phenomenon as an example of the 'extent to which changes in the nature of literary production and consumption require us to refine our assumption that women "resist" through reading. Readers of *Divine Secrets* register dissatisfaction and desire, yes. But these are then ever-more-rapidly rerouted – by the culture around them and by their own mental predilections – into unthreatening forms.'[39] Likewise, the most challenging aspects of *Paradise*, those that might conceivably force a reconsideration of the workings of narrative itself, and the limits of individual identification as a basis for cultural understanding, are 'rerouted' into the less threatening prospect of simply being open to the possibilities of the novel and its vaguely-understood beneficent healing powers.

When Winfrey started her Book Club up again in 2003, this time choosing 'classics' rather than contemporary novels, she explained her choice of Steinbeck's *East of Eden* as the first in the new series by saying that she wanted to give her readers something to think about without making them feel like they were back in school. Rita Barnard points out, in an article in which she describes her work for *Oprah* online, as a 'literary guide' to Alan Paton's *Cry, the Beloved Country* (the selection that followed *East of Eden*), that both Steinbeck and Paton are in fact among the more likely authors to have been encountered by students in high school (clearly the kind of 'school' to which Winfrey was referring). Paton's novel, says Barnard, is 'a book with a long pedagogical track record and one of two South African works ... that I can expect many of my American students to have read before they begin their university education'.[40] That Professor Barnard should have been invited to serve as a 'literary guide' to the novel, encouraged to bring 'university-quality instruction'[41] to Oprah's readers, suggests that there really was a difference between the old club and the new one, between an author-centred pedagogy and one that acknowledged the need for a third party, someone with verifiable critical expertise, when it came to dealing with the 'classics'.

What Barnard found, though, as she fielded the questions forwarded to her, was that although there were some questions that dealt explicitly with the literariness of the text (questions about symbolism, for instance), and that employed what we think of as a more literary critical vocabulary, there were also 'ways in which the emotional and woman-centered hermeneutic fostered by the earlier Book Club may have shaped readers' responses'.[42] Further, 'there were also several questions that we, as literary academics, might fault for assuming that fiction and reality are seamlessly connected'.[43] In other words, these questions suggested that readers were treating the 'classics' precisely as they would treat any other Oprah book. At the same time, it is worth noting that Barnard does not dismiss these questions as utterly useless, nor does she let pass the opportunity to encourage the questioners to think more deeply about their own interpretative practices: 'I also suggested, as gently as I could, that characters were not people, that one should perhaps not ask why John Kumalo holds back his power, but rather why Paton *presents* John Kumalo as holding back: a formulation more likely to produce a critical probing of Paton's suspicious treatment of black militancy in the novel.'[44] This is what happens in a real seminar, as opposed to the mock variety staged at Princeton: students are encouraged to think through their initial responses, rather than simply expressing them, to ask questions *about* the questions they are asking, and to progress from concerns about 'relateability' to more critical analyses of the workings of the text. Clearly the online Q&A format, and the relative freedom granted to Professor Barnard to answer questions as she saw fit, conspired to give more room here to genuinely literary critical concerns, and allowed the 'literary guide' to override, temporarily at least, some of the most cherished assumptions in the Oprah tradition (for example, that characters sort of *are* real people).[45]

What emerges from this discussion overall is the fact that struggles over the value of different kinds of questions, and different ways of reading, are often grounded in an almost painful awareness of the inseparability of professional and non-professional modes of interpretation. After all, every scholar, every critic, is also or once was a novice, a 'general' reader, and most reading group participants have experienced at least some formal education and may well have taken literature courses. Both settings are fundamentally communal in nature; both depend on ways of reading that are developmental and geared toward resolution. The graduate seminar and the encounter group threaten to merge rather easily; hence the struggle to keep them separate, even while calling on each to legitimate, in some sense, the operations of the other. In the end, a question like the one that forms part of the epigraph to this essay, 'what other historical events need telling from a woman's point of view?' is neither a good nor a bad question; it is, however, a leading question, a question designed to evoke a particular kind of response in a particular setting. It lends itself to earnest self-disclosure and consideration of 'the female perspective', and it also has the potential to be a serious critical tool. What a question like this can *accomplish* depends very much on who wields it and how.

Notes

1. This question is from the Reader's Guide provided in the Ballantine Reader's Circle edition of the novel. The guide was prepared by Ron Fletcher, a teacher at Boston College High School in Massachusetts.
2. Margaret Atwood, 'Foreword', in *The Book Group Book*, ed. Ellen Slezak (Chicago: Chicago Review Press, 2000), xi.
3. While it is difficult to get a handle on a contemporary phenomenon so decentralized, there are a number of resources. In *Book Clubs: Women and*

the Use of Reading in Everyday Life (Chicago: University of Chicago Press, 2003) Elizabeth Long bases her analysis on first-hand observation of groups in Houston, TX, while Jenny Hartley's *Reading Groups* (Oxford: Oxford University Press, 2001) offers a detailed survey of reading groups in Britain. For examples of 'how to' books see Ellen Slezak (ed.), *The Book Group Book* (Chicago: Chicago Review Press, 2000) and Rachel Jacobsohn, *The Reading Group Handbook* (New York: Hyperion, 1998), which include accounts of existing groups, book lists, and advice from book group participants. Such books both reflect and help shape the existing culture. This is in addition to the wealth of journalistic reporting and anecdotal evidence.
4. Atwood, 'Foreword', xi.
5. For examples of 'the personal turn' in feminist criticism, see Gayle Greene and Coppelia Kahn, eds, *Changing Subjects: the Making of Feminist Criticism* (New York: Routledge, 1993) and Diane Freedman, Olivia Frey, and Francis Murphy Zauhar, eds, *The Intimate Critique: Autobiographical Literary Criticism* (Durham: Duke University Press, 1993).
6. Nancy Miller, *Getting Personal: Feminist Occasions and other Autobiographical Acts* (New York: Routledge, 1991), 14.
7. See Oprah.com.
8. This quote and the one that follows are taken from the standard back cover copy. Each guide is authored by an individual whose credentials are also given in a bio on the back cover. A list of books in the series is available at www.continuumbooks.com.
9. Gerard Genette, *Paratexts: Thresholds of Interpretation* (Cambridge: Cambridge University Press, 1997), 2.
10. There are some reader's guides to 'classics', particularly online. I have also purchased a Penguin edition of *Jane Eyre* that features the logo of the Great Books Foundation along with the phrase 'recommended for discussion' and the information that a discussion guide is available online, which is simply a reminder that the contemporary phenomenon under discussion here has its roots in other, long-established projects designed to promote reading among the general public. [Editor's note: Please see Daniel Born (Chapter 4 above) to better understand the historical ideologies and philosophies of the Great Books Foundation.]
11. For a fuller discussion of this trend in popular fiction, see Trysh Travis, 'Heathcliff and Cathy: the Dysfunctional Couple', *Chronicle of Higher Education* (11 May 2001): 13–14.
12. Anxious dissociation from reading group culture is not limited to academics by any means. The highly publicized clash between Jonathan Franzen and Oprah Winfrey in 2001, which some believe led to the demise of the first incarnation of Oprah's Book Club, came about when he expressed mixed feelings about her selection of his book, *The Corrections*. In an interview with Terry Gross (*Fresh Air*, National Public Radio, WHYY Philadelphia, 15 October 2001) Franzen suggested that his resistance was based in part on his perception that Oprah's selections tend to be less edgy than he feels his own work to be and that her readers are all female.
13. Examples include: Jeffrey Louis Decker, 'Saint Oprah', *Modern Fiction Studies* 52, 1 (Spring 2006): 169–78; Mark Hall, 'The "Oprahfication" of Literacy: Reading "Oprah's Book Club"', *College English* 65, 6 (July 2003): 646–67; and

Cecilia Konchar Farr, *Reading Oprah: How Oprah's Book Club Changed the Way America Reads* (Albany: State University of New York Press, 2005).
14. Examples include a University of Wisconsin course titled 'Reading Oprah's Book Club' taught in the English department under the rubric of Literature and Contemporary Life (Fall 2000) and a University of Illinois course titled 'The Oprah Effect: Classes, Masses, and Public Spheres' taught in the English department under the rubric of Literature and Experience (Spring 2002).
15. These questions are taken from a 'Readers Guide' in the Penguin edition.
16. Dennis Baron, 'I Teach English – and I Hate Reader's Guides', *Chronicle of Higher Education* 4 (2002): 5.
17. It is worth noting that it is really the 'high school mentality' of these questions that comes under attack. In other words, resistance to the reading guide may reflect not just a general hierarchy in the academy but also a more focused critique by the professoriate of the limitations of high school English instruction.
18. William McGinley, Katanna Conley, and John Wesley White, 'Pedagogy for a Few: Book Club Discussion Guides and the Modern Book Industry as Literature Teacher', *Journal of Adolescent and Adult Literacy* 44, 3 (Nov 2000): 208.
19. This is, in fact, a good example of a 'bad' question from a teaching standpoint in the sense that it is likely to produce descriptive rather than analytic essays.
20. Travis, 'Heathcliff and Cathy', 13.
21. Ibid., 14.
22. Ibid.
23. Elizabeth Long, 'Textual Interpretation as Collective Action', *Discourse* 14, 3 (1992): 116.
24. Janice Peck, 'TV Talk Shows as Therapeutic Discourse: the Ideological Labor of the Televised Talking Cure', *Communication Theory* 5, 1 (February 1995): 58.
25. Ibid., 59.
26. Ibid., 67.
27. Jane Shattuc, *The Talking Cure: TV Talk Shows and Women* (New York: Routledge, 1997), 95.
28. Ibid., 98.
29. This quote and all subsequent quotes from the Oprah Winfrey Show are taken from transcripts provided by Burrelle's Information Services, Box 7, Livingston, NJ, 07039.
30. Laurie Haag, 'Oprah Winfrey: the Construction of Intimacy in the Talk Show Setting', *Journal of Popular Culture* 26, 4 (Spring 1993): 119.
31. For a fuller discussion of the racial politics of this discussion see Timothy Aubrey, 'Beware the Furrow of the Middlebrow: Searching for Paradise on the Oprah Winfrey Show', *Modern Fiction Studies* 52, 2 (Summer 2006): 350–73. For more general discussions of race and Oprah's Book Club, see Kimberley Chabot Davis, 'Oprah's Book Club and the Politics of Cross-Racial Empathy', *International Journal of Cultural Studies* 7, 4 (2004): 399–419, and Decker, 'Saint Oprah'.
32. Aubrey, 'Beware the Furrow of the Middlebrow', 360.
33. Ibid., 369.
34. John Young, 'Toni Morrison, Oprah Winfrey, and Postmodern Popular Audiences', *African American Review* 35, 2 (Summer 2001): 187.

35. Ibid., 181.
36. Trysh Travis, 'Divine Secrets of the Cultural Studies Sisterhood: Women Reading Rebecca Wells', *American Literary History* 15, 1 (2003): 150.
37. Rebecca Wells, *Divine Secrets of the Ya-Ya Sisterhood* (New York: Harper Perennial, 1996), 356.
38. Travis, 'Divine Secrets', 150.
39. Ibid., 155.
40. Rita Barnard, 'Oprah's Paton, or South Africa and the Globalization of Suffering', *Safundi: the Journal of South African and American Studies* 7, 3 (July 2006): 4.
41. Ibid. 5.
42. Ibid., 8.
43. Ibid.
44. Ibid.
45. At the same time, as Barnard goes on to illustrate, the power of her critical perspective and her ability to seize on the 'teaching moments' offered by the Q&A could not in fact override the very different kind of teaching that Oprah Winfrey was doing, and politicized critique of the novel was 'rapidly lost in the welter of voices that constitute Oprah's megatext' (Barnard, 'Oprah's Paton', 9).

9
Marionettes and Puppeteers? The Relationship between Book Club Readers and Publishers

Danielle Fuller, DeNel Rehberg Sedo and Claire Squires

Introduction

The recognizable orange, white and black colour scheme catches the attention of patrons passing by the local library bulletin board for reading groups.[1] The brochure's headline, 'PENGUIN READERS' BOOK OF THE MONTH', jumps out from the various pamphlets on display. The front text tells us that Penguin asked 'hundreds of librarians nationwide' (in the UK) to recommend contemporary novels that they believed would appeal to reading groups. Inside the brochure we find six Penguin titles for their 2005 'Book of the Month' programme, ranging from Esther Freud's *The Sea House* to *The Jane Austen Book Club* by Karen Joy Fowler. The programme, according to Penguin, includes novels that 'appeal to each member of the wide-ranging library reading groups that they will be running and supporting for the next six months'.[2]

The relationship Penguin is trying to build via this campaign with librarians – and through them, with book club readers – is but one example of the changing milieu of print culture not only in the UK, but also in Canada and the US. Book historians and communication scholars have documented a series of major shifts in the twentieth-century book publishing industries of the US, the UK and Canada: the demise of small publishing houses or their amalgamations into multi-national media conglomerates;[3] the resulting changes in business operations and staffing practices;[4] evolving audience/reader considerations;[5] and social and technological changes both within the industry, and in society more widely.[6] However, none have considered in detail how these shifts affect book club readers in particular. In this chapter we provide a critique of the relationship between book club readers and publishers, and an analysis of reading and community as a commodified social practice.

Using the findings from interviews with book club members, an online study of readers in both face-to-face and virtual book clubs, and interviews with publishers and other cultural workers in both Canada and the UK, we examine the complex framework of book distribution, marketing, consumption and reception in the three nation-states at the end of the twentieth and the beginning of the twenty-first centuries. The chapter argues that the relationship fostered by publishers is one that book club readers sometimes readily accept and are sometimes resistant towards. The title of this chapter, with book club members questionably posited as 'marionettes' and publishers as 'puppeteers',[7] hints at this. We also propose that through an analysis of the relationship between publishers and book club readers, the broader processes of literary commodification are brought into focus.

What does the 'book club movement'[8] represent for book publishers and booksellers? Although published figures estimate that there are upwards of 500,000 book clubs in the United States, 50,000 in Great Britain and 40,750 clubs in Canada, no one really knows how many contemporary book clubs exist because there is no formal registry system, and the groups and membership of them are fluid.[9] A 1999 Gallup poll in the United States found that 6 per cent of US residents are members of book clubs.[10] Based on these findings, there may be upwards of 17,230,933 US readers who are members of book clubs. Readers also meet online in Internet chatrooms, on listservs and in blogs. Others participate in book clubs broadcast through television and radio channels. It should be no surprise, then, that publishers and booksellers are keen to tap into this potentially lucrative market.

Changing markets, changing marketing

While book clubs are the contemporary iteration of literary societies of previous centuries, modern media and technology have converged to create and respond to imagined and real communities of readers.[11] The social structure of book groups aids communication with and between members of the groups, and indeed, between groups themselves.[12] Publishers and booksellers attempt to identify and capture this somewhat elusive audience of readers. Simultaneously, publishers and retailers try to create new consumer groups through books they identify as 'good' book club books. Interestingly, however, the small independent bookstores in North America and the UK appear to have more influence with book club members than the much-lamented 'big box' booksellers such as Borders, Chapters and Waterstones. Before expanding on these insights, let us position the book club 'market' within the current publishing and bookselling environment.

Educational reforms of the late nineteenth and early twentieth centuries in Canada, the US and the UK played a significant role in garnering a larger market for book publishers in all three countries. With the rise of the educated working classes came expanding markets interested in self-education and a resultant hunger for books. As Squires has pointed out elsewhere, 'the expansion of the reading public brought about by the educational reforms had the effect of widening culture to a mass audience'.[13] The reactions of both modernist writers and publishers suggest a desire to preserve the intellectual hierarchy from the masses, which, in subsequent decades, was made manifest through the expression of anxiety about the deleterious effects of mass readership on literature.[14] Commenting on the new reading public's effect on the publishing industry in 1934, the publisher Geoffrey Faber wrote:

> Literature now is in the hands of the mob; and the mob is stampeded. It moves in a mass, this way or that, and all its thinking is done for it. For those who will hit the taste of the masses the reward is very large. Hence, an ever growing temptation to write for the herd, to publish for the herd, to buy for and sell to the herd… The whole nation reads to order. Books are, increasingly, written to order.[15]

During the succeeding decades, the debates around market-based publishing and the marketing activity that it provokes have intensified. Indeed, the discussions evoked by the environment of mergers and convergence are reminiscent of the concerns expressed by Faber and his contemporaries. Contemporary authors argue that the recent trend of multinational conglomerations swallowing independent houses has resulted in industry pressure to create and promote best-sellers at the expense of mid-list titles and 'serious' literature.[16]

Elizabeth Long suggests that the anxiety about commercialization in publishing has foundations in the cultural elite's fear of losing power, and she suggests that the expanding marketplace is a result of the growing reading public.[17] Similarly, Janice Radway demonstrates that the historical foundations of the Book-of-the-Month Club are entrenched in cultural authority conflicts between the 'literary' few and the ever-growing masses.[18] While the lamentations sound similar across the decades, the economic realities of the publishing industry of the early twenty-first century are influenced by a more commercialized, market-focused workforce; new technologies; a different retail environment; and, consequently, an evolving interaction between publishers and society.[19]

The publishing industry's transition from small to mid-sized, family-owned presses before World War II to the market domination of a handful of multinational, multimedia companies in the 1990s was a result of market deregulation in the US and the UK in the 1970s and 1980s. Deregulation provided large publishers with an 'increased availability of long- and short-term equity and debt financing', which allowed large firms or their parent companies to take over small and medium-sized houses.[20] As a result, the markets of all three countries have come to be dominated by an oligopolistic group of multinational, multimedia companies with strong negotiating power in the marketplace. The economies of scale available to large firms such as Bertelsmann and HarperCollins, who own a range of publishing imprints in Canada, the US and the UK, mean they have the ability to offer discounts to their customers, and to influence the positioning of books inside bookselling superstores. Changes in publishing and retailing have thus also determined which books get into the spotlight. With the advent of conglomeration, increased marketing and promotional pots of money are made available to decidedly few, but carefully selected, titles.[21]

Online bookstores such as Amazon, with its heavy discounting policies, have changed consumer expectations about prices. They have also altered the experience of book-buying, and the processes by which readers learn about new books – while simultaneously providing readers with a massively increased range of access to different titles. Ironically, alongside the impact of bigger marketing and promotional budgets, advances in technology have forced booksellers and publishers to return to an earlier era when one-to-one relationships were created between publisher and reader, or at least, bookseller and reader. Booksellers of any size often keep a database of customer preferences, and those bookstores that have sufficient staff make contact with individual customers. Of course, this contemporary relationship is largely facilitated by computer communication.

Book club choice

Do book club readers respond to publishers' direct marketing efforts? Examining the processes of book selection within book clubs suggests that book club title choice is a practice that illustrates how the reader's individual agency is influenced by the collective interpretative community. Marketing may have an impact, but other factors are also at play. Canadian singer Jan Arden represented a popular misconception about how readers select books when she commented that, 'People are like cattle. They go to the top 30 books and think that if everyone else thinks something's good, then it must be good, and they buy it.'[22] Arden's reflections on reader behaviour were made during an interview after her appearance on the Canadian Broadcasting Corporation's television book discussion programme, *By the Book*. She had been invited on to the show to review Ian McEwan's *Atonement*, a book that certainly fit into Arden's conception of a visible 'top 30' since it was a best-seller and had been short-listed for the Booker and Whitbread prizes. Arden's comments, and Hartley's generalization that book club readers 'want to read what everyone else is reading',[23] may have some merit – in some groups and with some readers. However, we suggest that title selection is more complicated than reading the best-seller lists. Book club readers frequently choose books because other readers have told them that a certain book might be an appropriate 'book club book'.[24]

Long has argued that reading group book selection is a process to 'legitimate choices and to predict the outcome of [book club member's] reading experience'.[25] Text selection can determine levels of particular interpretative experiences: 'Reading group members, like readers of formulaic fiction, do what they can to ensure they will be satisfied by each book, but since they cannot rely on the security of a formula, they must discover by some other means what kind of reading experience to expect.'[26] The group's 'legitimate choices' and their expectations, occur differently in each group, and evolve over time with the group's history of selection and experiences in interpretation.[27]

Long identified four group methods for title selection that 'tend to bring groups into different kinds of dialogue with agencies of cultural authority'.[28] They are: (1) formal, or committee choice; (2) consensual choice; (3) direct voting; and (4) individual member choice. Although studies by Hartley and Rehberg Sedo indicate that contemporary Canadian and UK book groups appear to depend less on cultural authorities than those Long studied in Texas,[29] her analysis of the modes of negotiation offers a useful means of categorizing the selection process.

Like most small groups, book club processes change occasionally, and clubs seem to continually look for ways to improve the process within the group itself. A 'cross-cutting tendency towards egalitarianism' may arise because 'reading groups are voluntary associations that can continue only as long as their members find them pleasurable'.[30] On a functional level, the only consistent stipulation is that most groups require the book to be in paperback and that there must be sufficient copies available for every group member.[31] Most groups are conscious of the cost of books for those who purchase them, but availability is more important. If a book is not available to all members, it can create great frustration and may mean the death of discussion. If a book is too long, some of the groups feel the time pressure to finish it takes the enjoyment out of reading. In addition, some group members may feel uncomfortable coming to their book club if they have been too busy to read the book.

The books that book groups read cannot be neatly categorized. From a preliminary glance at any book club lists found in the plethora of 'how to' book club books or in libraries, for example, it would appear that almost any piece of classic or contemporary fiction would fit into the category of a book club book.[32] Is there then a 'good' book club book?

In many book clubs, readers will 'pitch' titles to their groups, articulating reasons why a particular title is an appropriate book club read. As Rehberg Sedo has demonstrated elsewhere,[33] the title selection decisions that readers make, and their sense of the meaning of those decisions, confirm Stanley Fish's argument that 'the act of recognizing literature is not constrained by something in the text, nor does it issue from an independent and arbitrary will; rather, it proceeds from a collective decision as to what will count as literature'.[34] Readers depend on each other to confirm the choices, because a title will be accepted as a worthy read 'only so long as a community of readers or believers continues to abide by it.'[35]

Long identified three characteristics of judgement used by book club readers.[36] First, a book is valued for its literary worth, an evaluation that is dependent upon notions of literary value and aesthetics learned through school and/or university, as other cultural theorists maintain.[37] Second, other book clubs and 'trusted others' such as a friend, family member, or the media have determined its suitability.[38] And finally, the book needs to speak to each individual's life.

According to studies by Hartley and Rehberg Sedo, 'good' book club books fit well into a category that Radway's Book-of-the-Month editors identified as 'appropriate' serious fiction: 'On the one hand, there is the assumption ... that fiction should be technically complex and self-consciously *about* significant issues. On the other ... such fiction should be pleasurable to read, a stipulation that differs little from that made regularly by readers of best-sellers and genre fiction who desire always to be entertained.'[39]

In other words, book club books need to be challenging, or at least considered somewhat 'highbrow'. They *also* need to be pleasurable to read. Although none of the selections on book club lists that we have seen would be considered 'lowbrow' by literary critics, the books chosen as good book club books suggest that book club members develop an 'omnivorous' taste for books.[40] The selection of books permeates the highbrow/middlebrow classification boundaries constructed by cultural authorities such as academics and literary reviewers.

Recommendation and commodification

The process of recommendation and choice is an important issue within book clubs in part because of the overproduction of literature in the late twentieth and early twenty-first centuries. There are roughly 600,000 titles published worldwide each year.[41] Approximately 3500 of those titles are novels (not including genre and paperback fiction) from the US alone.[42] The number of books published each year in the UK has been quoted as high as 161,000 in 2005, whereas in 1990, 61,000 books were published.[43] In Canada, 8020 'trade books' and those classified by Statistics Canada as 'other' were published in English in 2000–01.[44] Another 920 were published in French.[45] The marketplace for fiction is extremely overcrowded, with more novels published every year. Large publishing houses are aware of the purchasing power possessed by book clubs, and so have allocated the human resources to plan, analyse and use marketing research that will facilitate the process of communicating with this segment of readers. In other words, publishers – and to a lesser extent booksellers – are using reading groups as a marketing resource. By promoting titles directly to reading groups, publishers are commodifying the process of word-of-mouth recommendation that is foundational to the social structure of book clubs. In 1993, Random House in the US targeted book clubs with a pamphlet entitled 'Reading Group Recommendations' featuring 15 Vintage paperback titles. Late that same year, Doubleday created a guide for Margaret Atwood's *The Robber Bride*, which was written specifically for book club readers and distributed through bookstores.[46] Then, in 1995, articles began appearing in the publishing industry press outlining the potential of the book club market segment.[47] In 1998, Random House in the UK began producing reading guides for 'classic' titles on their Vintage list, including Louis de Bernières's *Captain Corelli's Mandolin*. According to a marketing and sales representative at HarperCollins Canada, as early as 1999, more than 250 kits comprising publisher's guides, a newsletter and bookmarks aimed at book groups were sent to libraries and book stores across Canada.[48] Jane Friedman of Vintage Books is quoted in a 1995 *Globe and*

Mail article as saying about her organization's publication of reading group guides, 'For the first time in publishing history, we've figured out how to reach the true book addicts.'[49]

According to marketing representatives Karen Cossar and Steve Osegood of HarperCollins Canada, and Randy Chan of Random House Canada, it was not always easy for publishers to reach 'true book addicts'.[50] Advertising was not particularly successful until direct online marketing was adopted on a large scale by the big houses. Reading group guides partially fulfilled the objective of communicating with avid readers. The problem with the reading group guides, however, lay in their distribution. For example, a Transworld marketer found that the guides were not prominently displayed in bookstores and hence were not picked up by enthusiastic readers.[51] Moreover, the production and printing costs of the guides were prohibitively high: some figures given by various publishing houses quote upwards of $2 CDN per copy, a little more than £1.[52] When one considers that industry standards for promotion (advertising, tour costs, and catalogue production) are $1 CDN/per book/per print run, then the cost of producing reading guides seems exorbitant.[53]

An alternative to the high cost of producing, printing and distributing paper reading group guides are reading group reference websites. These virtual reviewer/recommendation sites fall into two broad categories: publisher-supported or independent. RandomHouse Canada, for example, hosts a website called 'Bookclubs.ca', which highlights titles they have chosen as book club-friendly titles from their relevant imprints. Another example is Penguin UK (www.readers.penguin.co.uk), which is heavily promoted through libraries, newspaper advertising and through reading events that Penguin supports financially. These large houses, along with publishers such as Simon & Shuster, Inc. (http://community.simonandschuster.com/) and HarperCollins (www.harpercollins.com/readersgroups.asp), offer book club members easy access to other readers, information about new books and author access. There are also opportunities to receive monthly electronic newsletters through e-mail alerts, and short notices through Twitter.

Proliferating at the end of the 1990s, and evolving with the addition of new genres, communication tools and recommendation services, sites such as www.readinggroupsguides.com and www.readinggroupchoices.com reflect the changing nature of text selection and recommendation among and within reading groups, as many members turned to the Internet as a research resource.

The Reading Group Guides website is one of seven author/reader sites under the umbrella company named the Book Report Network. For a fee of $100 US, publishers are able to submit reading guide copy to the website. Guaranteeing at least 100,000 hits per month, the company charges publishers and authors centre-page advertising rates of $750/month or $500/month for top right-side ad placement.[54] The company also sells advertorials[55] and special promotions. Tellingly, the first three titles highlighted in the August 2005 'We Recommend' section of the web page were all from the Bertelsmann family: Laura Pedersen's *Heart's Desire* (Ballantine); *Up from Orchard Street* (Bantam) by Eleanor Widmer; and *A Sudden Country* (Random House) by Karen Fisher. None of the publishers' names appear on the first page, but if a reader clicks the book's title, she is taken to a inside page providing purchasing information which includes the publisher name, promotional copy, discussion questions and jacket-type promotional text. A link to Amazon.com is also prominently displayed.

Banking on the timeless fascination that readers appear to have for authors, publishers in the US and Canada use author 'visits' as a way to acquire valuable demographic information. In addition to the previously mentioned HarperCollins webpage and Random House of Canada's Bookclubs.ca 'Connecting Authors with Book Clubs', Simon & Shuster's SimonSays.com sponsored a programme titled 'Author@cces' until 2007. On their website, Vintage/Anchor – divisions of Random House – share some of their in-house book club knowledge with booksellers offering 'facts' about reading groups, advice for targeting these readers, and comments from reading group members from across the US who have shared their experiences with the publishers. Booksellers are encouraged to participate in their 'Writers on Reading®' programme, which, according to promotional copy, 'is a reading group program which brings together booksellers, authors, and publishers with members of reading groups and book lovers in a setting where they can exchange ideas, enjoy stimulating conversation, and discover wonderful books'.[56] Promising 'significant publisher support', booksellers can, according to Vintage and Anchor Books, expect a '… creative and successful event that translates into happy repeat customers and increased sales'.

Sponsorship of face-to-face events such as Writers on Reading® appears to be more common in the UK than in North America. Penguin UK's interactive approach to their relationship-building with book club readers includes partnership with Orange, a telecommunication firm, and the bookseller Waterstones. Together, the organizations subsidize the Penguin Orange Reading Group prize, which garners a significant amount of media coverage. Newspapers run stories about the winning reading group, the runner-up groups, the panel of judges, the sponsors, and the books and authors mentioned in the prize entries.

Reader event days in the UK are another way in which publishers are able to connect directly with readers, and book club readers in particular, as these events are largely promoted to and attended by women who are already reading group members. Both Bloomsbury and Penguin in the UK support these events. On a smaller scale, and representing much more work from authors, are individual book group meetings. Both small and large publishers in North America and the UK encourage authors to visit individual book clubs as a way of grassroots marketing. For some authors, this is an enjoyable task, though whether or not an author finds discussing their work with individual readers pleasurable, meeting with groups is a laborious process. Still, it can be considered financially successful for authors whose publishers are (1) not large enough to provide a substantial promotional budget, (2) not willing to bank on an unknown author, or (3) unwilling to dedicate time, money, and effort for any variety of reasons.[57]

The 'early' years of marketing to book clubs tended to be an unsystematic endeavour. Members of marketing teams – often members of book clubs themselves or in close relations with friends and family members who participated in reading groups – would identify potential backlist titles that were 'accessible literary fiction'. Alternatively, editors would alert marketing staff when they thought a manuscript might be a 'good book club book' rather than responding directly to customer requests or interests.[58] In recent years, however, publishers have become much more sophisticated in tracking reading group tastes, practices and preferences.

In *Marketing Literature*, Squires shows how and why the years 1945–2000 saw an intense commodification of fiction.[59] She argues that 'the reversal of the traditional book economy of long-termism and the backlist towards a short-term, mass-market logic' had a profound influence on the publishing practices and industry philosophies during the latter half of the past century.[60] Reading groups do not only represent a specific market for new titles. Because of their wide-ranging reader tastes, publishers have found a way to ensure the survival of their backlist titles. Indeed, according to a marketing representative at HarperCollins Canada, backlist sales are the only way to truly track whether specific marketing to book clubs is effective.[61]

Penguin appears to have been the first house in Canada to begin the daunting task of collecting information about book club readers, but this is difficult to confirm because of the competitive and secretive nature of the business. Our records show that Random House Canada began collecting data on book clubs, and subsequently distributing e-mail marketing newsletters to subscribers, in early 2002. Information about reading group readers was, and still is, collected through publisher websites largely in the form of contests and invitations to readers to receive e-mail alerts and electronic newsletters.

Through analysis of scholarly publications such as Hartley's *Reading Groups*, trade press publications such as Mickey Pearlman's *What to Read*, and the information gathered through the contest applications, publishers with sufficient human and economic resources have been able to create databases of readers. These databases contain information on readers' reading preferences – both personal and book club picks – in addition to age, gender, education level, marital status and number of children living in the home. Of course, the coveted e-mail and postal addresses also form part of the record.

HarperCollins US collects both individual and group composition information for their 'Invite the Author' programme. When signing up, the reader is asked where the group meets, how many are in the group and where they buy their books. In addition, the reader is asked, 'Are you or have you been the leader of a reading group?'[62] By identifying these natural 'opinion leaders' or 'trusted others', as Rehberg Sedo has called these reading group cultural authorities, HarperCollins is able to communicate directly with those readers who have access to and are most likely to be respected by other readers inside and outside their own clubs. In sum, the publisher has identified a person who may spark the fire of a new best-seller book club book.

Sophisticated marketing research carried out by the large international houses has resulted in diverse reading group market segmentation that enables publishers to capitalize on the international appeal of specific genres. The marketing staff at HarperCollins Canada, for example, are members of an international book club task force that includes their colleagues in the US and the UK.[63] Sharing data collected in each other's markets, the individual marketing teams are able to identify potential transnational titles and share marketing techniques. While not evident in conversations with publishers, informal longitudinal analysis of the major publishers' websites indicates that there has been an evolution in the assumptions about what book clubs read. From promoting only contemporary fiction and classics, publishers have moved to highlighting books that might be considered obscure in order to capture those readers who do not, in their own words, want to 'read what everybody else is reading'. Other lucrative markets that have been identified are African American and religious book clubs.

The extensive book club site at readers.penguin.co.uk connects readers with clubs throughout the UK and across the Internet, and offers discounts to those who buy reading group titles directly through their site. They also promote 'Penguin UK's Group of the Month', through the following process: 'Each month we get a reading group to read and review a Penguin book. We send them enough copies of the book so that everyone can read the book together (and keep the books afterwards). In exchange we ask the group to send us a report on what they thought of the book and what type of discussion questions were raised.'[64] At a very low cost, Penguin UK accomplishes several marketing goals: (1) they are able to track and analyse reader discourse; (2) their database of reading groups expands; and (3) they acquire promotional text and discussion questions from a book club member, which is potentially perceived as more trustworthy than marketing copy. These efforts, combined with their already successful branding as a 'cherished national institution' (in the UK), aims to make reading group books synonymous with Penguin.[65] How successful they are remains to be seen.

In January 2005, CBC Arts online writer Li Robbins warned her audience against book club members. She wrote: 'Beware of book club fanatics: marionettes gently dancing for the publishing industry's puppeteers. These people want to tell you what to read, when, and how to read it.'[66] She argued that publishers have identified word-of-mouth marketing as the most successful means of promoting a book, and that they are using book club readers as their primary tool to create hype around chosen titles. 'What better conduit than book clubs?' she asked. Indeed, what better conduit? Robbins was correct in identifying that publishers have recognized the social and economic power of book clubs. However, Robbins was incorrect in her scathing generalization that 'Book clubs are being gently led to the well for a long drink of whatever publishers want them to swallow.' While the commodification of book club reader recommendation has proven to be successful for some publishers and some titles, book club readers offer some resistance by employing their own personal methods of reading selection. Most publishers promote primarily their contemporary fiction titles to book clubs, but in an online survey conducted in 2003, Rehberg Sedo found that in addition to contemporary fiction, clubs chose classical fiction, biographies and genre fiction.[67]

Arts Council England-funded www.bookgroup.info is an example of organized resistance. The site's creators were given funding specifically because they did not promote any one publisher while fulfilling the Arts Council's funding criteria for literature, which are (a) to fund new and existing writers and (b) to encourage readers to engage with literature.[68] The website mimics publisher book club reference pages, but because the producers communicate their independence they may be successful in reaching book club members who are not passive reader-consumers. Book clubs tend to be particular about the books and genres that they read and they have their own means and rules about how to choose and evaluate books.[69]

Many book club readers want to distinguish themselves from everyone else by reading titles that are obscure and that do not appear on other people's lists.[70] Book clubs and book club readers should be considered as agents who are influenced not only by the current ruling structures of economics and power within society, but also by their club's histories. While Long argues that 'most reading groups accept *unquestioningly* the systems of classification and evaluation generated by traditional cultural authorities',[71] we argue that this conclusion negates the 'trusted other', who is most often a reading woman's friend or family member whose book judgement she values. These people often include book club members outside the reader's club, supporting Hartley's argument that word of mouth is 'the powerful and distinctive engine of the reading group movement'.[72] Moreover, readers will often exchange lists with friends in other regions, provinces and countries looking for books that 'really worked well for ... book club this year'. Book club members, then, in addition to being part of a larger book club community, become their own cultural intermediaries and authorities. Of course, this is the engine that publishers are trying to fire.

A book club's search for what to read next can be viewed as an eternal quest, a pleasurable process in and of itself.[73] Groups formulate their own tastes as an interpretative community, which not only integrates each individual's preferences, but also works to shape them. Although the reader might bring titles to her group, it does not necessarily mean that the group will choose them. Each book club works to create their own specific book club genre. In other words, the readers learn a certain cultural taste based on the history of books chosen by the group, and will look for those types of books to read both as individuals and, often, within the group.

Mary Trentadue, a bookseller in Vancouver, British Columbia, Canada, believes book club readers in general are passive when it comes to searching for club reads. In an interview she said: 'I'd say largely most of them don't really care what they read as long as they're reading some good fiction, as long as that is what they want to read. But most, a lot of people, want to be told what to do.'[74] Indeed, in an online survey, Rehberg

Sedo found that 50 per cent of readers in virtual clubs and 43 per cent of those in face-to-face clubs use publisher-produced reading guides to choose their book club picks.[75] These findings, and the difficulties encountered by publishers, suggest that Trentadue's comments may be valid. Nevertheless, the eclectic reading lists of thousands of book clubs demonstrate that not all readers want to be told what to read. Some readers may not have the time or the skills to conduct research, and will seek advice from trusted others who certainly can include booksellers and publisher websites. Another reason for taking direction may be that the readers are participating in a culture in which it is important to give to one another and to share emotional experiences, a social interaction which has its own challenges and burdens. The situation of book club members and the social agency that they demonstrate is best understood as operating at the interface of ruling and non-ruling relations of power.[76] Readers want to demonstrate their cultural capital by choosing books that are viewed by cultural authorities as 'worthy' literary titles, and they must actively consider the tastes and practices that have been collectively determined within their book club.

Although publishers and book retailers have attempted to commodify the processes of choice enacted by reading groups, this activity has been fraught with challenges and difficulties. These have ranged from early failures in ineffective marketing and distribution to the more profound issue of incorporating what is essentially a social practice into the practice of business. The processes of choice undertaken by individual readers and reading groups are diverse, diffuse and frequently wilful, even if patterns emerge, and commodification can intervene. The marionettes cannot always be manipulated as the puppeteers would wish them to be.

Conclusions

Publishers readily acknowledge the purchasing power of book club members. There are also, however, more altruistic reasons for relationship-building between publishers and reader-consumers. Almost all the marketing individuals we spoke with – workers in both independent houses and the large multinationals – stress their own passion for reading and their belief that direct marketing to book clubs promotes reading (as opposed to specific titles) as an important social activity. This also makes commercial sense since publishers believe that communicating directly with book clubs in support of reading ultimately invites book buying that will (they hope) raise the profile and profits of their own company. This gestures towards the paradoxical workings of the culture industries, in which commercial and cultural forces are combined, often with a certain degree of difficulty.

In this chapter we have suggested that virtual and face-to-face book clubs are manifestations of social practices. Through book clubs, readers not only commune with the book, but also with fellow readers. There is a certain 'grassroots' feel to the contemporary reading group movement, where social networks count for more in terms of recommendation than the interventions of big business. Yet, social networks or communities are formed through book clubs where issues of literary taste are informed and reinforced by cultural hierarchies that are themselves influenced by marketing. Nonetheless, some readers actively resist marketing efforts in order to distinguish themselves from other readers and other book clubs.

Thinking about the relationship between publishers and book clubs allows us to reconfigure the relationship between readers, publishers and books at the turn of the twenty-first century. If we think of publishers purely in their role as producers of books, we, and they, will tend to interpret their initiatives aimed at book clubs purely in terms of profit. If, however, we consider a model of publishing that places readers at its centre, then the practices of publishers might start to orient themselves towards the various and variable desires of all readers. The element of responsiveness to book clubs that some publishers can afford in both human resources and economic capital might be seen as part of this process. If we switch attention from the world of production to the world of consumption, placing readers at the very centre of the publishing process, it is perhaps possible that a more responsive and diverse literary marketplace will come into being. Publishers will respond and attempt to control fluctuations in taste, but in order to produce materials that are desirable to their readers they must continually hold in balance the reactive and proactive nature of the enterprise. This, essentially, is why reading groups are so important to publishers: they indicate the absolute centrality of readers to books and the publishing industry.

Notes

1. Book clubs are commonly referred to as reading groups in the UK. Because of the cross-regional nature of this study, we will use the terms interchangeably throughout this chapter.
2. Penguin Readers' Brochure.
3. See, among many others, Danielle Fuller, *Writing the Everyday: Women's Textual Communities in Atlantic Canada* (Montreal and Kingston: McGill-Queen's University Press, 2004); Christopher Gasson, *Who Owns Whom in British*

Book Publishing (London: Bookseller Publications, 2002); Roy MacSkimming, *The Perilous Trade: Publishing Canada's Writers* (Toronto: McClelland & Stewart, 2003); Simone Murray, *Mixed Media: Feminist Presses and Publishing Politics* (London: Pluto, 2004); André Schiffrin, *The Business of Books: How International Conglomerates Took Over Publishing and Changed the Way We Read* (London: Verso, 2000); Aritha Van Herk, 'Publishing and Perishing with no Parachute', in *How Canadians Communicate*, ed. David Taras, Frits Pannekoek and Maria Bakardjieva (Calgary, AB: University of Calgary Press, 2003).

4. Jon Bekken, 'Books and Commerce in an Age of Virtual Capital: the Changing Political Economy of Bookselling', in *Citizenship and Participation in the Information Age*, ed. Roma Harris and Manjunath Pendakur (Aurora, Ontario: Garamond Press, 2002); Claire Squires, *Marketing Literature: the Making of Contemporary Writing in Britain* (Basingstoke: Palgrave Macmillan, 2007).
5. Danielle Fuller, *Writing the Everyday*, 46–58; Elizabeth Long, 'The Cultural Meaning of Concentration in Publishing', *Book Research Quarterly* 1, 4 (1985–1986): 3–27.
6. Pierre Bourdieu, *The Field of Cultural Production* (New York: Polity Press, 1993); Giles Clark and Angus Phillips, *Inside Book Publishing*, 4th edn (London: Routledge, 2008); David Hesmondhalgh, *The Cultural Industries* (London: Sage Publications, 2002).
7. Li Robbins, 'Book Club Virgin (and Proud of It): the Scorn of the Solitary Reader', CBC, at www.cbc.ca/arts/books/bookclubvirgin.html (accessed 6 December 2009).
8. Jenny Hartley, *Reading Groups* (Oxford: Oxford University Press, 2001), ix.
9. Ibid., vii.
10. Darren K. Carlson, 'Poll Shows Continuing Strong American Reading Habits', in *Nonfiction More Popular than Fiction: Book Discussion Groups not a Large Factor Yet* (Princeton, NJ: Gallup News Service, 1999).
11. For discussion on imagined communities, see Benedict Anderson, *Imagined Communities: Reflections on the Origin and Spread of Nationalism*, revised edn (London: Verso, 1991). See also Rehberg Sedo's Introduction, Snape (Chapter 3) and Howie (Chapter 4) above.
12. Rehberg Sedo, 'Badges of Wisdom, Spaces for Being: a Study of Contemporary Women's Book Clubs', PhD dissertation, Simon Fraser University (2004), 143–68.
13. Squires, 'Novelistic Production and the Publishing Industry in Britain and Ireland', in *Companion to the British and Irish Novel 1945–2000*, ed. Brian Shaffer (Oxford: Blackwell, 2004), 181.
14. John Carey, *The Intellectuals and the Masses* (London: Faber and Faber, 1992); Queenie D. Leavis, *Fiction and the Reading Public* (London: Chatto & Windus, 1932).
15. Geoffrey Faber, *A Publisher Speaking* (London: Faber and Faber, 1934), 29.
16. Jason Epstein, *Book Business: Publishing Past, Present, and Future* (New York: W.W. Norton & Company, 2001); Fred Kobrak and Beth Luey, *The Structure of International Publishing in the 1990s* (New Brunswick: Transaction Publishers, 1992); Schiffrin, *The Business of Books*; Thomas Whiteside, *The Blockbuster Complex: Conglomerates, Show Business & Book Publishing* (Irvington, NY: Wesleyan University Press; distributed by Columbia University Press, 1981).
17. Long, 'The Cultural Meaning of Concentration in Publishing', 9.

18. Janice Radway, *A Feeling for Books: The Book-of-the Month Club, Literary Taste and Middle-Class Desire* (Chapel Hill: University of North Carolina Press, 1997). See also the seminal work of Lawrence W. Levine, *Highbrow/Lowbrow: the Emergence of Cultural Hierarchy in America*, The William E. Massey, Sr. Lectures in the History of American Civilization (Cambridge, MA: Harvard University Press, 1988) for a discussion of the historical foundations of a cultural hierarchy in the US as a market reaction, especially pages 230–1; John Seabrook, *Nobrow: the Culture of Marketing, the Marketing of Culture* (New York: Vintage, 2001).
19. Squires, *Marketing Literature*.
20. Clark and Phillips, *Inside Book Publishing*, 15.
21. Laura Miller, *Reluctant Capitalists: Bookselling and the Culture of Consumption* (Chicago: University of Chicago Press, 2006).
22. Stephen Cooke, 'Approachable Arden Shares Love of Books', *Sunday Herald*, 9 December 2001.
23. Hartley, *Reading Groups*, 38.
24. Rehberg Sedo, 'Readers in Reading Groups: an On-Line Survey of Face-to-Face and Virtual Book Clubs', *Convergence: the International Journal of Research into New Media Technologies* 9, 1 (2003): 66–90; 'Badges of Wisdom', 200–3.
25. Elizabeth Long, 'The Book as Mass Commodity: the Audience Perspective', *Book Research Quarterly* 3, 1 (1987): 19.
26. Ibid.
27. Hartley, *Reading Groups*; Long, *Book Clubs: Women and the Uses of Reading in Everyday Life* (Chicago: University of Chicago Press, 2003); Rehberg Sedo, 'Badges of Wisdom'.
28. Long, 'The Book as Mass Commodity', 15.
29. Hartley, *Reading Groups*; Rehberg Sedo, 'Badges of Wisdom'.
30. Long, 'The Book as Mass Commodity', 14.
31. This finding is different from that of a 2009 ReadingGroupGuide.com survey, which claims that only 15 per cent of groups read paperback only. The for-profit website's survey is accessible through www.readinggroupguides.com/surveys/survey_results.asp.
32. Martha Burns and Alice Dillon, *Reading Group Journal: Notes in the Margin* (New York: Abbeville Publishing Group, 1999); Harry Heft and Peter O'Brien, *Building a Better Book Club* (Toronto: Macmillan Canada, 1999); David Laskin and Holly Hughs, *The Reading Group Book: the Complete Guide to Starting and Sustaining a Reading Group, with Annotated Lists of 250 Titles for Provocative Discussion* (New York: Plume, 1995); Victoria Golden McMains, *The Readers' Choice: 200 Book Club Favorites* (New York: Quill, 2000); Kira Stevens and Ellen Moore, *Good Books Lately: the One-Stop Resource for Book Groups and Other Greedy Readers* (New York: St Martin's Griffin, 2004); Mickey Pearlman, *What to Read: the Essential Guide for Reading Group Members and other Book Lovers*, 2nd edn (New York: HarperCollins, 1999).
33. Rehberg Sedo, 'Badges of Wisdom'.
34. Stanley Fish, *Is there a Text in This Class? The Authority of Interpretive Communities* (Cambridge, MA: Harvard University Press, 1980), 11.
35. Ibid.
36. Long, 'The Book as Mass Commodity', 20.
37. Tony Bennett, Michael Emmison and John Frow, *Accounting for Tastes* (Cambridge: Cambridge University Press, 1999); Pierre Bourdieu, *Distinction: a*

Social Critique of the Judgement of Taste, trans. Richard Nice (1979; Cambridge, MA: Harvard University Press, 1984); Paul DiMaggio, 'Classification in Art', *American Sociological Review* 52 (1987): 440–55.

38. Rehberg Sedo, 'Badges of Wisdom'.
39. Radway, *A Feeling for Books*, 528, emphasis in original.
40. For a discussion on 'omnivorous' reading, see Bennett et al., *Accounting for Tastes*, 187–95.
41. 'The Evidence in Hand: Report of the Task Force on the Artifact in Library Collections', Council on Library and Information Resources, http://www.clir.org/pubs/reports/pub103/appendix1.html (accessed 21 December 2010).
42. M.J. Rose, 'Everything Old is New Again: Reinventing the Publishing Model', Poets & Writers: From Inspiration to Publication, http://www.pw.org/mag/rose0205.htm (accessed 22 July 2005).
43. Robert McCrum, 'E-Read All About It', *Guardian*, at http://books.guardian.co.uk/print/0,3858,5374656-110368,00.html (accessed 15 January 2006).
44. 'Profile of Book Publishing and Exclusive Agency, for English Language Firms', Canadian Statistics, http://www40.statcan.ca/l01/cst01/arts02.htm (accessed 21 December 2010).
45. 'Profile of Book Publishing and Exclusive Agency, for French Language Firms', Statistics Canada, http://www40.statcan.ca/l01/cst01/arts05.htm (accessed 22 December 2010).
46. See Ivy (Chapter 8 above) for an analysis of contemporary reading guides.
47. Linda Leith, 'Ladies of the Club: Spontaneous by Nature, Reading Groups Betray Few Common Traits, except that they're Social, Self-Educating and Very Likely Sisterly', *Quill & Quire* (May 1995): 8–9.
48. Fiona Lamb, personal communication, 11 November 1999.
49. Val Ross, 'Gathered Together in Literature's Name', *Globe & Mail*, 14 January 1995.
50. Personal communication, 5 May 2004.
51. Elizabeth Dare, personal communication, 18 May 2001.
52. Joy Gugeler, personal communication, 4 February 2003; Lynn Cadence, personal communication, 3 February 2003.
53. Joy Gugeler, email communication, 13 October 2003.
54. This information was found at the following webpage, but is no longer available: www.tbrnetwork.com/advertising/advertising_aug2004.pdf (accessed 24 August 2005).
55. Advertorials is a marketing term for advertisements that appear as if they were editorials.
56. 'Reading Group Center', http://www.randomhouse.com/vintage/read/booksellers.html (accessed 26 August 2005).
57. Loranne Brown, personal communication, 10 May 2001; Catherine Gildiner, personal communication, 12 February 2003.
58. Cadence, personal communication; Randy Chan, personal communication, 13 February 2003; Dare, personal communication; Lamb, personal communication; Liz Smith, personal communication, 18 May 2001.
59. Squires, *Marketing Literature*, 20–7.
60. Ibid., 26.
61. Steve Osgoode, personal communication, 5 May 2004.

62. This information was retrieved from a survey in which Rehberg Sedo participated at the following webpage, but it is no longer available: www.harpercollins.com/survey.net (accessed 26 August 2005).
63. Osgoode, personal communication.
64. 'Group of the Month', Penguin, at http://readers.penguin.co.uk/nf/shared/WebDisplay/0,,70753_1_2,00.html (accessed 12 September 2009).
65. Raymond N. MacKenzie, 'Penguin Books', in *British Literary Publishing Houses, 1881–1965*, ed. Jonathan Rose and Patricia Anderson (Detroit: Gale Research, 1991).
66. Robbins, 'Book Club Virgin'.
67. Rehberg Sedo, 'Readers in Reading Groups', 82.
68. 'Open Book', BBC.
69. Hartley, *Reading Groups*; Long, *Book Clubs*; Rehberg Sedo, 'Badges of Wisdom'.
70. These conclusions are informed by Bourdieu, *Distinction*. Considering Bourdieu's thesis, one might conclude that the formal education system influences the value that readers place on literature; their expectations of literary interpretation; and how cultural capital gained from the educational setting can be transferred into other settings.
71. Long, 'The Book as Mass Commodity', 18, our emphasis.
72. Hartley, *Reading Groups*, ix.
73. Rehberg Sedo, 'Badges of Wisdom'.
74. Mary Trentadue, personal communication, 10 January 2000.
75. Rehberg Sedo, 'Readers in Reading Groups'.
76. See Dorothy E. Smith, 'Feminist Reflections on Political Economy', *Studies in Political Economy* 30, Autumn (1989): 37–59. This elaboration of the concept of power situates political, legal, economic and institutional structures that organize society as the ruling relations of power. Non-ruling civic and domestic relations of power are those that are negotiated among and between individuals and groups.

Bibliography

Adams, Thomas R. and Nicolas Barker, 'A New Model for the Study of the Book', in *A Potencie of Life: Books in Society*, ed. Nicolas Barker, London: British Library, 1993, 5–43.
Adkins, Lisa and Beverley Skeggs, *Feminism after Bourdieu*, Oxford and Malden, MA: Blackwell, 2004.
Adler, Mortimer J. (ed.), *The Great Conversation*, Great Books of the Western World, Vol. I, Chicago: Encyclopedia Britannica, 1952.
——, *Philosopher at Large: an Intellectual Biography*, New York: Macmillan, 1977.
——, *The Paideia Proposal: an Educational Manifesto*, New York: Macmillan, 1982.
——, 'Reforming Education: the Opening of the American Mind', ed. Geraldine Van Doren, New York: Macmillan, 1988.
——, *A Second Look in the Rearview Mirror: Further Autobiographical Reflections of a Philosopher at Large*, New York: Macmillan, 1992.
Aftab, Tahera, 'Reform Societies and Women's Education in Northern India in the Later 19th Century', *Journal of the Pakistan Historical Society* 35, 2 (1987): 121–35.
Allen, James Sloan, *The Romance of Commerce and Culture: Capitalism, Modernism, and the Chicago-Aspen Crusade for Cultural Reform*, Chicago: University of Chicago Press, 1983.
Allen, Katie, 'Ross Confident of Book Club Future', *thebookseller.com*, 2009, at http://www.thebookseller.com/news/ross-confident-book-club-future.html.
Altick, Richard D., 'Varieties of Readers' Response: the Case of Dombey and Son', *Yearbook of English Studies* 10 (1980): 79.
Anderson, Benedict, *Imagined Communities: Reflections on the Origin and Spread of Nationalism*, revised edn, London: Verso, 1991.
Ang, Ien, 'Feminist Desire and Female Pleasure: on Janice Radway's *Reading the Romance*', in *Living Room Wars: Rethinking Media Audiences for a Postmodern World*, London: Routledge, 1996.
Ashmore, Harry, *Unseasonable Truths: the Life of Robert Maynard Hutchins*, Boston: Little, Brown, 1989.
Atwood, Margaret, 'Introduction', in *The Book Group Book*, ed. Ellen Slezak, Chicago: Chicago Review Press, 2000.
Aubrey, Timothy, 'Beware the Furrow of the Middlebrow: Searching for Paradise on the Oprah Winfrey Show', *Modern Fiction Studies* 52, 2 (2006): 350–73.
Augst, Thomas, 'Introduction: American Libraries and Agencies of Culture', in *The Library as an Agency of Culture*, ed. Thomas Augst and Wayne A. Wiegand, Lawrence, KS: American Studies, 2001, 5–22.
Austin, B.F., *Woman, Her Character, Culture and Calling a Full Discussion of Woman's Work in the Home, the School, the Church and the Social Circle, with an Account of Her Successful Labors in Moral and Social Reform*, Ottawa: Canadian Institute for Historical Microreproductions, 1980.
Baker Miller, Jean, *Toward a New Pyschology of Women*, Boston: Beacon Press, 1976.
Barnard, Rita, 'Oprah's Paton, or South Africa and the Globalization of Suffering', *English Studies in Africa* 47 (2004): 85–108.

Baron, Dennis, 'I Teach English – and I Hate Reader's Guides', *Chronicle of Higher Education* 4 (2002): 5.
Belasco Smith, Susan, 'Serialization and the Nature of *Uncle Tom's Cabin*', in *Periodical Literature in Nineteenth Century America*, ed. Kenneth M Price and Susan Belasco Smith, Charlottesville: University of Virginia Press, 1995, 69–89.
Bekken, Jon, 'Books and Commerce in an Age of Virtual Capital: the Changing Political Economy of Bookselling', in *Citizenship and Participation in the Information Age*, ed. Roma Harris and Manjunath Pendakur, Aurora, Ontario: Garamond Press, 2002, 231–49.
Benjamin, Jessica, *The Bonds of Love: Psychoanalysis, Feminism and the Problem of Domination*, London: Virago, 1990.
Bennett, Tony, Michael Emmison and John Frow, *Accounting for Tastes*, Cambridge: Cambridge University Press, 1999.
Berg, Temma, '"What Do You Know?"; or, the Question of Reading in Groups and Academic Authority', *LIT: Literature Interpretation Theory* 19, 2 (2008): 123–54.
Bessman Taylor, Joan, 'Readers' Advisory – Good for What?' *Reference & User Services Quarterly* 46, 4 (2007): 33.
——, 'Readers' Advisory – Good for What? Non-Appeal, Discussability, and Book Groups (Part 2)', *Reference & User Services Quarterly* 47, 1 (2007): 26.
——, 'When Adults Talk in Circles: Book Groups and Contemporary Reading Practices', PhD dissertation, University of Illinois at Urbana-Champaign, 2007.
Birkets, Sven, *The Gutenberg Elegies: the Fate of Reading in an Electronic Age*, Boston: Faber and Faber, 1994.
Birley, Derek, *Land of Sport and Glory: Sport and British Society 1887–1910*, Manchester: Manchester University Press, 1995.
Blair, Karen, *The Clubwoman as Feminist: True Womanhood Redefined, 1868–1914*, New York: Holmes & Meier Publishers, 1980.
Boddy, Ernest H., 'The Dalton Book Club: a Brief History', *Library History* 9 (1992): 97–105.
Bourdieu, Pierre, *Distinction: a Social Critique of the Judgment of Taste*, trans. Richard Nice, Cambridge, MA: Harvard University Press, 1984 [1979].
——, *The Field of Cultural Production*, New York: Polity Press, 1993.
Boyko-Head, Christine, 'Stay at Home Writers: the Women's Literary Club of St. Catherine's', paper presented at the Popular Culture Conference, San Diego, CA, 1999.
Brantlinger, Patrick, *The Reading Lesson: the Threat of Mass Literacy in Nineteenth Century British Fiction*, Bloomington: Indiana University Press, 1998.
Brewer, John, 'Reconstructing the Reader: Prescriptions, Texts and Strategies in Anna Larpent's Reading', in *The Practice and Representation of Reading in England*, ed. James Raven, Helen Small and Naomi Tadmor, Cambridge and New York: Cambridge University Press, 1996, 226–45.
Brown, Mary Ellen, *Soap Opera and Women's Talk*, London: Sage, 1994.
Browning, Elizabeth Barrett, *Aurora Leigh*, New York and Boston: C.S. Francis & Co., 1857. [Susan B. Anthony Collection, Library of Congress.]
Burbules, Nicholas C., 'Rethinking Dialogue in Networked Spaces', *Cultural Studies – Critical Methodologies* 6, 1 (2006): 107–22.
Burns, Martha and Alice Dillon, *Reading Group Journal: Notes in the Margin*, New York: Abbeville Publishing Group, 1999.

Burwell, Catherine, 'Reading Lolita in Times of War: Women's Book Clubs and the Politics of Reception', *Intercultural Education* 18, 4 (2007): 281–96.

Bush, Julia, *Edwardian Ladies and Imperial Power*, London: University of Leicester Press, 2000.

Carey, John, *The Intellectuals and the Masses*, London: Faber and Faber, 1992.

Carlson, Darren K., 'Poll Shows Continuing Strong American Reading Habits', in *Nonfiction More Popular than Fiction; Book Discussion Groups not a Large Factor Yet*, Princeton, NJ: Gallup News Service, 1999.

Chabot Davis, Kimberly, 'Oprah's Book Club and the Politics of Cross-Racial Empathy', *International Journal of Cultural Studies* 7, 4 (2004): 399–419.

——, 'White Book Clubs and African American Literature: the Promise and Limitations of Cross-Racial Empathy', *LIT: Literature Interpretation Theory* 19, 2 (2008): 155–86.

Charmaz, Kathy, 'The Grounded Theory Method: and Explication and Interpretation', in *More Grounded Theory Methodology: a Reader*, ed. B.G. Glaser, Mill Valley, CA: Sociology Press, 1994.

——, *Constructing Grounded Theory: a Practical Guide through Qualitative Analysis*, London: Sage, 2010.

Chartier, Roger, *The Order of Books: Readers, Authors, and Libraries in Europe between the Fourteenth and Eighteenth Centuries*, trans. Lydia G. Cochrane, Stanford, CA: Stanford University Press, 1994.

Chodorow, Nancy, *The Reproduction of Mothering: Pyschoanalysis and the Sociology of Gender*, Berkeley: University of California Press, 1978.

——, *Feminism and Psychoanalytic Theory*, New Haven: Yale University Press, 1989.

Clark, Giles and Angus Phillips, *Inside Book Publishing*, 4th edn, London: Routledge, 2008.

Clark, Peter, *British Clubs and Societies, 1580–1800: the Origins of an Associational World*, New York: Oxford University Press, 2000.

Clee, Nicholas, 'The Book Business', *New Statesman*, 21 March 2005, at http://www.newstatesman.com/200503210047.

Colclough, Stephen, *Consuming Texts: Readers and Reading Communities, 1695–1870*, Basingstoke and New York: Palgrave Macmillan, 2007.

Collins, John Churton, 'The National Home Reading Union and its Prospects', *Contemporary Review* (August 1890): 193–211.

Collins, Philip Arthur William, *Charles Dickens: the Critical Heritage*, London: Taylor & Francis e-Library, 2003.

Collins, Wilkie, *My Miscellanies*, London: S. Low, 1863.

Cooke, Stephen, 'Approachable Arden Shares Love of Books', *Sunday Herald*, 9 December 2001, B6.

Council on Library and Information Resources, 'The Evidence in Hand: Report of the Task Force on the Artifact in Library Collections', at http://www.clir.org/pubs/reports/pub103/appendix1.html.

Curran, James, 'Literary Editors, Social Networks and Cultural Tradition', in *Media Organizations in Society*, ed. James Curran, London: Arnold, 2000.

Cusk, Rachel, 'The Outsider', *Guardian*, 20 August 2005, at http://books.guardian.co.uk/review/story/0,12084,1551867,00.html.

Darnton, Robert, *The Literary Underground of the Old Regime*. Cambridge, MA and London: Harvard University Press, 1982.

——, 'First Steps Towards a History of Reading', in *The Kiss of Lamourette: Reflections in Cultural History*, New York: W.W. Norton, 1990, 154–91.
Davidson, Cathy N., 'Towards a History of Books and Readers', *American Quarterly* 40, 1 (1988): 7–17.
——, *Reading in America: Literature & Social History*, Baltimore: Johns Hopkins University Press, 1989.
——, *Revolution and the Word: the Rise of the Novel in America*, expanded edn, New York: Oxford University Press, 2004.
Day, Leanne, 'Brisbane Literary Circle: the Quest for Universal Culture', *Journal of Australian Studies* 23, 63 (1999): 87–93.
De Lauretis, Teresa, ed., *Feminist Studies, Critical Studies: Theories of Contemporary Culture*, London: Macmillan, 1986.
Decker, Jeffrey Louis, 'Saint Oprah', *Modern Fiction Studies* 52, 1 (Spring 2006): 169–78.
Dick, Archie L., '"To Make the People of South Africa Proud of Their Membership of the Great British Empire": Home Reading Unions in South Africa, 1900–1914', *Libraries & Culture* 40, 1 (2005): 1–24.
Dickens, Charles, *The Letters of Charles Dickens*, ed. Graham Storey and Kathleen Tillotson, 40, Oxford: Oxford University Press, 1995.
——, *Little Dorrit*, ed. Stephen Wall and Helen Small, Harmondsworth and New York: Penguin, 1998.
DiMaggio, Paul, 'Classification in Art', *American Sociological Review* 52 (1987): 440–55.
Duncombe, John, *The Feminiad, a Poem (1754)*, Los Angeles: Augustan Reprint Society, 1981. [William Andrews Clark Memorial Library, University of California.]
Dzuback, Mary Ann, *Robert M. Hutchins: Portrait of an Educator*, Chicago: University of Chicago Press, 1991.
Epstein, Jason, *Book Business: Publishing Past, Present, and Future*, New York: W.W. Norton & Company, 2001.
Epstein, Joseph, 'The Great Bookie: Mortimer Adler, 1902–2001', *Weekly Standard*, 23 July 2001.
Faber, Geoffrey, *A Publisher Speaking*, London: Faber and Faber, 1934.
Fast, Rosabel, 'The Impact of Sponsorship: the University of Manitoba's Rural Adult Education Program, 1936–1945', M.Ed., University of Alberta, 1991.
Fergus, Jan, *Provincial Readers in Eighteenth-Century England*, Oxford: Oxford University Press, 2006.
Fish, Stanley, *Is there a Text in This Class? The Authority of Interpretive Communities*, Cambridge, MA: Harvard University Press, 1980.
——, *Doing What Comes Naturally: Change, Rhetoric, and the Practice of Theory in Literary and Legal Studies*, Oxford: Clarendon Press, 1989.
Fister, Barbara, 'Reading as a Contact Sport: Online Book Groups and the Social Dimensions of Reading', *Reference & User Services Quarterly* 44, 4 (2005): 303–9.
Fitch, J.G., 'The Chautauqua Reading Circle', *Nineteenth Century* 24 (1888): 487–500.
Flax, Jane, *Disputed Subjects: Essays on Psychoanalysis, Politics and Philosophy*, New York: Routledge, 1993.
Flint, Kate, *The Woman Reader 1873–1914*, Oxford: Oxford University Press, 1993.

Flynn, Elizabeth and Patrocinio Schweickert, eds, *Gender and Reading: Essays on Readers, Texts and Context*, Baltimore: Johns Hopkins University Press, 1986.

Forster, John, *The Life of Charles Dickens*, London and Toronto, New York: J.M. Dent & Sons; E. P. Dutton & Co., 1927.

Fowler, Karen Joy, *The Jane Austen Book Club*, New York: Putnam, 2004.

Freedman, Diane P., Olivia Frey and Frances Murphy Zauhar, eds, *The Intimate Critique: Autobiographical Literary Criticism*, Durham: Duke University Press, 1993.

French, Doris, *Ishbel and Empire: a Biography of Lady Aberdeen*, Toronto: Dundurn Press, 1988.

Freud, Esther, *The Sea House*, London: Hamish Hamilton, 2003.

Freund, Elizabeth, *The Return of the Reader: Reader-Response Criticism*, London: Methuen, 1987.

Fuller, Danielle, *Writing the Everyday: Women's Textual Communities in Atlantic Canada*, Montreal and Kingston: McGill-Queen's University Press, 2004.

Fuller, Danielle and DeNel Rehberg Sedo, 'A Reading Spectacle for the Nation: the CBC and "Canada Reads"', *Journal of Canadian Studies* 40, 1 (2006): 5–36.

Gaskell, Elizabeth Cleghorn, *Wives and Daughters. A Novel*, New York: Harper & Brothers, 1866.

Gasson, Christopher, *Who Owns Whom in British Book Publishing*, London: Bookseller Publications, 2002.

Genette, Gerard, *Paratexts: Thresholds of Interpretation*, Cambridge: Cambridge University Press, 1997.

Geraghty, Christine, *Women and Soap Opera: a Study of Prime Time Soaps*, Cambridge: Polity Press, 1991.

Gilligan, Carol, *In a Different Voice: Psychological Theory and Women's Development*, Cambridge, MA: Harvard University Press, 1982.

Gilmore-Lehne, William J., *Reading Becomes a Necessity of Life: Material and Cultural Life in Rural New England, 1780–1835*, Knoxville: University of Tennessee Press, 1989.

Gilmore, Michael T., *American Romanticism and the Marketplace*, Chicago: University of Chicago Press, 1985.

Gladwell, Malcolm, *The Tipping Point: How Little Things Can Make a Big Difference*, Boston: Little Brown, 2000.

Glaessner, Verina, 'Gendered Fictions', in *Understanding Television*, ed. A Goodwin and G. Whannel, London: Routledge, 1990.

Glaser, B.G., 'The Constant Comparative Method', in *More Grounded Theory: a Reader*, ed. B.G. Glaser, Mill Valley, CA: Sociology Press, 1994.

González, Norma Linda, 'Nancy Drew: Girls' Literature, Women's Reading Groups, and the Transmission of Literacy', *Journal of Literacy Research* 29, 2 (1997): 221–51.

Great Books Foundation Archive, Chicago.

Greene, Gayle and Coppelia Kahn, eds, *Changing Subjects: the Making of Feminist Literary Criticism*, New York: Routledge, 1993.

Greenwood, Thomas, 'The Great Fiction Question', in *Library Year Book*, London: Cassell, 1897, 107–16.

Gregory, Patricia, 'Women's Experience of Reading in St. Louis Book Clubs', PhD dissertation, Saint Louis University, 2000.

Griffin, Kathy, *Official Book Club Selection: a Memoir According to Kathy Griffin*, New York: Ballantine Books, 2009.

Griffin, Linda, 'An Analysis of Meaning Creation through the Integration of Sociology and Literature: a Critical Ethnography of a Romance Reading Group', PhD dissertation, University of Houston, 1999.
Gruber Garvey, Ellen, 'The Power of Recirculation: Scrapbooks and the Reception of Nineteenth-Century Books', in *New Directions in American Reception Study*, ed. Philip Goldstein and James L. Machor, Oxford and New York: Oxford University Press, 2008, 211–31.
Guest, Harriet, *Small Change: Women, Learning, Patriotism, 1750–1810*, Chicago: University of Chicago Press, 2000.
Haag, Laurie L., 'Oprah Winfrey: the Construction of Intimacy in the Talk Show Setting', *Journal of Popular Culture* 26, 4 (1993): 115–22.
Habermas, Jürgen, *The Structural Transformation of the Public Sphere: an Inquiry into a Category of Bourgeois Society*, Studies in Contemporary German Social Thought, Cambridge, MA: MIT Press, 1989.
Haldane, Elizabeth, *From One Century to Another: the Reminiscences of Elizabeth S. Haldane*, London: Maclehose, 1937.
Hall, R. Mark, 'The "Oprahfication" of Literacy: Reading "Oprah's Book Club"', *College English* 65, 6 (2003): 646–67.
Hammerton, A. James, 'Gender and Migration', in *Gender and Empire*, ed. Philippa Levine, Oxford: Oxford University Press, 2004, 156–80.
Hammond, Brean S., *Professional Imaginative Writing in England, 1670–1740: Hackney for Bread*, Oxford: Clarendon, 1997.
Hanson, Clare, *Hysterical Fictions*, Basingstoke: Macmillan, 2000.
Hartley, Jenny, *Reading Groups*, Oxford: Oxford University Press, 2001.
——, *The Reading Groups Book*, 2002–2003 edn, Oxford: Oxford University Press, 2003.
Hedrick, Joan D., *Harriet Beecher Stowe: a Life*, New York: Oxford University Press, 1994.
Heft, Harry and Peter O'Brien. *Building a Better Book Club*, Toronto: Macmillan Canada, 1999.
Hesmondhalgh, David, *The Cultural Industries*, London: Sage Publications, 2002.
hooks, bell, *Talking Back: Thinking Feminist, Thinking Black*, Boston: Sheba Feminist Publishers, 1989.
Howie, Linsey, 'Speaking Subjects: a Reading of Women's Book Groups', PhD dissertation, La Trobe University, 1998.
Howsam, Leslie, *Old Books & New Histories: an Orientation to Studies in Book & Print Culture*, Toronto: University of Toronto Press, 2006.
Hughes, Linda K. and Michael Lund, *The Victorian Serial*, Victorian Literature and Culture Series, Charlottesville: University Press of Virginia, 1991.
Hutchins, Robert Maynard, *The Higher Learning in America*, New Haven: Yale University Press, 1936.
Hutchinson, Roger, *Empire Games: the British Invention of Twentieth Century Sport*, Edinburgh: Macmillan, 1996.
Hyman, Sidney, 'Mortimer J. Adler (1902–2001): a Century of Great Books', *Common Review* 1, 2 (2002): 34–9.
Jacobsohn, Rachel W., *The Reading Group Handbook*, New York: Hyperion, 1998.
Jeffries, Stuart, 'The Booksellers', *Guardian*, 26 February 2004, http://books.guardian.co.uk/print/03858,4867043-99930,00.html.

Jordan-Smith, Paul and Laurel Horton, 'Communities of Practice: Traditional Music and Dance', *Western Folklore* 60, 2,3 (2001): 103–9.
Jordan, Judith V., 'Empathy and Self Boundaries', in *Women's Growth in Connection: Writings from the Stone Center*, ed. J.V. Jordan, A.G. Kaplan, J.B Miller, I. Stiver and J.L. Surrey, New York: The Guilford Press, 1991, 67–80.
——, 'The Meaning of Mutality', in *Women's Growth in Connection: Writings from the Stone Center*, ed. J.V. Jordan, A.G. Kaplan, J.B. Miller, I. Stiver and J.L. Surrey, New York: The Guilford Press, 1991, 81–96.
——, Alexandra G. Kaplan, Jean Baker Miller, Irene Stiver and J.L. Surrey, *Women's Growth in Connection: Writings from the Stone Center*, New York: The Guilford Press, 1991.
Kellner, Douglas, 'Critical Pedagogy, Cultural Studies, and Radical Democracy at the Turn of the Millennium: Reflections on the Work of Henry Giroux', *Critical Studies/Critical Methodologies* 1, 2 (2001): 220–39.
Kelly, Frank K., *Court of Reason: Robert Hutchins and the Fund for the Republic*, New York: Free Press, 1981.
Kelly, Gary, 'Bluestocking Feminism and Writing in Context', in *Bluestocking Feminism: Writings of the Bluestocking Circle, 1738–1785*, ed. Gary Kelly, London: Pickering and Chatto, 1999.
Kobrak, Fred and Beth Luey, *The Structure of International Publishing in the 1990s*, New Brunswick: Transaction Publishers, 1992.
Konchar Farr, Cecilia, *Reading Oprah: How Oprah's Book Club Changed the Way America Reads*, New York: University of New York Press, 2005.
—— and Jaime Harker, *The Oprah Affect: Critical Essays on Oprah's Book Club*, Albany, NY: State University of New York Press, 2008.
Kristeva, Julia, *Revolution in Poetic Language*, trans. Margaret Waller, New York: Columbia University Press, 1984.
Lacy, Tim, 'Making a Democratic Culture: the Great Books, Mortimer Adler, and Twentieth-Century America', PhD dissertation, Loyola University, 2006.
Landvik, Lorna, *Angry Housewives Eating Bon Bons*, New York: Ballantine Books, 2003.
Laskin, David and Holly Hughes, *The Reading Group Book: the Complete Guide to Starting and Sustaining a Reading Group, with Annotated Lists of 250 Titles for Provocative Discussion*, New York: Plume, 1995.
Lazere, Donald, 'Literacy and Mass Media: the Political Implications', *New Literary History* 18, 2 (1987): 237–55.
Leavis, Queenie D., *Fiction and the Reading Public*, London: Chatto & Windus, 1932.
Lehmann, Chris, 'Literati: the Oprah Wars', *American Prospect Online*, 12 March 2001, at http://www.prospect.org/print/V12/21/lehmann-c.html.
——, 'Oprah's Book Fatigue: How Fiction's Best Friend Ran out of Stuff to Read', *Slate*, 10 April 2002, at http://www.slate.com/id/2064224/.
Leith, Linda, 'Ladies of the Club: Spontaneous by Nature, Reading Groups Betray Few Common Traits, Except that they're Social, Self–Educating and Very Likely Sisterly', *Quill & Quire*, May 1995: 8–9.
Levin, Jerome David, *Theories of the Self*, Washington: Hemisphere Publishing Company, 1992.
Levine, Lawrence W., *Highbrow/Lowbrow: the Emergence of Cultural Hierarchy in America*, The William E. Massey, Sr. Lectures in the History of American Civilization, Cambridge, MA: Harvard University Press, 1988.

Lindlof, Thomas R., 'Media and Audiences as Interpretive Communities', in *Communication Yearbook*, ed. James Anderson, Newbury Park, CA: Sage, 1988, 81–107.
Long, Elizabeth, 'The Cultural Meaning of Concentration in Publishing', *Book Research Quarterly* 1, 4 (1985–86): 3–27.
——, 'The Book as Mass Commodity: the Audience Perspective', *Book Research Quarterly* 3, 1 (1987): 9–27.
——, 'Textual Interpretation as Collective Action', *Discourse* 14, 3 (1992): 104–30.
——, 'Textual Interpretation as Collective Action', in *The Ethnography of Reading*, ed. Jonathan Boyarin, Berkeley: University of California Press, 1992, 180–211.
——, *Book Clubs: Women and the Uses of Reading in Everyday Life*, Chicago: University of Chicago Press, 2003.
Lovell, Terry, 'Subjective Powers? Consumption, the Reading Public, and Domestic Woman in Early Eighteenth-Century England', in *The Consumption of Culture 1600–1800: Image, Object, Text*, ed. Ann Bermingham and John Brewer, New York: Routledge, 1997, 23–41.
Lugones, Maria, 'Playfulness, "World"-Travelling, and Loving Perception', *Hypatia* 2, 2 (1987): 3–19.
Lyons, Martyn, 'Reading Models and Reading Communities', in *A History of the Book in Australia, 1891–1945: a National Culture in a Colonised Market*, ed. Martyn Lyons and John Arnold, St Lucia, Queensland and Portland, OR: University of Queensland Press, 2001, 370–88.
Macdonald, Dwight, 'The Book-of-the-Millennium Club', in *Against the American Grain: Essays on the Effect of Mass Culture*, New York: Vintage, 1962, 243–61.
Machor, James L., *Readers in History: Nineteenth-Century American Literature and the Contexts of Response*, Baltimore: Johns Hopkins University Press, 1993.
—— and Philip Goldstein, *Reception Study: from Literary Theory to Cultural Studies*, New York: Routledge, 2001.
Mackenzie, John M., *Propaganda and Empire: the Manipulation of British Public Opinion 1880–1960*, Manchester: Manchester University Press, 1984.
MacKenzie, Raymond N., 'Penguin Books', in *British Literary Publishing Houses, 1881–1965*, ed. Jonathan Rose and Patricia Anderson, Detroit: Gale Research, 1991, 251–61.
MacSkimming, Roy, *The Perilous Trade: Publishing Canada's Writers*, Toronto: McClelland & Stewart, 2003.
Manguel, Alberto, *A History of Reading*, New York: Viking, 1996.
Mattson, Kevin, *When America Was Great: The Fighting Faith of Postwar Liberalism*, New York: Routledge, 2004.
Mayer, Milton, *Robert Maynard Hutchins: a Memoir*, Berkeley: University of California Press.
McCrum, Robert, 'Don't Judge a Book-Reading Group by its Cover', *Guardian*, 24 July 2005, at http://books.guardian.co.uk/news/articles/0,6109,1534954,00.html.
——, 'E-Read All About It', *Guardian*, 15 January 2006, at http://books.guardian.co.uk/print/0,3858,5374656-110368,00.html.
McGinley, William, Katanna Conley and John Wesley White, 'Pedagogy for a Few: Book Club Discussion Guides and the Modern Book Industry as Literature Teacher', *Journal of Adolescent and Adult Literacy* 44, 3 (2000): 204–14.
McHenry, Elizabeth, '"Dreaded Eloquence": the Origins and Rise of African American Literary Societies and Libraries', *Harvard Library Review* 6, 2 (1995): 32–56.

——, *Forgotten Readers: Recovering the Lost History of African American Literary Societies*, New Americanists, Durham: Duke University Press, 2002.

McLuhan, Marshall, *The Mechanical Bride: Folklore of Industrial Man*, Madera, CA: Gingko Press, 2002 [1951].

McMains, Victoria Golden, *The Readers' Choice: 200 Book Club Favorites*, New York: Quill, 2000.

McMillan, David W., 'Sense of Community', *Journal of Community Psychology* 24, 4 (1996): 315–25.

—— and David M. Chavis. 'Sense of Community: a Definition and Theory', *Journal of Community Psychology* 14 (1986): 6–23.

McNay, Lois, *Gender and Agency: Reconfiguring the Subject in Feminist and Social Theory*, Cambridge: Polity Press and Malden, MA: Blackwell, 2000.

McNeill, William H., *Hutchins' University: a Memoir of the University of Chicago 1929–1950*, Chicago: University of Chicago Press, 1991.

Miller, Laura, *Reluctant Capitalists: Bookselling and the Culture of Consumption*, Chicago: University of Chicago Press, 2006.

Miller, Nancy, *Getting Personal: Feminist Occasions and other Autobiographical Acts*, New York: Routledge, 1991.

Missner Barstow, Jean, 'Reading in Groups: Women's Clubs and College Literature Classes', *Publishing Research Quarterly* (Winter 2003): 3–17.

Moi, Toril, ed., *The Kristeva Reader*, New York: Columbia University Press, 1986.

Montagu, Elizabeth, 'Dialogue III', in *Women Critics, 1660–1820*, ed. the Folger Collective on Early Women Critics, Bloomington and Indianapolis: Indiana University Press, 1995, 102.

Montagu, Matthew, ed., *The Letters of Mrs. Elizabeth Montagu*, 4 vols, London: Cadell and Davies, 1809, Vol. I.

——, ed. *The Letters of Mrs. Elizabeth Montagu*, 4 vols, London: Cadell and Davies, 1809–13.

Moore, Henrietta L., *A Passion for Difference: Essays in Anthropology and Gender*, Bloomington: Indiana University Press, 1994.

Morley, Malcolm, 'Little Dorrit, on and off', *Dickensian* 49–50 (1954): 136–40.

Morris, R.J., 'Clubs, Societies and Associations', in *The Cambridge Social History of Britain, 1750–1950*, ed. F.M.L. Thompson, Cambridge: Cambridge University Press, 1990, 395–443.

Morrison, Theodore, *Chautauqua: a Centre for Education, Religion and the Arts*, Chicago: University of Chicago Press, 1974.

Mulhern, Francis, 'English Reading', in *Nation and Narration*, ed. Homi K. Bhabha, London; New York: Routledge, 1990, 250–64.

Murray, Heather, 'Great Works and Good Works: the Toronto Women's Literary Club 1877–1883', *Historical Studies in Education/Revue d'histoire de l'education* 11, 1 (1999): 75–95.

——, *Come, Bright Improvement! The Literary Societies of Nineteenth-Century Ontario*, Toronto: University of Toronto Press, 2002.

Murray, Simone, *Mixed Media: Feminist Presses and Publishing Politics*, London: Pluto, 2004.

Nafisi, Azar, *Reading Lolita in Tehran*, London: Fourth Estate, 2004.

Noble, Elizabeth, *The Reading Group*, New York: Perennial, 2005.

Orange, Donna M., *Emotional Understanding: Studies in Psychoanalytic Epistemology*, New York: The Guilford Press, 1995.

Passmore Edwards, John, *A Few Footprints*, London: Clement's House, 1905.
Paton, John Lewis, *John Brown Paton: a Biography*, London: Hodder & Stoughton, 1914.
Patten, Robert L., 'Dickens as Serial Author: a Case of Multiple Identities', in *Nineteenth Century Media and the Construction of Identities*, ed. Bill Bell, Laurel Brake and David Finkelstein, London: Palgrave Macmillan, 2001, 137–53.
Pearlman, Mickey, *What to Read: the Essential Guide for Reading Group Members and Other Book Lovers*, 2nd edn, New York: HarperCollins, 1999.
Peck, Janice, 'TV Talk Shows as Therapeutic Discourse: the Ideological Labor of the Televised Talking Cure', *Communication Theory* 5, 1 (1995): 58–81.
Pecoskie, Jen (J.L.), 'The Solitary, Social, and "Grafted Spaces" of Pleasure Reading: Exploring Reading Practices from the Experiences of Adult, Self-Identified Lesbian, Gay, Bisexual, and Queer Readers and Book Club Members', PhD dissertation, University of Western Ontario, 2009.
Pennington, Montagu, ed., *Memoirs of the Life of Mrs. Elizabeth Carter, with a New Edition of Her Poems*, London: Rivington, 1808.
——, ed., *Letters from Mrs. Elizabeth Carter to Mrs. Montagu, between the Years 1755 and 1800*, 3 vols, London: Printed for F.C. and J. Rivington, 1817.
——, ed., *A Series of Letters between Mrs. Elizabeth Carter and Miss Catherine Talbot, from the Year 1741 to 1770, to Which Are Added Letters from Mrs. Elizabeth Carter to Mrs. Vesey, between the Years 1763 and 1787*, 4 vols, London: F.C. and J. Rivington, 1817.
Phegley, Jennifer, *Educating the Proper Woman Reader: Victorian Family Literary Magazines and the Cultural Health of the Nation*, Columbus: Ohio State University Press, 2004.
Poole, Marilyn, 'The Women's Chapter: Women's Reading Groups in Victoria', *Feminist Media Studies* 3, 3 (2003): 263–81.
Price, Kenneth M. and Susan Belasco Smith, 'Introduction', in *Periodical Literature in Nineteenth-Century America*, ed. Kenneth M. Price and Susan Belasco Smith, Charlottesville: University Press of Virginia, 1995.
Price, Leah, 'Reading: the State of the Discipline', *Book History* 7, 1 (2004): 303–20.
——, 'Essay – You Are What You Read', *New York Times Book Review* (2007): 19.
Prinsloo, P.J.J., 'Die Pietermaritzburgse Debat En Letterkundige Vereniging, 1908–1918', *Hisoria (South Africa)* 40, 1 (1995): 72–89.
Proust Marcel, *On Reading*, Preface and trans John Sturrock, Harmondsworth: Penguin, 1994.
Quarter, Jack, 'James John Harpell: an Adult Education Pioneer', *Canadian Journal for the Study of Adult Education* 14, 1 (2000): 89–112.
Radford, George, *The Faculty of Reading: the Coming of Age of the National Home Reading Union*, Cambridge: Cambridge University Press, 1910.
Radner, Hilary, 'Extra-Curricular Activities: Women Writers and the Readerly Text', in *Women's Writing in Exile*, ed. Mary Lynn Broe and Angela Ingram, North Carolina: University of North Carolina Press, 1989, 251–68.
Radway, Janice, *Reading the Romance: Women, Patriarchy, and Popular Literature*, Chapel Hill and London: University of North Carolina Press, 1991 [1984].
——, *A Feeling for Books: The Book-of-the-Month Club, Literary Taste and Middle-Class Desire*, Chapel Hill: University of North Carolina Press, 1997.

Rehberg Sedo, DeNel, 'Readers in Reading Groups: an On-Line Survey of Face-to-Face and Virtual Book Clubs', *Convergence: the International Journal of Research into New Media Technologies* 9, 1 (2003): 66–90.

——, 'Badges of Wisdom, Spaces for Being: a Study of Contemporary Women's Book Clubs', PhD dissertation, Simon Fraser University, 2004.

Renan, Ernest, 'What is a Nation?' in *Nation and Narration*, ed. Homi K. Bhabha, London and New York: Routledge, 1990, 8–22.

——, *Introduction to the History of Sir George Ellison*, Lexington: University Press of Kentucky, 1996.

Robbins, Li, 'Book Club Virgin (and Proud of It): the Scorn of the Solitary Reader', CBC, at www.cbc.ca/arts/books/bookclubvirgin.html.

Rooney, Kathleen, *Reading with Oprah: the Book Club that Changed America*, Fayetteville: University of Arkansas Press, 2005.

Rose, Jonathan, *The Intellectual Life of the British Working Classes*, New Haven: Yale University Press, 2001.

——, 'How Historians Study Reader Response: Or, What Did Jo Think of *Bleak House*?' in *Literature in the Marketplace*, ed. John O. Jordan and Robert L. Patton, Cambridge: Cambridge University Press, 2003, 195–212.

Rose, M.J., 'Everything Old is New Again: Reinventing the Publishing Model', *Poets & Writers: from Inspiration to Publication*, at http://www.pw.org/mag/rose0205.htm.

Ross, Catherine Sheldrick, Lynne McKechnie and Paulette M. Rothbauer, *Reading Matters: What the Research Reveals about Reading, Libraries, and Community*, Westport, CT: Libraries Unlimited, 2006.

Ross, Val, 'Gathered Together in Literature's Name', *Globe & Mail*, 14 January 1995, 1, 2.

Rubin, Joan Shelley, *The Making of Middlebrow Culture*, Chapel Hill: University of North Carolina Press, 1992.

Ruggles Gere, Anne, *Intimate Practices: Literacy and Cultural Work in U.S. Women's Clubs, 1880–1920*, Urbana and Chicago: University of Illinois Press, 1997.

Schiffrin, André, *The Business of Books: How International Conglomerates Took over Publishing and Changed the Way We Read*, London: Verso, 2000.

Schweickart, Patrocinio P., 'Reading Ourselves: Toward a Feminist Theory of Reading', in *Gender and Reading: Essays on Readers, Texts, and Contexts*, ed. Patrocinio P. Schweickart and Elizabeth A. Flynn, Baltimore and London: Johns Hopkins University Press, 1986, 31–63.

Scott, John C., 'The Chautauqua Vision of Liberal Education', *History of Education* 34, 1 (2005): 41–59.

Seabrook, John, *Nobrow: the Culture of Marketing, the Marketing of Culture*, New York: Vintage, 2001.

Shattuc, Jane, *The Talking Cure: TV Talk Shows and Women*, New York: Routledge, 1997.

Sicherman, Barbara, 'Sense and Sensibility: a Case Study of Women's Reading in Late Victorian America', in *Reading in America*, ed. Kathy Davison, Baltimore: Johns Hopkins University Press, 1989, 201–25.

——, *Well-Read Lives: How Books Inspired a Generation of American Women*, Chapel Hill: University of North Carolina Press, 2010.

Silva, Elizabeth B., 'Gender, Home and Family in Cultural Capital Theory', *British Journal of Sociology* 56, 1 (2005): 83–103.

Slater, Michael, ed., *Dickens 1970: Centenary Essays*, London: Chapman & Hall for the Dickens Fellowship, 1970.
Slezak, Ellen, ed., *The Book Group Book*, 3rd edn, Chicago: Chicago Review Press, 2000.
Smith, David, 'Women are Still a Closed Book to Men: Research Shows Men Mainly Read Works by Other Men', *Observer*, 29 May 2005, at http://books.guardian.co.uk/news/articles/0,6109,1495060,00.html.
Smith, Dorothy E., 'Feminist Reflections on Political Economy', *Studies in Political Economy* 30 (Autumn 1989): 37–59.
Snape, R., *Leisure and the Rise of the Public Library*, London: Library Association Publishing, 1995.
——, 'The National Home Reading Union', *Journal of Victorian Culture* 7, 1 (2002): 86–110.
——, 'An English Chautauqua: the National Home Reading Union and the Development of Rational Holidays in Late Victorian Britain', *Journal of Tourism History* 2, 3 (2010): 213–34.
Springhall, John, *Youth, Empire and Society: British Youth Movements 1883–1940*, London: Croom Helm, 1977.
Squires, Claire, 'Novelistic Production and the Publishing Industry in Britain and Ireland', in *Companion to the British and Irish Novel 1945–2000*, ed. Brian Shaffer, Oxford: Blackwell, 2004, 177–93.
——, *Marketing Literature: the Making of Contemporary Writing in Britain*, Basingstoke: Palgrave Macmillan, 2007.
St Clair, William, *The Reading Nation in the Romantic Period*, Cambridge: Cambridge University Press, 2004.
Stevens, Kira and Ellen Moore, *Good Books Lately: the One-Stop Resource for Book Groups and Other Greedy Readers*, New York: St Martin's Griffin, 2004.
Surrey, Janet L., 'The Self-in-Relation: a Theory of Women's Development', in *Women's Growth in Connection: Writings from the Stone Centre*, ed. J.V. Jordan, A.G. Kaplan, J.B. Miller, I. Stiver and J.L. Surrey, New York: The Guilford Press, 1991, 51–66.
Swanton, M.J., 'A Dividing Book Club of the 1840s: Wadebridge, Cornwall', *Library History* 9, 3 and 4 (1992): 106–21.
Taylor, John Russell, *Hitch: the Life and Times of Alfred Hitchcock*, New York: Pantheon Books, 1978.
'The 102 Great Ideas: Scholars Complete a Monumental Catalog', *Life*, 26 January 1948, 92–102.
Thompson, Ann, 'A Club of Our Own: Women's Play Readings in the Nineteenth Century', *Borrowers and Lenders: the Journal of Shakespeare and Appropriation* 2, 2 (2006), at http://www.borrowers.uga.edu/cocoon/borrowers/request?id=781461.
Thornham, Sue, *Feminist Theory and Cultural Studies: Stories of Unsettled Relations*, London: Arnold, 2000.
Tietjens Meyer, Diana, *Subjection and Subjectivity: Psychoanalytic Feminism and Moral Philosophy*, New York: Routledge, 1994.
Tomlinson, John, *Cultural Imperialism*, London: Pinter, 1991.
Travis, Trysh, 'Heathcliff and Cathy, the Dysfunctional Couple', *Chronicle of Higher Education* (2001): 13–14.
——, 'Divine Secrets of the Cultural Studies Sisterhood: Women Reading Rebecca Wells', *American Literary History* 15, 1 (2003): 134–61.

Van Eijck, Koen and Kees Van Rees, 'Media Orientation and Media Use: Television Viewing Behaviour of Specific Reader Types from 1975 to 1995', *Communication Research* 25, 5 (2000): 574–616.

Van Herk, Aritha, 'Publishing and Perishing with no Parachute', in *How Canadians Communicate*, ed. David Taras, Frits Pannekoek and Maria Bakardjieva, Calgary, AB: University of Calgary Press, 2003, 121–41.

Verba, Ericka Kim, 'The Circulo De Lectura De Senoras (Ladies' Reading Circle) and the Club De Senoras (Ladies' Club of Santiago, Chile: Middle- and Upper-Class Feminist Conversations (1915–1920)', *Journal of Women's History* 7, 3 (1995): 6–33.

Vickery, Amanda, *The Gentleman's Daughter: Women's Lives in Georgian England*, New Haven: Yale University Press, 1998.

Wadsworth, Sarah A., 'Social Reading, Social Worth and the Social Function of Literacy in Louisa May Alcott's "May Flowers"', in *Reading Women Literary Figures and Cultural Icons from the Victorian Age to the Present*, ed. Jennifer Phegley and Janet Badia, Toronto: University of Toronto Press, 2006, 149–67.

Weedon, Chris, *Feminist Practice and Poststructuralist Theory*, Cambridge: Blackwell, 1987.

Wells, Rebecca, *Divine Secrets of the Ya-Ya Sisterhood: a Novel*, New York: HarperCollins, 1996.

Whiteside, Thomas, *The Blockbuster Complex: Conglomerates, Show Business & Book Publishing*, Middletown, CT and Irvington, NY: Wesleyan University Press, 1981.

Winter Sisson, Michelle Diane, 'The Role of Reading in the Lives of African American Women Who Are Members of a Book Club', PhD dissertation, University of Georgia, 1996.

'Worst Kind of Troublemaker', *Time*, 21 November 1949, 58–64.

Wright, David, 'Watching the Big Read with Pierre Bourdieu: Forms of Heteronomy in the Contemporary Literary Field', working paper (2007), at http://www.cresc.ac.uk/publications/watching-the-big-read-with-pierre-bourdieu-forms-of-heteronomy-in-the-contemporary-literary-field.

Young, John, 'Toni Morrison, Oprah Winfrey, and Postmodern Popular Audiences', *African American Review* 35 (2001): 181–204.

Zboray, Ronald J. and Mary Saracino Zboray, *Everyday Ideas: Socioliterary Experience among Antebellum New Englanders*, Knoxville: University of Tennessee Press, 2006.

Index

Aberdeen, Lady and the Earl of Aberdeen 71–3
academic readers *see* reader
Adler, Mortimer 14, 17, 18, 81, 86
adult education 5, 95, 141
  see also education
advertisements 48, 52, 54, 198n.
Africa 65, 66, 145
Amazon.com 7, 189
Anderson, Benedict 5, 196n.
Ang, Ien 126, 132, 137nn., 139n.
Atwood, Margaret 101, 159, 166, 187
audiences 41, 45, 53, 124, 126, 137n.
Australia 12, 14, 18, 45, 65–70, 74, 104, 141
  Australasian 68–9

Barthes, Roland 131–2
BBC 64, 125, 127, 130
Big Read (UK) 125, 127, 130
Big Read (US) 8–9
blogs and litblogs 7, 9, 15, 22n., 105, 182
Bluestockings 12, 25, 27, 35, 40–1, 42n., 43n.
  Boscawen, Frances 25
  Carter, Elizabeth 25–40
  Montagu, Elizabeth 25–40, 42n., 43nn.
  Robinson Scott, Sarah 25–9, 31–3, 35–9, 42n., 43nn.
  Talbot, Catherine 26, 28–30, 32–41
  Vesey, Elizabeth 25, 27, 29
book awards
  Booker 129, 185
  British Book Awards 7
  Orange Reading Group Prize (Penguin Orange Prize) 129, 130, 139, 189
  Richard and Judy's Best Read of the Year 7, 129
  Whitbread 185
  Young Adult literary awards 105–8, 110, 111, 113, 119
    Michael L. Printz Prize for Excellence in Young Adult Literature 110–12
    National Book Award for Young People's Literature 110–12
    Newbery Medal 110–12
  see also Big Read (UK)
book clubs (book groups, reading clubs, reading groups)
  African American book clubs, literary societies 3, 10, 191
  cultural practices of 2, 5–7, 9–10, 12–15, 19, 60, 72, 74, 102–3, 106, 117–19, 124–5, 126, 134, 140, 144, 153–5, 160, 193, 194–5
  hierarchy of taste in 18, 19, 25, 30, 34, 41, 67, 187, 190, 193–5
  movement 3, 9, 25, 64, 70, 85–6, 182, 193, 195
  and readers' ideology of instruction and self-improvement 10, 26, 33, 72–3, 84, 96, 148, 159; *see also* distinction.
  religious (church) 63, 83, 192
  trust in 107–8, 115, 173, 186, 191–4
  see also literary societies; reading circles
book discussion *see* dialogue
book history 15–16, 20
  Adams and Barker's New Model of Book History 16
  circuit model of 15–16
book market, marketing, marketplace 11, 14, 19, 29, 53–4, 83, 89, 113, 124, 136, 139n., 160, 162, 165, 182, 184, 195, 197n., 198n.

214 *Index*

book reviews, reviewers 1, 7, 11, 48, 49, 53, 54, 55, 102, 104, 105, 107, 109, 110, 118, 120, 124, 126, 127, 128, 133, 135, 185, 187, 188, 192
book selection 7, 16, 19, 28, 54, 57, 60, 101, 105, 107–9, 119, 124, 130, 138n., 140, 151, 169–70, 176, 178n., 184–8, 192, 194
booksellers, bookstores 11, 19, 37, 160, 161, 182, 184, 187, 188, 189, 193, 194
Bourdieu, Pierre 17, 49, 102, 107, 108, 126–8, 137n., 199n.
British Empire 60, 68, 75, 76, 77

Canada 3, 12, 14, 19, 65, 66, 67, 70–4, 79n., 104, 114, 181, 182, 183, 184, 187, 188, 189, 190, 191, 193
Canadian Broadcasting Corporation (CBC) 185, 192
Chartier, Roger 16
Chautauqua Literary and Scientific Circles 6, 60, 68, 71
class articulations, distinctions and negotiations 35, 40, 42n., 45, 46, 72, 76, 85, 102, 126, 153, 175, 193
  high–low (popular) 64, 67, 174
  middle class 3, 4, 9, 64, 69, 70, 71, 129–30, 175
  upper class 25, 42n., 175
  working class 35, 37, 44, 54, 61, 63, 64, 66, 67, 69, 73, 126, 183
collective reading *see* reading practices
community
  epistolary 16, 25–41; *see also* correspondence, reader to reader; letters
  ethnic 173–4
  geographical 5, 9, 65, 68, 69, 73, 75
  imagined 5, 14, 75–7, 145, 182, 196n.
  interpretative 40, 85, 86, 113, 118, 122n., 186

  online 1, 7, 12, 13, 18, 19, 102, 120, 121n., 124, 160, 182, 184, 194, 195
  reading as engaging 57, 68, 75, 140, 173
  virtual 26, 41; *see also* online (*above*)
Collins, Wilkie 46–7
correspondence
  author to reader, reader to author 26, 54
  reader to reader 65, 66, 70, 129; *see also* epistolary community
  see also letters
consumers 37, 124, 162, 174, 182, 184, 193, 194
convergence (media convergence) 2, 7, 15, 55, 182, 183
cultural authority 7, 10, 18, 36, 32, 102–9, 116–18, 120, 122n., 125, 163, 169–70, 172–4, 176, 183, 185, 193
cultural capital 3, 102, 104, 107–8, 126–7, 130, 190, 197n.
cultural consumption, reading as 102, 108, 123
cultural tastes *see* reading tastes
Curran, James 127–8, 130

Darnton, Robert 15, 24n.
Dewey, John 83, 89, 94, 96
dialogue, discourse, discussion, book talk 5, 7, 9, 10, 11, 13, 17, 18, 19, 25, 28, 34, 41, 54, 61, 68, 82, 85, 87, 90, 101, 102, 109, 110, 118, 124, 134–5, 140, 142, 143, 148–56, 160–4, 166, 168–70, 177, 185, 189, 192
  as an educational process 9, 11, 17, 34, 41, 61, 84–7, 90, 108, 110, 119, 142, 148, 149–50, 152–3
  gendered 25, 28, 34, 41, 134–5, 142, 148–56, 159
  online 7, 18, 102–10, 113–19, 121n., 124, 137n.
  personal 6–7, 13, 27, 106, 109, 125–6, 131, 135, 141–3, 146, 148, 150–1, 160, 167, 168, 170, 172, 174

pleasures of reading with others   142, 148
prescribed   6, 7, 13, 14, 60, 84–7
on radio   182
resistant, dissident   154–5, 159, 162
Shared Inquiry™   85–6
Socratic discussion method   85
Talmudic discussion method   85
on television   7, 135, 167–77
as therapy   167–8, 173
diaries and journals   15, 32, 45
Dickens, Charles   2, 4, 17, 46, 48–57, 61, 62
discussion boards, forums, websites *see* dialogue, discourse, discussion, book talk, online
distinction   37–8, 76, 80, 126, 137n., 160, 163, 171, 172, 193

education   2, 3, 5–6, 8, 9–10, 11, 12, 14, 17–18, 19, 28, 32, 37, 39, 41, 45, 47, 60, 63, 64, 67, 71–4, 76–7, 82–5, 87, 89, 91, 95, 96, 106, 108–10, 114, 115, 119, 125, 126, 152, 177, 191, 199n.
 African American literary societies   3
 educational reform   14, 73, 89, 90–1, 92, 94, 96, 183
 higher education   10, 17, 89, 90–1, 92–4, 163, 171, 173, 176
 literacy   3, 12, 17, 47, 102, 119, 125, 136, 138n.
 pedagogy   19, 85, 90, 110, 159, 163, 176
 self-education   12, 64, 183
enlightenment   8, 11, 42n., 44–5
Enlightenment, the   13, 153
Erskine, John   7, 86, 87, 91, 98

feminism, feminist   25, 104, 132
feminist criticism   18, 47, 103, 132, 137n., 146, 148, 153–6, 160, 162, 178n.
Fish, Stanley   113, 122n., 186
Flint, Kate   44
Franzen, Jonathan   130, 138n., 178n.

friendship   11, 12, 32, 34, 41, 45, 57, 74, 106, 145, 164

genre   15, 27, 28, 29, 30, 35, 41, 46, 104, 106, 109, 114, 119, 120, 126, 128, 131, 132, 133, 135, 165, 186, 187, 188, 191, 192, 193
 autobiography   89, 92
 biography   17, 29, 46, 52, 66, 89, 92, 128, 163, 192
 classical fiction, classics   31, 37, 56, 86, 161, 176, 191, 192
 contemporary fiction   35, 160, 186, 191, 192
 essays   33, 38, 63, 66, 70, 84
 fan fiction   7, 22, 165
 fiction, literary fiction   7, 8, 10, 22n., 32–40, 46, 47, 49, 70, 103, 119, 124, 128, 130, 131, 134, 136, 139n., 144, 160, 162, 164, 165, 166, 170, 174, 175, 176, 185–7, 190, 193; *see also* genre, novels (*below*)
 genre fiction   126, 131, 132, 135, 136, 192
 history   6, 25, 32, 33, 38, 46, 90, 128, 163
 memoir   6, 17, 31, 36, 39, 40, 77, 134, 139
 mystery   103, 106, 133
 non-fiction   8, 36, 110
 novels   6, 10, 29, 30, 35, 36, 37, 42n., 46, 47, 48, 63, 72, 120, 127, 128, 130, 134, 135, 164, 165, 174, 176, 181, 187
 plays   22n., 33, 38, 72
 poetry   22, 25, 33, 39, 40, 47, 61, 62, 63, 70
 romance   27, 37, 106, 113, 126, 131, 132, 135, 154
 satire   34, 36, 54
 science fiction   106
 young adult fiction   102–20
Gioia, Dana   8, 22n.
Giroux, Henry   106, 110
Great Books   81–8, 90, 92–3, 95, 96, 98
 Great Books Foundation   13, 14, 17, 18, 85–6, 94–5, 178n.
 Junior Great Books   85

Great Britain 5, 14, 60, 61, 64, 66, 67, 68, 73, 76, 77, 182
  see also United Kingdom (UK)

Habermas, Jürgen 13, 44
Howsam, Leslie 14, 19
humanities 82, 89, 90, 91, 128
Hutchins, Robert Maynard 14, 17, 81–98

identity 28–31, 120
  collective 140, 148, 155, 168
  imagined 77
  imperial 77
  individual 11, 71, 75, 77, 101, 140, 148, 168
  national 68, 72, 75, 76
  social 11, 168
India 65, 70
Internet 7, 106, 121n., 165, 182, 188, 192
  chat rooms, forums 1, 106, 124, 125, 137n.
  see also community, online

Kellner, Douglas 110, 114, 120
King, Stephen 17, 52–3
Kristeva, Julia 132, 152, 154–5

legislation 14
letters 1, 5, 12, 16, 17, 26, 27, 28–30, 33, 38, 39, 41, 42n., 53–4, 66, 184, 194
  see also community, epistolary; correspondence
librarians 10, 46, 63, 101, 102, 104, 107, 108, 110, 119, 120, 125, 136, 181
libraries
  Association for Library Service 110
  circulating 3, 29
  LibraryThing.com 7
  public 45, 63, 77, 78n., 101, 102, 109, 110, 119, 125, 181
  New American Library *see* publishers
  subscription 29, 72
litblogs *see* blogs and litblogs
literacy *see* education

literary salons 1, 2
  see also salons
literary societies (book societies and reading societies) 2, 3–4, 21n., 58n., 182
Long, Elizabeth 10, 102, 103, 106, 138n., 167, 177n., 183

Manguel, Alberto 75, 123, 132
marginalia 15
marketing 11, 14, 19, 83, 89, 139n., 162, 165, 182–4, 187, 188, 190, 191–2, 194–5
McCarthyism 97
McCrum, Robert 123, 129, 130
McHenry, Elizabeth 20n., 102
McLuhan, Marshall 83, 84, 85
media 2, 7, 11, 18, 19, 97, 105, 124, 127, 128, 130, 132, 181, 182, 184, 186, 189
middlebrow 174, 187
  see also reading tastes, cultural hierarchy, cultural tastes
Morrison, Toni 170–5
multidisciplinarity (interdisciplinarity) 1, 11, 15–16, 19, 90–3, 141
Murray, Heather 70, 71, 102

National Endowment for the Arts 8, 9, 22n.
National Home Reading Union 6, 11, 17, 21n., 45, 60–77
  Australasian Home Reading Union 68
  Canadian Home Reading Union 73
  South African Home Reading Union 70
newspapers 5, 34, 54, 92, 105, 127, 128, 188, 189

One Book, One City programs 8
Oprah Winfrey 6, 53, 86
  Oprah's Book Club 6, 7, 9, 18, 86, 121n., 127–30, 138n., 159–62, 166, 168–77, 179n., 180n.

peace 52, 83, 94, 95, 97, 98, 103, 115

Index 217

pedagogy *see* education
place
 as context for reading,
  discussion 2, 3, 8, 10, 13, 18,
  19, 41, 106, 124–5, 132, 134,
  136, 151, 171–2
 cultural expressions of 32, 52
 ideal 133–4
 literary expressions of 45, 53, 56,
  135
 sense of 55, 60, 63–74, 117, 119
 see also space
Price, Leah 1, 22n.
public sphere 13, 26, 44, 124
publishers 7, 11, 18, 19, 104, 107,
  128, 130, 160, 161, 181–95
 Ballantine 161, 166, 177n., 189
 Bantam 189
 Bertelsmann 184, 189
 Bloomsbury 130, 190
 Continuum 160, 178n.
 Doubleday 187
 HarperCollins 130, 184, 187, 188,
  189, 190, 191
 New American Library 164
 Penguin Group 56, 86, 129, 130,
  178n., 179n., 181, 188, 189,
  190, 192
 Random House 130, 187, 188,
  189, 190
 Simon & Shuster 124, 188, 189
 Vintage/Anchor 187, 189

radio 100n.
 and books 15, 49, 105, 178n., 182,
  192
Radner, Hilary 131, 132, 138n.
Radway, Janice 103–4, 113, 121n.,
  126, 131–2, 135, 154, 183, 186
reader
 expert, professional 17, 25, 28, 29,
  41–1, 63–4, 104–7, 118, 119,
  162, 170, 172, 177
 ideal 35, 130, 134, 135, 136
 lay 60, 64, 160, 162, 163, 166,
  172, 177
 redemptive 126
reader-response criticism, reception
 studies 24n., 36, 122n., 125

reading circles 6, 12, 13, 45, 57, 60,
  64, 68–72, 76, 77
 see also book clubs
reading guides 18, 160, 161, 162–6,
  178n., 179n., 187, 188, 194
reading practices
 collective, shared 2, 9, 13, 15, 26,
  28–9, 40, 45, 47, 50, 52, 86,
  117–18, 122n., 134–5, 142–8,
  168–72, 184, 186, 194
 critical 35, 39, 51, 85, 114, 125–6,
  134, 166
 with family, shared reading 10,
  14, 26, 30, 45, 47, 55, 57, 64,
  76, 186, 190, 193; *see also*
  community, epistolary
 gendered 13, 18, 26, 32, 34, 37,
  41, 42nn., 64, 69–70, 103–4,
  117, 123, 129–30, 133–5, 136,
  142, 162, 173
 guided 18–19, 25, 60, 113,
  160–77, 179n.; *see also*
  prescribed reading (*below*)
 as intellectual engagement 5, 19,
  33, 64, 74, 84–6, 171
 pleasure reading 19, 26, 40, 57,
  69, 86, 131–2, 134, 144, 167,
  169, 171
 prescribed reading 6, 14, 17, 37,
  45, 60–5, 71–2, 85–6
 reading aloud 13, 48, 52, 64, 72
 reading resistance 31, 34, 35,
  118–19, 126, 128, 131, 135,
  163, 179n., 192
 re-reading 49–50, 51
 reading for self-improvement *see*
  education, self-education
 solitary reading 2, 16, 18, 30, 41,
  75, 134, 138n., 140, 164, 194
Reading at Risk 8–9
reading tastes, cultural hierarchy,
 cultural tastes 13, 19, 22,
  25, 28, 30, 34, 35–9, 41, 45–7,
  67, 126, 127, 131, 183, 186,
  187, 190, 193, 194, 195, 197n.
 high-, middle-, low-brow 19,
  46, 67, 123–5, 127–8, 130,
  136, 163, 174, 186–7; *see also*
  middlebrow

research methods
  archival 15, 17, 26–8, 42n., 65–7, 78n., 160
  case studies 17, 101–2, 103
  ethnographic 18, 105, 131; *see also* participant observation (*below*)
  experimental 17, 44, 48–57
  grounded theory 141
  interviews 17, 18, 19, 124, 127, 137, 141, 142, 182
  literary criticism 29, 55, 159–60, 163, 172; New Critics 85
  memoir study 17, 26–8, 35, 77, 134–5
  participant observation 18, 105
  questionnaires 104, 108, 141
  quantified history 44
  reading reception 15, 17, 24n., 49; *see also* reader-response criticism, reception studies
  survey 18, 19, 105, 141, 177n., 192, 193, 197n.
  textual analysis 15, 17, 124, 166
Richard and Judy's Book Club 7, 18, 126, 127, 128, 129
  Richard Madeley and Judy Finnigan 7
ritual 5, 10, 140
Rose, Jonathan 44, 54
Ruggles Gere, Anne 4, 21n.

salons 3, 26, 29, 41, 159
  see also literary salons

self-improvement 10
  see also education, self-education
serial, serialization 11, 17, 44, 49, 52–7, 166
series 6, 55, 160–1, 164, 166, 176, 178n.
Sicherman, Barbara 4
social capital *see* cultural authority; cultural capital
South Africa 12, 14, 65, 66, 67, 69–70, 73, 74, 76, 176
space 3, 5, 7, 10, 13, 16, 20, 26, 76, 80, 89, 90, 102, 103, 105–7, 114–15, 118, 128, 132, 140, 148, 169, 175
St Clair, William 44, 45, 58n.
Stein, Gertrude 87–8
Syntopicon 17–18, 81–4, 96, 98

television 49, 124, 125, 167–8
  and books 1, 6, 7, 13, 15, 18–19, 101, 105, 123–4, 125–6, 136, 168–77, 182, 185
Travis, Trysh 103–4, 166–7, 175–6
Twitter 7, 188

United Kingdom (UK) 6, 7, 18, 19, 104, 114, 123, 127, 129, 181, 182, 183, 184, 185, 187, 188, 189, 190, 191, 192, 195n.
  see also Great Britain
United States of America (US) 4, 6, 7, 8, 19, 86, 97, 101, 104, 105, 106, 111, 114, 127, 181, 182, 183, 184, 187, 189, 191, 197n.

Studies of f2f groups have included gender studies as these groups are predominantly female. The internet discussion groups can mask gender identity.

F2F also raises issues to do with speaking up and those who do not speak are noticed (p.149) - this can be intimidating - not an issue with internet groups.